GEOFFREY CHAUCER

Troilus and Criseyde
IN MODERN VERSE

GEOFFREY CHAUCER

Troilus and Criseyde
IN MODERN VERSE

Translated, with Notes, by

Joseph Glaser

Introduction by

Christine Chism

Hackett Publishing Company, Inc.
Indianapolis/Cambridge

17 16 15 14   1 2 3 4 5 6 7

For further information, please address
   Hackett Publishing Company, Inc.
   P.O. Box 44937
   Indianapolis, Indiana 46244-0937

   www.hackettpublishing.com

Interior design by Elizabeth L. Wilson
Cover design by Brian Rak
Composition by William Hartman

Library of Congress Cataloging-in-Publication Data

Chaucer, Geoffrey, –1400.
    Troilus and Criseyde in Modern Verse / Geoffrey Chaucer ;
    translated, with notes, by Joseph Glaser ; introduction by
    Christine Chism.
        pages cm
        Includes bibliographical references.
        ISBN 978-1-62466-193-8 (pbk.) —
        ISBN 978-1-62466-194-5 (cloth)
        1. Troilus (Legendary character)—Poetry. 2. Cressida
    (Fictitious character)—Poetry. 3. Trojan War—Poetry.
    4. Troy (Extinct city)—Poetry. I. Glaser, Joseph, translator.
    II. Title.
    PR1895.W7 2014
    821'.1—dc23   2014008023

Contents

Introduction

Geoffrey Chaucer wrote *Troilus and Criseyde* as a fully mature poet, and it is his greatest finished work, a five-part study in human mutability and stubbornness. It survives in sixteen manuscripts, dating from the fifteenth and sixteenth centuries, one of which was owned by Henry IV. There were also three early printed editions. Chaucer wrote the poem between 1382 and 1386, during one of the most poetically productive periods of his life. At that time, alongside *Troilus and Criseyde,* Chaucer was translating into English prose an influential treatise of late antique philosophy, *The Consolation of Philosophy* by Boethius (ca. 480–525). Boethius' discussions of the conflicts between free will and predestination imbue Book 4. More largely, the Boethian question of how to deal with the vagaries of changing fortune sharpens the ethical urgency of Chaucer's drama of love in a time of war. In the early parts of the 1380s, Chaucer also wrote *The Parliament of Fowls* (1380–1382) and a number of narrative poems and lyrics, including "Complaint to Adam Scriveyn," "Complaint of Mars," "Complaint of Venus," "Palamon and Arcite" (later used as "The Knight's Tale" in the *Canterbury Tales*), "The Former Age," "Fortune," "Lak of Stedfastnesse," "Truth," "Gentilesse," and the beginning of *The Legend of Good Women*.

Taken as a group, these works dramatize the torment of change—whether changes of heart or changes of fortune—which is the central theme of *Troilus and Criseyde.* In *Troilus and Criseyde* Chaucer undertakes to tell the double sorrow of Troilus, of the sufferings he underwent first by falling in love and then by losing his love. Along the way, Chaucer also dilates upon a counter-story that is not as fully realized in the poem's sources—of how Criseyde is enticed and manipulated toward love with Troilus, a love to which she slowly and then joyously accedes—and then the more troubling story of how, as circumstances alter, she forgets him and binds herself to another. The pas de deux through which these lovers meet and part is punctuated throughout by the reminder that they are loving in the city of Troy, under siege and verging upon destruction, and that events larger than the lovers will encroach on their best choices and their strategies in ways that cannot be resisted.

Trojan Fortunes in Richard II's London

It seems no accident that Chaucer was translating Boethius, writing *Troilus and Criseyde,* and turning out lyrics like "Lak of Steadfastness" and "Fortune" during one of the most politically troubled decades of the late fourteenth century. The governance of the realm was at issue as it had not been since the beginning of the fourteenth century. Richard II took the throne in 1377 at the age of ten, and a number of continual councils were appointed to administer the governance of the realm for fear that the king's powerful uncles, and particularly John of Gaunt, would seize the regency. The decade was punctuated with civic upheavals, beginning with the Rising of 1381, a general insurrection of laborers and city dwellers, who rose against the landowning hereditary nobility and the richly endowed clergy and advocated the abolishment of feudal social structures and the restructuring of the realm as a polity of equals under the rule of a single king. They passed into London through Aldgate, the great eastern gate of the city, over which Chaucer was living at the time. They burned the Savoy Palace of John of Gaunt, not only the king's uncle but the most powerful magnate in the land; they beheaded the archbishop of Canterbury, Archbishop Sudbury, and the lord high treasurer, Robert Hales, and displayed their heads upon London bridge. The insurgents were dispersed and their leader, Wat Tyler, was killed by a mixture of trickery, force, and precocious leadership from Richard II himself. After the rising had been put down, Richard began exerting his own authority in ways that would make him less dependent on the strong baronial influences that had dominated the politics of previous decades. He began fostering a number of protégés and constituents, bound to him by personal endowments and friendship. Sidelining his uncles and cousins among the greater magnates of the realm, Richard II filled his court with new allies such as Robert de Vere, for whom he created a title (the Duke of Ireland), and Michael de la Pole, whom he made chancellor of the realm. He also fostered ties with certain factions of merchant oligarchs from the city of London, such as the one led by former mayor Nicholas Brembre. Finally, he gathered a number of lettered companions and civil servants drawn from both gentry and nobility, including several of Chaucer's circle of chamber knights, civil servants, and fellow bureaucrats.

Richard's tactics to garner independent authority did not go unnoticed; they alarmed the House of Commons and they infuriated several among the king's uncles, the greater magnates, whose networks of influence were threatened. A baronial faction, led by the Duke of Gloucester and the Earl of Arundel began to assemble into a party that would challenge Richard's power not only over Parliament and the realm, but even his own house-hold; they would come to call themselves the Lords Appellant. Through-out the early 1380s, they skirmished with Richard and his favorites in Parliament, over taxation and the possibility of new campaigns in France, part of the ongoing Hundred Years' War. In 1386 when Michael de la Pole appeared before Parliament to propose greatly elevating war taxes, Parliament demanded instead that Richard remove him from the office of chancellor or face deposition. After a brief, vocal resistance, Richard submitted, not only to the removal of his friend but also to a commis-sion that took control of his finances for a whole year. The power plays between the king, the Lords Appellant, Parliament, and the city of London would come to a head in the Merciless Parliament of 1388, when those of Chaucer's fellow civil servants who had allied themselves too exclusively to the king's party were purged from office at the behest of the triumphant Lords Appellant and a number of them were executed. Although Chaucer was occupationally tied to Richard II's affinity, or circle of high-ranking associates and retainers, and had worked under Nicholas Brembre as con-troller of customs, he survived these political upheavals by propagating relationships with several of the factions and by deftly distancing himself from their skirmishes. In 1385 he became justice of the peace for the shire of Kent and a year later, as he was finishing *Troilus and Criseyde,* he was elected as a knight of the shire of Kent, an office whose duties often kept him out of London.

During this time, it is probably no coincidence that Chaucer's imagi-nation was drawn to the matter of Troy. Among the king's supporters exe-cuted by the Lords Appellant in 1388 was former London mayor Nicholas Brembre, who was somewhat hysterically accused of conspiring to rename London Little Troy (Parva Troia) while setting himself up as a tyrannical duke over the city. The analogy of London with Troy was conventional in British historiographies deriving from Geoffrey of Monmouth's twelfth-century account of the founding of Britain by Trojan refugees. London as Troy also surfaces in other late-fourteenth-century literary works, notably *St. Erkenwald.* However, it is clear that the events of the 1380s gave the analogy between London and Troy a dangerous, political edge. Chaucer situates his little poem ("Go, little book. Go, [little] my tragedy" [5.1786]) within a suspended moment before the fall of that besieged and fated city and in disregard of the larger epic literary traditions that require its destruction. In contrast to foundational histories such as Virgil's *Aeneid* or Geoffrey's *History,* Chaucer's poem arrests the fall of Troy before its vast historical consequences—Rome, France, Britain—can domino through the ages into Chaucer's turbulent, familiar London. In that suspension of history Chaucer tells a story of an intimate interlude governed by the movements of hearts and not armies, personal letters and not nations, to show how change writes itself as painfully upon private lives as it does upon a whole era.

Anachronism and the Uncanny World of *Troilus and Criseyde*

The poem's strategy of interpolating a love story into a war story makes a statement about the type of literature in which Chaucer was interested: one in which the pragmatic and ideal join hands and the battlefield adjoins urban boulevard and private bower. Chaucer plays with genre and style throughout the poem—is it history, epic, romance, tragedy, philosophical treatise, or an interweaving of all five? Joseph Glaser's translation draws attention to the breathless shifts in register throughout the poem: at one moment courtly archaism and at the next slangy urbanity. This stylistic shifting reflects the poem's deeper temporal ambiguity as its antique Trojan plot verges repeatedly on the contemporary. Chaucer's Troy is medieval and therefore distant to us, but its inhabitants are driven by familiar emotions: loneliness, fear, joy, anxiety, and pain. The poem conveys how it might have felt to live among the gentry in a medieval city, with their affinities, parties, and intrigues, their hopes, and their losses. It is possible to read the poem and imagine with hallucinatory vividness the precise color of the dusk of Criseyde's bedroom, while she mulls her future with her heart in the balance, or the exact way the light falls across Troilus' bed the morning after the lovers' first tryst, while Pandarus sidles in for a report in pursuit of who knows what vicarious gratification. But the poem is also, as the narrator keeps reminding us, profoundly alien, a thing constructed from a clash of sources, suspended across several millennia of destruction, scandal, and forgetfulness.

The illuminator for one of the poem's most beautiful manuscripts, Cambridge Corpus Christi College Ms. 61 (ca. 1399–1413), highlights the poem's juxtaposition of the historical and literary to the contemporary and everyday. The frontispiece of CCCC 61 shows Chaucer standing at a high red-draped lectern, performing his poem to a court audience. He holds no book in his hands, he extemporizes or chants from memory, and his clothing is remarkably plain in contrast to the ornate company that surrounds him. In the foreground, groups of richly dressed gentlefolk mingle and disport themselves, some listening and some occupied with each other. In the left corner, a woman in enormous blue sleeves listens raptly, while her companion in a formfitting blue gown clasps her shoulder and gestures in conversation. To the right, two prosperous looking men in red and pink seem absorbed in their own confabulation. A carefully drawn man stands behind them, chin thoughtfully in his hand, as he gazes at the poet. Facing the poet is a small crowd of listeners, one of whom is dressed completely in gold and seems to be crowned, and there is a gold-crowned woman beside him—is it Richard II and his queen? Farther back, other nobles turn away from the poet, talking among themselves. The foreground is clearly an outdoor court setting, filled with poetry, gossip, and business all at the same time and inhabited exclusively by aristocracy.

It is the background in the top half of the frontispiece, however, that highlights the poem's anachronism most starkly. There, the world inside the poem cascades toward its external audience. Behind the poet, a green forest and a rocky ravine cut across the page at a diagonal, separating the poetic landscape from the poet's courtly, distracted listeners. Above the ravine, the scene seems to depict a significant moment from *Troilus and Criseyde*, perhaps the prisoner exchange at the beginning of Book 5. At the center, a beautiful blonde or crowned woman in blue and white accompanies a tall noble in red in a sortie from a massive, pink, elaborately gothic palace or town. Behind them their retinue is already half returning to the palace. The palace is not empty, however; it is haunted by the central couple's doubles. High above the palace a similar couple in blue and red are perched on adjacent turrets, while in a framed window over the gate, another tiny couple in blue and red gaze into each other's eyes, like echoes of bygone rendezvous. From the left, the welcoming party is led by a showy prince in gold (is it Diomedes?) who kneels and offers a gold and white hat or crown, while the rest of his party looks on inscrutably. Behind them, in the top right corner on a steep double-pronged crag, looms a dark fortress, not a military encampment but a stolid bastion of war. At the extreme upper edge, a dark blue sea laps in little inlets at the plain of gold. This top part of the frontispiece thus paints a one-shot narrative picture, with the pink and glowing Trojan past of the lovers' happiness to the right and their foreboding, deceptively welcoming future to the left. At the center, Troilus and Criseyde—still momentarily joined—stand resplendent and poised for tragedy.

While the contrast between the left and the right halves of the frontispiece is startling, the lack of contrast between its upper and lower halves is even more so. The world of the poem and the world of the audience are nearly indistinguishable. The nobles within the story look like the nobles listening to the story. They are dressed in similar colors, similarly occupied with their companions. Ancient Troy looks like Chaucer's courtly milieu. Conversely, the poet could almost be performing in the scene in Criseyde's

parlor in Book 2, where Pandarus interrupts a company of noblewomen
reading romances aloud, talking, and singing love songs to each other.
The similarity between the world of the poem and the world of the courtly
audience seems to close a courtly circle against all commoners and invest
Chaucer's poem with impeccable aristocratic potential. It is probably no
accident that this manuscript was planned as a very lavish and cost-inten-
sive production, with spaces left for 96 or 97 pictures, in addition to the
frontispiece, across the five books of the poem.

The frontispiece illuminates another of the poem's most intriguing fea-
tures: its extraordinary narrator, the mediator who binds Trojan past to
courtly medieval present. He stands in the center of the page and a little
to the right—the only person who stands out as different—marked off by
his plain robes and his beautifully draped lectern. The narrator of *Troi-
lus and Criseyde* functions as performer, arbiter, and, at times, victim of
his own poetic narrative. He visibly negotiates the interface between his
readers, the poetic world he constructs, and the various sources that he
collates, usurps, and resists. Like his character counterpart Pandarus, also
a supreme rhetorical manipulator, the narrator depicts himself as alien
to the plot he instigates, a reader rather than a practitioner of ennobling
love and one who does not want to draw the judgments toward which his
misogynist sources lead him. He defamiliarizes his story by reminding
us that however much his characters use Christian expressions, use four-
teenth-century colloquialisms, and inhabit a thoroughly medieval urban
world, they are also ancient pagans (see especially 5.1849–55), and he is
fabricating them from sources he finds both supportive and constraining.
One moment, the narrator inserts antiquarian footnotes on his characters'
foreign customs, pagan beliefs, and unexpected features—for instance, the
Palladium festival, Mercury as Troilus' psychopomp, or Criseyde's joined
eyebrows. The next moment, the narrator falls in love with Criseyde him-
self, bending over backward to protect her from the calumny that preoc-
cupies the sources on which he draws. As a result, the narrative is by turns
engrossing and alienating. As the poem oscillates between epic hyperbole
and sentimental empathy, the reader experiences the connections Chaucer
is weaving between the epic and the intimate and between the illustrious
past and the quotidian present. The poem thus creates a complex, dimen-
sional reading experience in which we are often aware of the narrator's
intrusive, inconsistent, and sometimes perplexing choices.

While some scholars attribute *Troilus and Criseyde*'s flagrant anachro-
nism to the supposed inability of medieval writers to conceive of histori-
cal differences between the past and the present, it is clear that Chaucer
and many other medieval writers exhibit historical consciousness. At the

beginning of Book 2, which is dedicated to Clio, the muse of history, and introduces Criseyde, the narrator asserts how the past may be very different in its forms of speech and love while still connecting to contemporary experience:

> You know as well the forms of speech may change
> Within a thousand years. Words come and go.
> What once was common now seems quaint and strange,
> Or so we think; and yet men once spoke so
> And sped in love as well as we, you know.   (2.22–26)

Given this passage's awareness of historical distance and the capacity to reach across it, it is clear that Chaucer anachronizes with deliberate inconsistency. The inconsistent anachronism draws readers into Chaucer's narrative without allowing them to feel uncritically at home there. For instance, it is difficult for modern readers to understand (and keep from judging) when Troilus in Book 1 refuses, against all logic and self-interest, to tell Criseyde that he loves her. Recourse to literary conventions of medieval *fin amor* or courtly love can help readers with this, but even then his behavior is extreme enough to verge on parody. In Book 3, Troilus, face to face with a bed full of Criseyde, freezes and nearly faints, inducing Pandarus physically to throw him into bed with her—how can we not see that as humorous? Should we not? It is difficult to know how to interpret these extremities of emotion. Chaucer's other writings prove that he is not above humor, even in the midst of tragedy. At the same time, Troilus can be intensely sympathetic, as when he perambulates Troy hallucinating Criseyde in all the places they used to haunt or pleads desperately with Criseyde to allow him to steal her away from the city in Book 4 and then caves in, respecting her wishes without quite believing her when she swears she will return.

By constantly playing off narrative intimacy against alienation, Chaucer intensifies and defers answering the questions that the text raises. For example, the narrator plumbs his characters' innermost thoughts in some of the most exquisite interior reflections in medieval literature, only, at crucial moments, to render the characters' intentions opaque, seemingly even to themselves. Did Criseyde really come to love Diomedes in sympathy after his deadly wounding at Troilus' hands? The narrator refuses to say. Did Troilus really transcend the sorrowing, traitorous world at which he laughs on his way to the utmost sphere? Who knows? The narrator tells us only that Mercury led him to an unknown destination in the afterlife. What did Pandarus mean by jumping into Troilus' bed for a debrief after

xiv   Introduction

the night of the tryst in Book 3 and why does the poem mix such overt homoeroticism precisely into the section of the poem most preoccupied with heteroerotic bliss? More fundamentally, to what extent is Troilus and Criseyde's love really ideal at all, when it was brought about by Pandarus' guileful manipulation? Does Criseyde really have any choice either in falling in love or forgetting her love? She shows agency as a character and makes choices but she is also repeatedly an object of trade between men. Her father first abandons her and then reclaims her like left luggage. Her supposed male protectors—Pandarus, Troilus, and Diomedes—are clearly pursuing their own interests, which sometimes but not always coincide with hers. The narrator is no help. At times he may withhold comment (5.1093–99), taking refuge in the silence of his sources. At other times he may build to a misogynist judgment (such as Criseyde signifying all women's fickleness) only to swerve breathlessly and state that he writes not in sympathy with true men betrayed by false women, but rather paradoxically "for women who have been betrayed / By lying folk—God give those grief, amen!" (5.1780–81). The result of the narrator's suspended and inconsistent judgments is that the reader is continually challenged to assess his or her own interpretations and emotional identifications. Ultimately, the narrator creates the uncanny half-at-home world of Troy to ethically engage his readers, while denying them certainty of judgment.

RICARDIAN POETRY AND THE POEM'S AUDIENCES

Who were this poem's intended readers and who actually read it? The frontispiece to CCCC 61 pictures Chaucer reading to an audience of noble lords and ladies, including a gold-clad prince or king and a queen. However, we don't know whether the *Troilus and Criseyde* frontispiece was a flattering tribute to Chaucer's literary power and courtly popularity or whether it reflected historical reality. We don't know to what extent Richard II was interested in poetry, or whether Chaucer ever performed his poetry at Richard's court, or, if he did, whether ladies would have been among his audience. No household records indicate whether Richard II actually patronized writers and poets or even read what Chaucer and John Gower, Chaucer's contemporary and fellow poet, dedicated to him. Out of the almost 500 surviving household records of Chaucer's payment for services ranging from diplomat to controller of customs, clerk of the works for royal tournaments, and justice of the peace for the shire of Kent there is not a single record of any reward for poetry or literary production.

Yet despite mixed evidence for widespread royal patronage or a courtly literacy, many scholars argue that there was a distinctive Ricardian literary culture in which various members of the royal court and Richard's

London protégés participated. Richard II counted poet and diplomat Sir John Clanvowe among the familiars of his intimate chamber. John Clanvowe knew Chaucer, testified in a heraldic trial, Scrope v. Grosvenor (1385–1390), along with him, and based his poem *The Book of Cupid* on Chaucer's *Parliament of Fowls;* both poets were influenced by French traditions of poetic dream vision. Richard II appointed another poet and politician, Thomas Usk, as undersheriff of London. Usk wrote *Testament of Love* and was an ambitious politicker between the court and the city while Chaucer was the controller of customs; they undoubtedly knew each other. The two writers to whom Chaucer submitted *Troilus and Criseyde* for correction at its end, "moral Gower" and "philosophical Strode," were lawyers and poets, and Strode occupied a mansion above Aldgate while Chaucer also had a residence there. John Gower's most important work in English, the *Confessio Amantis,* was apparently written at Richard II's request in 1386; he revised it in 1393 and changed the dedicatee to Henry of Lancaster, the future King Henry IV. The *Confessio Amantis* extols the utility of poetry for wise governance, but Richard was not good at taking counsel. When Chaucer went on an embassy to Lombardy in 1378, he made Gower one of his legal executors. Gower and Chaucer stole plots from each other and rewrote each other's stories, but we don't always know which way the lines of influence ran. Ralph Strode was an Oxford schoolman and fellow of Merton College who in 1373 was elected common pleader of the city of London (if the scholar and the lawyer are the same man; records are unclear). In 1381 both Strode and Chaucer stood surety for the London merchant John Hende in a dispute over lands. Strode left two philosophical treatises and is also described as a poet by early biographers though none of his poetry has survived. Finally, among the men known to Chaucer who combined royal and civic service with poetic production, we might consider the clerks of the London Guildhall, where most of the early manuscripts of Chaucer and Gower were produced. In their work as scribes, Guildhall clerks read and responded to contemporary poetry and actively incorporated their reading practices into the works they copied.

These men and others formed Chaucer's literary and intellectual circle while they worked for the king, the court, or the city of London in the 1380s, a time both of great civic unrest and literary productivity. In sum, while Richard II is not on record for having patronized poets for their poetry, he certainly seems to have sought them out as protégés, companions, and civil servants, and they clearly influenced each other poetically throughout their bureaucratic associations. Associates like these fellow bureaucrats with literary or philosophical interests may have been Chaucer's first real audience for *Troilus and Criseyde.*

By contrast, the poem's imagined audiences are more ecumenical, encompassing a range of noble, civic, and professional interests. In certain ways the poem does aim at aristocratic sympathies. It is centered on Troilus, a prince who is the epitome of noble virtue. Troilus' experience of love follows a conventional literary program for a type of ennobling love that had a long medieval history. Known by scholars as courtly love and described in medieval romances, satires, and instruction books as *amour courtois* or *fin amor,* this idealized form of love yoked unflagging erotic desire to equally unflagging chivalric service. The lover was typically a young noble and his beloved was a noblewoman rendered unavailable through higher status, powerful relatives, threatening enemies, or marriage. After the lover fell in love and swore chivalric service to his beloved, his ensuing sentimental journey could make or break his reputation. Lancelot and Guinevere and Tristan and Isolde are famous exemplars of courtly love. Although courtly love probably did not exist historically and in fact runs counter to much that we know of aristocratic marital and amatory practice, it was a literary obsession for at least four hundred years and by Chaucer's time had been imaginatively reworked by poets and writers across Europe. Arguably deriving from Arabic courtly Andalusian lyrical forms such as the *muwashshahat,* it appeared in troubadour lyric poetry in the eleventh century and acquired a sheen of Ovidian pragmatism and humor in Andreas Capellanus' twelfth-century *Art of Courtly Love.* It then effloresced in the twelfth-century romances of Chrétien de Troyes and the lays of Marie de France and underwent a lavish allegorical investigation in the thirteenth-century *Romance of the Rose* at the hands of Guillaume de Lorris and Jean de Meun. These writers treated courtly love as ennobling—a test of chivalric character, prowess, and truth. A hallmark of the noble classes, ultimately, as James A. Schultz has argued, courtly love was the love of courtliness itself.[1]

Whether courtly love ever existed historically is almost beside the point. It seems indisputable that medieval writers found it a useful way to explore the subjectivities of their heroes and heroines, innovate in literary forms, and compel the interest of their readers. Chaucer's poem is a good example of the kind of generic experimentation that ideals of courtly love could spark. He gives us a courtly lover in Troilus, but literalizes the conventional paralysis of the love smitten by making Troilus more than usually self-absorbed and helpless to act on his own behalf. This necessitates the intervention of Pandarus, who, out of love for Troilus, but also with quite

---

1. James A. Schultz, *Courtly Love, The Letters of Courtliness, and the History of Sexuality* (Chicago and London: University of Chicago Press, 2006), xxii.

a lot of brutal pragmatism and humor, takes over the management of rapprochement, even when it requires trickery, force, and the enlistment of unwitting bystanders. So a romance of chivalric love comes into dialogue with parody, burlesque, and the language of trade and professionalism, and this extends the appeal of the poem from aristocrats themselves to those in service to the aristocracy.

With Pandarus comes a connection to the professional world in which Chaucer himself circulated. Pandarus is a fixer, brilliant at rhetorical improvisation and social manipulation. When asked to come up with a fictitious litigation case pending against Criseyde, he doesn't even blink: "'Why drag this out?' he said. 'Here's what befell.' / He rang out the whole process like a bell" (2.1614–15). The joyous immediacy of skill seems not only Pandarus' but Chaucer's own. But matters of business, like extremities of aristocratic self-absorption, have a dark side. In Book 3, idealized love begins to assume the language of procurement, literalizing Pandarus' name. Pandarus arranges an assignation with Criseyde and the grateful Troilus promises to arrange similar procurements (perhaps of his sisters) should Pandarus wish it. With the satisfaction of a bargain well concluded, both men then turn to other business: "Thus each man thought that he was well repaid. / The world could not improve on what he'd earned" (3.421–22).

Pandarus also allows Chaucer to meditate on his own role as writer and mediator of his poem to his readers, as Pandarus carries letters between the lovers and arranges their meetings. When the lovers are finally in bed together, he withdraws to the fire to take up "his book / As if that was the only place he'd look" (3.979–80). In a literal sense, Pandarus is the author of Troilus and Criseyde's romance, and he claims readerly access to all its eventualities as well, from inculcation to assignation, consummation, and afterglow. Only when Criseyde has indisputably abandoned Troilus does the poem underscore the limits of Pandarus' authorship and the end of his rhetorical dexterity: "His wits, so much at fault, were overthrown. / Without a word he stood as still as stone" (5.1728–29). Pandarus can manipulate anyone in Troy, and his unshakable friendship with Troilus keeps him within certain chivalric bounds. But the beginning of Criseyde's autonomous choice to negotiate her own circumstances in Book 4 signals the end of Pandarus' (and Troilus') hold on the situation.

In addition, while Troilus solicits aristocratic sympathy and Pandarus professional admiration (or concern), Criseyde broadens the social import of the poem by engaging women and the vulnerabilities of gentlefolk operating in close-knit urban networks. In Book 1 Criseyde is merely a vision of beauty caught in the mirror of Troilus' desiring gaze, but Book 2 gives us a Criseyde who is a self-possessed, thinking, speaking character, who may or may not find a liaison to her advantage. As a widow, she is sexually experienced, and as a ward of the state under Hector's protection, she is as safe and independent as an unmarried woman in Troy who must keep her honor and good name can be:

> . . . my own woman, well at ease—
> Thank God for that—concerning my estate.
> I'm free to graze wherever I may please,
> No fear of other ties or harsh debate.
> No husband now can say to me, 'Checkmate!'   (2.750–54)

However, despite this relative independence, like any gentlewoman, Criseyde is vulnerable to gossip. Chaucer's Troy is like a medieval city and it is difficult for twenty-first-century westernized readers to realize how socially networked medieval towns and villages could be. While courts were hotbeds of high-profile gossip, cities could be just as scrutinizing. Medieval cities were governed by guilds of merchants and artisans who enforced regulations on buying and selling practices, product quality, and the use of public space. However, to a much larger extent than now, citizens and foreigns (those who had not secured admission to a guild) did their own policing by staffing the neighborhood watch, and the hue and cry, a general call for assistance that inhabitants were bound to obey. Citizens enforced social mores themselves with customs such as charivari or prosecutions through urban and ecclesiastical courts. Parishes subdivided cities into many local jurisdictions, so that a medieval city operated like a conglomerate of close-knit neighborhoods, with all the mutual surveillance and light-speed scuttlebutt resulting from such proximity. When Troilus worries about communicating his love for Criseyde to a single other human being, and when Criseyde is absolutely aghast at Pandarus' proposition because she fears "What men would think of it" (2.461), it is the cruel efficiency of these courtly and urban gossip mills that they fear. Criseyde's sense of vulnerability to gossip and loss of reputation is polarizing and appealing. Along with her playfulness, humor, and anxious attention to duty, it sympathetically aligns readers with her so that the ensuing actions of Book 2 can be all the more absorbing.

In contrast to Troilus' sudden-onset lovesickness in Book 1 Criseyde's induction into love is gradual enough to seem more psychologically realistic. Book 2 details the delicate internal and circumstantial processes by which Criseyde is propelled, is coaxed, and coaxes herself into love with Troilus. We see her proceed from initial fear to pondering the possibilities, with the first sight of Troilus home from the battlefield, flushed and bashful in his heroism, and the thought—potent as a love potion—that such a one loves her. As time progresses, we see Antigone's blissful love song that preconditions Criseyde for joyous surrender, Pandarus' aggressive thrusting of Troilus' letter into her bosom, and the nightingale-haunted dream of the bone-white eagle who painlessly tears out her heart and replaces it with its own. Chaucer goes out of his way to highlight not only the exquisite pleasures of this surrender but also its undercurrents of violence, rape, and trade. Chaucer's openness to the darker side of love invokes tales and experiences of women's suffering at men's hands—from Philomela, to Cassandra, to the women in Chaucer's immediate audience and beyond, under a range of patriarchies.

Yet the most powerful appeal of Criseyde to audiences may be the way Chaucer shows how she cannot fully know her own intentions or the boundaries of her control. Chaucer underscores this shadow between will and event in Book 3, when Troilus finally pounces upon his lady with mock violence and boasts:

> "O sweet, now may I rejoice,
> For you are caught, and we are all alone!
> Now yield yourself. You have no other choice."
> She answered in a low and tender voice:
> "Had I not already, sweetheart dear,
> Been yielded up, I never would be here." (3.1206–11)

Criseyde's passive construction means that neither she nor we are allowed to know who exactly did the yielding. Book 5, more unnervingly, also blurs Criseyde's agency in forgetting Troilus and transferring her affections to Diomedes. If she had a moment of choice, the narrator does not let us see it. Instead it is read from afar by signs: embarrassingly noncommittal letters, another unnerving animal dream, and Troilus' brooch on Diomedes' cloak. The closest we get to a decision comes after a long lament in which she remembers Troilus and her happiness in the city and resolves to return (5.697–765). Then Chaucer gives us a haunting image to describe her change of heart: "For Troy and Troilus both, as I must say / Shall knotless slide and drop down from her heart" (5.768–69). This visceral image entwines Troilus and Troy through their homophony and slides them through Criseyde's heart like a string without a knot on it. It reechoes the dream of the eagle's violent, painless heart exchange, but more painfully. For all of her intentions to return to Troy in the long speech that precedes it, Criseyde's heart has no power to keep hold; the ties that bind have somehow been unbound, and two months will reverse her intention to return. It is not clear how this reversal happens, despite her resolve. It would be easier for us to condemn her if she seemed more fully in control.

Why should Chaucer take such care to show that Criseyde is not fully in control—either in her taking up of Troilus' love or its erasure? I would argue that all the characters in the poem allow Chaucer to explore questions of intention, control, and outcome, but Criseyde in particular invites the reader to feel viscerally the importance of those questions. Criseyde makes intimate the poem's larger philosophical obsession with the limits of human agency within uncontrollable circumstances. This question appeals to a broader readership operating in a sphere that cuts across and encompasses issues of class sympathy, occupation, and gender. It is the same audience Chaucer imagines for much of the change-haunted poetry he is writing in the early 1380s. Ultimately, *Troilus and Criseyde* invokes an audience willing to address ethical questions of human action in a sphere where neither fate nor freewill can fully determine choices or outcomes. We might call such an audience humanist.

CHAUCER AND HIS SOURCES: COMPLICATING A TALE OF FEMININE FICKLENESS

At the time Chaucer was working on *Troilus and Criseyde* (ca. 1382–1386), he was a full-fledged medieval English humanist, following in the footsteps of Dante and Petrarch. He had digested for his own uses the most important available texts of classical Latin and medieval French and Italian literature. He was at the top of his form as a poet who read widely, translated extensively, and reimagined other people's stories to create highly complex and original works in English. His literary interlocutors include the thirteenth-century allegorical dream vision, *The Romance of the Rose,* by Jean de Meun and Guillaume de Lorris, whose section of the poem he had translated into English. Chaucer also went out of his way to read currently circulating work of his French and Italian predecessors and contemporaries. The French composer and poet Guillaume de Machaut influenced Chaucer's early poem *The Book of the Duchess.* Eustache Deschamps, a lyricist and satirist, pinioned virtually all Englishmen except Chaucer, whom he lauded as both a *grant translateur* (magnificent translator) and a poetic, philosophical, and cultural illuminator of Albion. In turn, Chaucer front-loaded parts of Deschamps' misogamist satire, the *Mirror of Marriage,* into the prologue of "The Wife of Bath" and other Canterbury tales debating marriage. Oton de Granson resided at the English royal court while Chaucer was active there, and Chaucer both called him the flower of French poets and referenced his ballades in the *Complaint of Venus*. Dispatched on several diplomatic embassies to Florence and Tuscany, Chaucer was the first Englishman we know who read Dante's *Divine Comedy*, which he then gently lambasted in his dream vision (*The House of Fame*) about literary reputation. He also read and made use of Petrarch's sonnets, one of which is translated into Troilus' complaint in Book 1. Finally, he discovered and made off with a number of works by Giovanni Boccaccio, whose poetry Chaucer incessantly usurped without attribution and rewrote to his own ends.

Boccaccio wrote the most important and immediate source of *Troilus and Criseyde, Il Filostrato*. Instead of citing Boccaccio, Chaucer attributes his story to an unknown and probably fictitious Latinate source called Lollius, whose supposed Latinity would endow his work with gravitas and authority. However, it is striking how often an overt citation of Lollius precedes sections of the narrative wholly original to Chaucer. In addition, Chaucer drew on two other versions of the Troilus episode: the twelfth-century poetic *Roman de Troie* of Benoît de Sainte-Maure (d. 1173) and the thirteenth-century Latin prose narrative of Guido delle Colonne (d. ca. 1290), *Historia Destructionis Troiae*, the *History of the Destruction of Troy*. Late antique accounts of the Trojan War by Dares the Phrygian and Dictys of Crete (supposed eyewitnesses of the war on the Trojan and Greek sides, respectively) stand behind all the aforementioned accounts, but they do not include the Troilus and Criseyde episode.

It is in Benoît's version that the story of the lovers first appears, and there it is very different. Benoît tells the story not of Troilus' passion but rather Diomedes'. Benoît structures the episode—first Calchas' desertion and then Briseida's (Benoît's name for Criseyde)—so that we can compare the father's treachery with the daughter's worse treachery. Beginning with Calchas' defection from Troy at Apollo's orders, it then quickly skips to the prisoner exchange of Calchas' daughter, Briseida, for Antenor. Briseida is presented as Troilus' lover from the onset, and we don't get the full story of their romance. As Diomedes receives Briseida and is smitten by love for her, Benoît sketches his three main characters, Diomedes, Briseida, and Troilus, in terms that clearly establish Troilus' superiority to Diomedes, Briseida's sliding heart, and Diomedes' arrogant violence. This introductory comparison of character portraits negatively implicates Briseida's imminent choice of an inferior lover over a superior one. Yet Diomedes' character flaws are quickly overshadowed by the intensity of his true love for Briseida. In fact, it is the spectacle of his arrogance completely subjugated by love that leads Briseida's heart toward him; she delights that he is in her power, perhaps as a compensation for her isolation and helplessness among the Greeks. Troilus' jealousy grows and he and Diomedes target each other in several battles, leading to an almost mortal wound for Diomedes. While pity for the wounded Diomedes completes the transfer of Briseida's heart, Troilus has one triumphant moment in which he condemns her to infamy. Looming over Diomedes' wounded body, Troilus scorns Briseida as a false lover and whore, and his taunts are heard by everybody, Greek and Trojan alike. Briseida herself, even as she swears that she will be true to Diomedes forever, decries her own choice in fierce self-condemnation, claiming that her calumny will resound to the ends of the earth. The episode ends with the embittered Troilus condemning all women, while all the women of the world themselves come to despise Briseida for shaming them. The misogyny of the episode makes it clear that Benoît is one of the sources, along with Guido delle Colonne's moralizing version, to which the *Troilus and Criseyde* narrator directs readers who are eager to find the condemnations of Criseyde that he refuses to utter.

Boccaccio has different agendas, more personal and heartfelt. He wrote *Il Filostrato* as a young man, around 1335, while he was mourning the departure to another city of his first great love, whom he calls Filomena. He takes Benoît's misogynist and Guido's moralizing versions (as well as some Italian prose versions) and shifts the emphasis from Diomedes to Troilus. He invents the account of Troilus' falling in love with Criseida and his silent unreciprocated affection, brought to careful fruition, as well as the whole story of the lovers' bliss before the events of the war intervene. Taking a leaf from Ovidian dramas of intermediaries and bauds, Boccaccio invents the character of Pandarus but makes him another young man, one of Troilus' friends, who has love troubles of his own. Pandarus is also Criseida's cousin rather than her uncle. As a result he has less authority over her and works more as a provocateur and facilitator of love than as a panderer, senior to her in authority and experience. Chaucer darkens Pandarus' character a little by showing him operating in loco parentis to Criseyde, counseling her on the running of her estate, and teasing her like a little girl, even as he urges Troilus' suit. By contrast, Boccaccio's Pandarus is a fellow player to Criseida in the game of love, and they interact as equals in amorous experience and inclination.

Boccaccio's Criseida is also far more urbane than Chaucer's. While Boccaccio's Criseida is also fearful of a besmirched reputation, she is less terrified than Chaucer's. In Boccaccio, she takes Troilus' high status into account as an asset and a problem: noblemen can be notoriously flighty in their liaisons with lesser women. After giving in to love for Troilus, Criseida herself plots their first private assignation, instructing Pandarus on its design rather than having to be tricked into it by him. Later, she will take on Diomedes with the same aplomb. In addition, Boccaccio's version indulges in more ambient misogyny; Pandarus and Troilus both comment cynically on the fickleness of women and the likeliness that Criseida's own appetites will do their work for them. Boccaccio also intimates that Troilus effectively betrays the war effort by falling in love and would be blamed by the king if word got out. By contrast, in Chaucer, Troilus' martial prowess is energized rather than enfeebled by love, and Chaucer removes all the misogynistic asides that litter Boccaccio's text. Finally, while relying on the events of Boccaccio's narrative and translating directly many of Boccaccio's stanzas, Chaucer enormously expands Boccaccio's text, adding to the characters' interior monologues, especially in Books 2, 4, and 5. Where Boccaccio's version was 5,704 lines long, Chaucer's is over 8,246 lines; Chaucer used about 2,730 of Boccaccio lines and the remaining 5,516 are original.

What Chaucer omits from Boccaccio often simplifies the ethical quandaries of Boccaccio's characters and as a result Boccaccio's text is more one-sided than Chaucer's. It is clear his sympathies are with Troilus, whose sorrows at the loss of his lover give voice to Boccaccio's similar sentiments at the absence of his beloved "Filomena." Boccaccio's narrator pleads to Filomena in the preface to the text, "If it comes to pass that you read [these rhymes], as many times as you find Troilus weeping and grieving for the departure of Criseida, that many times you may clearly recognize and know my own cries, tears, sighs, and distresses; and as many times as you find the beauty, the good manners, or any other thing praiseworthy in a lady written of Criseida, that often you can understand them to be spoken of you."[2] Boccaccio's *Il Filostrato,* as its title suggests, is about the man prostrated by love: his confusion and grief. It is less interested in the inner life of the woman. Boccaccio even edits out Criseida's remorse for her unfaithfulness to Troilus; she suffers no self-condemning realization of faithlessness nor its accompanying public infamy, as in Benoît. Conversely, Troilus' laments are transmuted from Benoît's vicious denunciation to helpless pleading. The entire poem invites its dedicatee, Filomena, to avoid Criseida's choice without shaming and condemnation and in the hopes that she will read it, understand, and return. In sum, Boccaccio modulates Benoît's fiercer misogyny into an urbane *Cosi fan tutte*—women are like that—even as he mourns his loss and hopes otherwise.

2. *Il Filostrato,* "Proem," in Geoffrey Chaucer, *Troilus and Criseyde with facing page Il Filostrato,* ed. Stephen A. Barney (New York and London: W. W. Norton, 2006), 7.

Comparing Chaucer's version of the story of Troilus and Criseyde to those of Benoît and Boccaccio enables us to see how Chaucer has complicated his sources. For one, Criseyde is more rounded than Boccaccio's Criseida and receives equal narrative space with Troilus. Where Book 1 is devoted to Troilus' induction into love, Book 2, equally long, details Criseyde's, an expansion of a whole book from three or four stanzas in Boccaccio. Chaucer is less one-sided in another sense as well. Throughout the first three books, Chaucer goes out of his way to show that although Troilus and Criseyde enter love at different tempos and in different situations, they have very similar experiences. They both fear that love will entrap them and endanger their independence. They both undergo a moment of thunderstruck gazing: Troilus is smitten by the sight of Criseyde alone, brilliant in black, standing at the temple, while Criseyde is equally smitten by the sight of Troilus returning flushed and triumphant from the day's battle. They write letters to each other with equal excesses of self-doubt and hope. They each undergo moments both of ecstatic bliss and fainting fear; they are both by turns paralyzed and predatory. Pandarus has to apply force toward each of them to bring them together, whether he is thrusting Troilus' letter into Criseyde's bosom or throwing Troilus bodily into bed with Criseyde. At the same time, Pandarus reaps from these transactions a self-rewarding intimacy, whether the delight of teasing Criseyde as much like a lover as an uncle or that of slipping into Troilus' bed on the morning after to hear how it went. This narrative evenhandedness means that we see Troilus, Criseyde, and Pandarus as characters in process as they move from mood to mood and circumstance to circumstance, struggling to exert control and struggling to give themselves over. When they finally come together in Book 3, the bliss is almost as much the narrator's and reader's as the characters', so effectively has the plot unfolded with the reciprocal intensity of a difficult game of chess.

However, we are not allowed to forget that despite this equivalence of experience, Criseyde has more to lose than Troilus in this liaison. He is the younger son of the king of the city, proven in its defense, and she is a gentle but not noble ward of the state, left fatherless and guilty by association by Calchas' treachery. Troilus has Pandarus in the palm of his hand, who as Criseyde's uncle and friend should by rights be protecting her honor, while Criseyde has only her own self-interest and Pandarus' secondary support. Both the lovers are terrified of the gossip of others, but for different reasons and with very different stakes: Troilus because of his history of public scorn for lovers and Criseyde because of the loss of her honor and reputation. Chaucer also repeatedly ratifies Criseyde's sense of vulnerability. He haunts her surrender to love with shadows of masculine violence, pandering, and rape. He alludes to the Ovidian story of Procne, Philomela, and Tereus. He literalizes Pandarus' ominous name by magnifying his manipulative tricks, such as the false litigation and Troilus' feigned illness, preying on Criseyde's fear and guilt. The moment of Criseyde's internal surrender is figured through the painless but violent dream of the heart-tearing eagle. Even Troilus' inner predator, when he finally catches her up in his arms, is menacing: "What does or can the simple skylark say / Whenas a hawk has clutched it in her foot?" (3.1191–92). In a multitude of ways, then, Chaucer takes the fearful Criseyde from his sources and gives her fearfulness probable cause.

He also intimates a significant corollary: Criseyde must look to those around her for survival; in a very literal sense her life depends on male protectors. Even when she most feels herself her "own woman" (2.750), she relies on Hector and Pandarus for surety and counsel. This ultimate dependence is also realized in her day-to-day existence. In one nuanced exchange after another, Chaucer dramatizes how she fashions herself through interactions with others, taking on roles and seizing cues as she tries to assess her situation. In these ways, Chaucer, unlike his sources, underscores how Criseyde's identity, security, and existence are intrinsically relational. This is a survival strategy, because the poem dramatizes how she is beholden not simply to one person but to many, at every level of her existence.

This relational form of identity keeps Criseyde always receptive to the complexities of her changing public situation in ways that Troilus, as a respected notable of the city, can afford not to be. Troilus takes on the service of love and follows the ideal forms and unswerving faith that *fin amor* dictates to the truly noble at heart, and he never strays from that path. Indeed, Troilus is extraordinary among literary courtly lovers, who are often associated with deception in the service of discretion, and the donning of various amorous masks, because he is virtually incapable of pretense. Criseyde's first question, upon hearing that he loves her is: "And can he speak of love?" (2.503), an allusion to the aristocratic skill of "love-talking" to which only the most elevated courtier could aspire and to the games of love that courtly and noble lovers played. Chaucer gives us a Troilus who can't or won't perform in this way, unlike Gawain in *Sir Gawain and the Green Knight,* or Lancelot, or any number of eminent lovers. He is true to himself almost to a fault, irrespective of his situation. Unlike Criseyde he is not obliged to pay heed to those around him, and thus we feel doubly honored when, throughout the poem, he proves almost faultlessly considerate. Troilus' truth is a luxury that very few people in Chaucer's Troy possess, and Chaucer shows that it is as much a consequence of Troilus' noble, masculine status as it is a virtue. It is also a very costly virtue, as the pathetic unfoldings of Books 4 and 5 underscore. Troilus is as unable to let go as Criseyde is to hold on, and both pay the price of their forms of subjectivity.

These changes to Chaucer's sources raise the ethical stakes when the lovers' situation is changed in Book 4 and when the Trojan War reenters the picture to end their happy, loving idyll. But Chaucer takes his problem even further. Troilus' unswerving love for Criseyde and hers for him are going to be crushed by history, but not history realized in the enormities of the Trojan War or the relentless trajectories of imperial foundation. Instead, their love will founder in the accidents of the everyday. For Criseyde, the situational inducements of life among the Greeks will let Troy and Troilus slide like a knotless string through her heart (5.769) and into oblivion. For Troilus, seeking epic denouements on the battlefield, it is the everyday life in a Troy without Criseyde that wears him down. Yet Criseyde's strategies of adaptation among the Greeks are precisely similar to those she deployed in Troy, under the blandishments of Pandarus and Troilus, when she left her identity as a widow of her husband and became Troilus' lover. To read her as a true woman in Troy but false when she delivers her heart to Diomedes is to ignore the continuities of endangerment and adaptation that Chaucer adds to his narrative. Conversely, to read Troilus as victimized by Criseyde's treachery and wholly vindicated by his helpless, self-brutalizing fidelity is to ignore all the intimations of amorous predation with which Chaucer associates him while he is wooing Criseyde, especially his deployment of Pandarus.

Why does Chaucer complicate in these ways the outbursts against feminine fickleness and masculine heartbreak that preoccupy his sources? Even more fundamentally, why does he choose this gender-polarizing tale, of all the possible tales he could reinvent? For 200 years the story of Troilus and Briseida/Criseida/Criseyde had been deployed as a case instance in a literary tradition of feminine changeability and masculine constancy. However, by dimensionalizing his characters over a long, sinuous narration, plumbing their thoughts, interactions, inconsistent reactions to changing circumstances, and strange choices, Chaucer charges them with a psychological realism rooted in relational process rather than character type. Chaucer invites us to see Troilus, Pandarus, and Criseyde in the exigencies of their means, rather than the summations of their ends. In so doing Chaucer implicates the strategies of reduction, division, and elision that render judgment possible at all.

CRISEYDE ON TRIAL—AND THE ENDINGS

An analogy: at the end of a long court trial in which a jury has heard cases presented by the prosecution and the defense and a series of witnesses cross-examined by opposing counsels, it is common for the judge to offer his or her summation of the evidence. This will be a statement, selecting the parts of the trial that seemed to the experienced judge to weigh most heavily. This summation is energizing. It filters the welter of evidence through the judge's legal expertise and helps the jury to come to an agreement on their decision. Yet different judges might have different summations—there might be minority reports and dissenting judgments. The possibility of appealing a case through different courts acknowledges this. Any verdict, therefore, is a product of filtering, privileging, and erasure of evidence. The accused and the accuser can only hope that these elisions are judicious because after the verdict is given and the sentence pronounced, the evidence is irrelevant unless the case is reopened. This forensic analogy helps pinpoint what Chaucer is facing when he takes up the polarized story of Troilus and Criseyde—a story that culminates in a judgment against women's fickleness in love or a vindication of men's truth in love.

However, Chaucer committed a poem, not a crime. Should a poem be reduced to its message? In Book 2, while drawing out Criseyde's curiosity about her as-yet-unknown admirer, Pandarus meditates on how the import of stories outweighs the bulk of what happens in them:

> "Although a kind of carping men delight
> To complicate their tales with arts and sleights,
> For all of that their constant aim, you'll find
> Is to advance some point they have in mind.
>
> "But since the end is every story's strength
> And since what I must say is for the good,
> Why should I paint or draw it out at length
> To such a friend? No, God forbid I should!"   (2.256–63)

Pandarus' literary sententiousness is comic here because it is self-implicating. He is perorating against exactly what he is doing—complicating his tale with arts and sleights, in the service of an ulterior motive, to whet Criseyde's interest. While Chaucer often uses Pandarus to explore the delights and world-shaping potency of fiction-making, here the rhetoric of reducing a tale to its point or reading a story through its ending amounts to an exposure. The real agenda has to be stripped of its cloaking arts and sleights and

emerge naked to the light of day. In the process, the story itself, recharac-
terized as decoration, dwindles to a message or agenda, its "constant aim"
(2.258). The only problem with this is that it destroys the tale by rendering
it a mere vehicle for some kernel of truth or intention that lurks within it.
Furthermore, any thought that does not conduce toward judgment and a
final closing of the case is rendered irrelevant. In fact, once the meaning
is extracted, the reader does not have to think further about the tale at all.

The question then becomes: Is Chaucer a storyteller like Pandarus? Is he
also trying to beguile, seduce, and trick us for mysterious and sinister ends
of his own? It is possible. Later, when he writes himself into the General
Prologue of the *Canterbury Tales,* Chaucer the pilgrim will group himself
with the clever swindlers, fixers, and middlemen. It is as though he raises
our suspicions to provoke us to try to see through his tales to the self-serv-
ing agendas we infer. However, it is equally possible that Chaucer plots this
way in order to raise consciousness about the reader's own judicial habits of
inferring, judging, and interpreting. He might be operating less like a con
artist and more like an agent provocateur. He invites suspicion and then
makes us look hard at what we suspect. *Troilus and Criseyde* for most of its
length seems to disarm judgment and instead work to provoke sympathy,
bemusement, philosophical reflection, and a sense of the might-have-been
that exceeds the tale's actual end. *Troilus and Criseyde* begs, in short, to be
read beyond and even against its ending.

When Chaucer fills his last book with the problems of reducing a tale to
an end, he restages for literature the poem's larger philosophical questions
concerning how choice and fate—or freedom and necessity, or human free
will and divine predetermination—can exist in the same universe. Troilus
is the one who asks this Boethian question most persistently, and Book 4
(lines 969–1088) is where it emerges most clearly. There, Troilus concludes
fatalistically and prematurely that fate trumps human choice, and he and
Criseyde accept the parliamentary decree for her departure. By dedicat-
ing Book 5 to the three implacable Fates, Chaucer makes the final book a
last stand for the question and he does it by exploiting the reading process
itself. From the beginning of the poem we have known that Criseyde will
prove untrue and Troilus will die of love. However, by every means the
narrator can assemble, we are persuaded to ignore that end and not view
the lovers deterministically as we read the poem. If the reader starts cas-
tigating Criseyde in Book 2, he or she will miss a great deal that Chaucer
goes out of his way to describe in his text. In Book 5, in a series of pain-
ful devolutions, Troilus pays the cost of paying too much heed to endings
when he deterministically re-envisions his past love exclusively through
its ending, and the devastating look backward finally destroys him. The

narrator himself seems to refrain from this in any way he can, inviting the reader to do the same. In a sense the reader has to try to forget the ending temporarily in order to experience the poem, and our inability to accomplish that completely creates the poem's most protracted narrative tension.

The narrator plays with the tension between narrative process and narrative conclusion when he repositions the character sketches of Diomedes, Criseyde, and Troilus not at the beginning of his tale, as in his sources, but at the poem's end (5.799–840). There the portraits seem inadequate and alienating, especially when weighed against the wealth of complicated insight we have already gleaned from the preceding narration. Are we meant to take these sketches as definitive because they come late, like verdicts, or trust our own previous experiences of the poem, or consider them simultaneously?

The need to question the predeterministic force of judgments and endings may even have been why Chaucer was drawn to such a misogynist story in the first place: he was rising to a challenge. When Criseyde achieves the unhappy prescience of her prophet/traitor father in Book 5, she envisions a future devoid of literary sympathy.

> "Alas, of me, until the world shall end,
> There never shall be written now or sung
> A kindly word. No author will defend
> One whose faults are rolled on every tongue."   (5.1058–61).

These lines are lifted from Briseida's self-condemnation in Benoît; they are nowhere to be found in Boccaccio. It is as though Chaucer read Benoît and the misogyny of his other sources and took those words as a challenge. Could a kindly word be written of Criseyde? Has Chaucer defended one whose faults are rolled on every tongue?

According to Robert Henryson, perhaps Chaucer defended Criseyde far too much. Henryson was a fifteenth-century Scottish poet who rewrote Chaucer as thoroughly as Chaucer rewrote Boccaccio. Henryson's *Testament of Cresseid* treats Chaucer's Book 5. Cresseid has been abandoned by Diomedes (Henryson gives the name as *Diomeid*) and become a prostitute. She outrages the gods by blaming them for her misfortunes, and they punish her by giving her leprosy. Begging in a leper colony outside Troy and blinded by the disease, she has a last unwitting encounter with Troilus when he rides from the city and is transfixed by her ruined face, which reminds him of his lost love. In Cresseid's memory he plies her with all the gold he is wearing and staggers sadly back into the city. Informed by her leper companions that noble Troilus gave her the gold, repentance finally strikes Cresseid and she realizes the true magnitude of her betrayal. Willing one last artifact to Troilus, a ring he had given her as a love token, she dies. Troilus recognizes the ring and builds her a beautiful tomb on which her epitaph stands as a warning to other women: "Here, fair ladies, Cresseid from the town of Troy, / At one time counted the flower of womanhood, / Under this stone, formerly a leper, now lies dead" (607–9).[3]

This is conclusion with a vengeance. Henryson's *Testament of Cresseid* completes the punishment that Chaucer refused to allot his heroine, with the added sting of prostitution, disease, blindness, death, repentance, and Troilus' distant pity. In sum, Henryson, who may have studied law as well as written poetry, reads beyond Chaucer's ending in order to make a more just ending. But is putting Criseyde on trial a distraction from the poem's deeper inquisitions? What would it mean to read beyond Chaucer's ending, not to end him but to pursue the questions his poem opens: to take the ending as a beginning? Troilus, leaving the world in his flight to the utmost sphere, laughs derisively at those who mourn him and, dying from love, scorns love just as he did in the temple at the Palladium, the first moment he entered the poem. Troilus' laugh returns him to his beginnings, even as he meets his ultimate fate. What else might be worth swerving aside from conclusions to reconsider—in the poem's long investigation of the processes of loving Criseyde and loving Troilus, along with the opportunistic interchanges, affectionate friendships, and exquisite readerly pleasures of the brittle, fated world of Troy? Read it and see.

---

3. Robert Henryson, *The Testament of Cresseid,* in *The Poems of Robert Henryson,* ed. Robert L. Kindrick (Kalamazoo, MI: Medieval Institute Publications, 1997). My translation.

Translator's Preface

I have always thought Chaucer's *Troilus and Criseyde* was a cracking good story, and it is. But it helps to gain a bit of perspective on things. In the course of making this translation I looked more closely at Chaucer's originals and what he made of them, and the differences throw his characteristic excellences into high relief. Two of his sources are plodding hack jobs—the *Journal of the Trojan War* by Dictys of Crete and the *History of the Destruction of Troy* by Dares the Phrygian—a pair of works that Chaucer may have known from a later, equally heavy-footed compilation in Latin, the *Iliad of Dares the Phrygian* by Joseph of Exeter. He used these books chiefly for background; none mentions the love affair between Troilus and Criseyde or the machinations of Pandarus, their enigmatic go-between.

For that story, Chaucer turned mainly to a very different source, Giovanni Boccaccio's suave and elegant Italian *Il Filostrato* (very roughly, *The Fellow Flattened by Love*); and here the comparisons become so useful that I've dropped footnotes throughout the translation to call attention to Chaucer's major departures.[1] There are a lot of them. Enough, in fact, to amount to a whole new treatment of the story. Steven Barney estimates that more than 5,500 lines of *Troilus and Criseyde*—two-thirds of the whole—are original to Chaucer.[2]

It's generally not hard to see when Chaucer is being Chaucer. The poem as we have it in Middle English is crisscrossed with his tracks, even when he's following *Il Filostrato* rather closely. For instance, he is immeasurably more pithy and concrete than Boccaccio. Where the smooth Italian has his Troilio regretfully muse, ". . . now you are caught in the snare which you

---

1. Like Shakespeare, Chaucer absorbed influences from everywhere. His other sources for *Troilus and Criseyde* were the *Roman de Troie* by Benoît de Sainte-Maure in French and a Latin translation of that work, the *Historia Destructionis Troiae* by Guido delle Colonne. But while he took several details from Benoît and Guido, he tellingly left behind their misogynistic remarks. See Barry Windeatt, *Troilus and Criseyde,* Oxford Guides to Chaucer (Oxford: Clarendon Press, 1992), 77–96.

2. Geoffrey Chaucer, *Troilus and Criseyde,* ed. Stephen A. Barney (New York and London: W. W. Norton, 2006), x.

xxxii   Translator's Preface

blamed others so much for being caught in,"³ Chaucer's Troilus growls, "Now you are caught. Now gnaw upon your chain" (1.509).

By the time he wrote *Troilus and Criseyde,* Chaucer's style was fully developed. He lards passages with homely sayings like "The [bear] leader may think one thing for his share; / 'But that won't make it happen,' says the bear" (4.1453–54). He embroiders his narratives with birds and beasts, including the memorable exemplum of Bayard the proud horse (1.218–24). He lets Pandarus call Troilus "fool" (1.618), "thief" (1.870), and "mouse's heart" (3.736), expressions Boccaccio would never allow. He stretches out the imaginative world of his sources in every direction, adding dawn songs, shifting seasons, gardens, nightingales, star lore, dream theory, thunderous rain, bedclothes, gutters, and over a hundred lines of muddled Boethian philosophy (4.958–1078)—to say nothing of the ancient history of Thebes and Troilus' Dantean final vision of the world from outer space (5.1807–25). And without apparent effort he finds the right style—grammar, words, images, and rhythms—to suit every change of matter.

"Beyond these harsh black waters as we sail, / Wind, O wind! The weather starts to clear" (2.1–2), he apostrophizes, echoing Dante in the epic mode. "Good Uncle, for God's love, hear me I pray, / . . . Come, sir! Now tell me what it is!" (2.309–10), begs Criseyde like the girl next door. "The swallow Procne, with her doleful lay, / When morning came bewailed her fate again" (2.64–65), sighs the narrator, remembering Ovid and the old myth of the nightingale. "No one but an infidel," Troilus reasons doggedly, "would hold / The present shapes what God has known of old" (4.1063–64).

Brief examples abound. Things go well during Criseyde's initial visit to Pandarus' house, and Chaucer's touch is suitably light:

> And after supper all of them arose
> At ease and well. Their hearts were fresh and gay.
> And lucky was the man who could propose
> A pleasing game or make her laugh some way.
> He sang; she played. He chattered like a jay.   (3.610–14)

But when the ladies are ready to go home, fate intervenes and the narrator shifts to a heroic or perhaps mock-heroic tone:

> O Fortune, skillful servant of the Fates!
> Divine influence from the heavens high!
> Under God, you rule us in all straits.   (3.617–19)

---

3. Barney edition, p. 36.

Then suddenly we're swept outside among the indifferent elements;

> The sickle moon in Cancer, slim and pale,
> With Jupiter and Saturn there as well,
> Caused such a rain from heaven now to hail,
> That every woman quailed, the truth to tell.
> They feared that smoking rain as they feared hell.   (3.624–28)

When Pandarus urges his niece to stay overnight, she thinks to herself in downright terms, "I'd rather be inside than wet out there" (3.641). But she answers him with studied and somewhat dishonest politeness, "I will, . . . my loving uncle dear. / Because you wish it, sir, it shall be so" (3.645–46).

At least five shifts of style, some quite subtle, in thirty-five lines! And other examples look out at us from almost every page. I doubt I did full justice to Chaucer's astonishingly lively and spot-on flying changes, but it was great fun to try.

Dealing with Chaucer's characters, notably Criseyde and Pandarus, was an even bigger challenge and again our options are defined largely by style and language, for the plot and setting of the story were already fixed in Boccaccio.[4] Naive, generally well-meaning Troilus may be a case of what you see is what you get, but Chaucer makes his other two principles as hard to pin down as anyone in literature. Is Criseyde the same tough-minded realist she was in Boccaccio? Sometimes it seems so. Everyone swears in *Troilus and Criseyde,* but Criseyde swears by far the most—somewhere in almost every early speech—and she never invokes God in any other way. She never even tries to seem religious.

> What shall I do? Why live as I have done?
> Shall I not love if that would please me best?
> I know, by God, that I am not a nun.   (2.757–59)

At other times, though, she seems vacillating and weak, too vulnerable to hold out against Pandarus' schemes. She was "slydynge of corage" (5.825, n. 33) we learn, an untranslatable phrase for *irresolute;* and the narrator tells us, "There was no more fretful lady in the town" (2.450).

And yet Chaucer often lets her seem to be genuinely dominated by her love of Troilus.

---

4. A notable exception to this is the lovers' meetings, which take place at Criseyde's house in Boccaccio but which Chaucer for his own reasons moves to Pandarus' house.

And like the newly startled nightingale,
Who stops her sound when she begins to sing,
If she should hear a shepherd in the dale,
Or among the hedges any noisy thing,
But once secure, then lets her sweet voice ring,
Right so Criseyde, free of dread and care,
Opened her heart and showed him what was there.   (3.1233–39)

"Had I not already, sweetheart dear, / Been yielded up," she says to Troilus at their first secret meeting, "I never would be here" (3.1210–11). And for the moment we believe her. It's only later that we wonder how that confession squares with her claims to know nothing of Pandarus' plans for that night.

Pandarus himself is more slippery yet. What to make of him? His cleverness and fluency are unmistakable and must come through in any acceptable translation. He can improvise his way around anything and speak in as many registers as Chaucer himself, but what is he trying to accomplish? He's been called a true friend, a pragmatic fixer, a benevolent meddler, a closet homosexual, a suck-up, a voyeur, and a would-be puppeteer who stage manages his friends' lives just because he can, or because he's jealous of them, or because he wants to feel superior, or . . . and on and on.

What's actually happening when he climbs in bed with Troilus or in that edgy morning-after scene when he twitches aside naked Criseyde's bed sheet and embraces her? Where is he and what is he doing when the lovers are making love for the first time? One thing is sure: Chaucer won't tell us. Just after the sheet-lifting scene, while we're still wondering what it is we just witnessed, he has his narrator remark: "I pass all that which I've no need to say" (3.1576), and pass on he does, here and elsewhere.

I've tried to preserve the wonderful darts and swerves of Chaucer's writing and the stubborn open-endedness of his characters because variety and open-endedness seem to me to be the essence of his art. As John Dryden famously remarked, discussing the range of pilgrims we meet in the *Canterbury Tales,* "there is such a variety of game springing up before me, that I am distracted in my choice, and know not what to follow. It is sufficient to say, according to the proverb, that here is God's plenty."[5]

Another notable feature of Chaucer's style that I've kept as well as I could is the seven-line, iambic pentameter rhyme royal stanza he invented, probably on the model of the eight-line ottava rima stanza Boccaccio employed in *Il Filostrato.* Though Chaucer had used this form before, in

---

5. Preface to the *Fables Ancient and Modern.*

"The Second Nun's Tale" and *The Parliament of Fowls,* it is most closely identified with *Troilus and Criseyde,* and has even been called the "Troilus stanza." It's a fine and flexible instrument, capable as we have seen of a wide range of effects. The interlocking rhymes—a, b, a, b, b—can work together to play off against the final couplet—c, c—but Chaucer more often divides them. He has a tendency (a weak one, it must be admitted) to come to a full stop after the first four lines; then the final three can become a unit or the fifth line can stand by itself, summing up the quatrain before giving way to a new departure in the couplet. This is what happens in the first stanza of the poem, which in this sense is as close to a typical Troilus stanza as Chaucer gets:

> Of Troilus' double sorrow I shall tell—
> Troilus, son of Priam, Troy's chief lord—
> In loving, how that knight's adventures fell
> From woe to weal, then back into discord.
> Before we part, I'll show all that occurred.
> Tisiphone, I ask you, help me to indite
> These woeful verses, weeping as I write.   (1.1–7)

But it would be quite wrong to suggest that Chaucer writes to a formula in versification any more than he does in any other facet of his work. He loves to take a known form—Boccaccio's traditional story of unfortunate lovers or the rhyme royal stanza—and spin it in unexpected and sometimes distinctly odd directions. If my version of the tale leaves you wondering about the meaning of it all, bemused and somewhat disoriented, then I've done at least part of my job as translator.

Suggestions for Further Reading

Benson, C. David, ed., *Critical Essays on Chaucer's* Troilus and Criseyde *and his major early poems* (Toronto; Buffalo: University of Toronto Press, 1991).

Chaucer, Geoffrey, *Troilus and Criseyde, with facing page Il Filostrato,* ed. Stephen A. Barney (New York: W. W. Norton, 2006).

Donaldson, E. Talbot, "The Ending of Troilus," in *Early English and Norse Studies Presented to Hugh Smith,* ed. Arthur Brown and Peter Foote (London: Methuen, 1963): 26–45.

Federico, Sylvia, *New Troy: Fantasies of Empire in the Late Middle Ages* (Minneapolis: University of Minnesota Press, 2003).

Gordon, R. K., ed., *The Story of Troilus* (Toronto: The University of Toronto Press, 1978).

Green, Richard Firth, "Troilus and the Game of Love," *Chaucer Review* 13 (1979): 201–20.

Lewis, C. S., "What Chaucer Really Did to *Il Filostrato,*" *Essays and Studies* 17 (1932): 56–75.

Mooney, Linne R., and Stubbs, Estelle, *Scribes and the City: London Guildhall Clerks and the Dissemination of Middle English Literature: 1375–1425* (York: York Medieval Press, 2013).

Nolan, Barbara, *Chaucer and the Tradition of the* Roman Antique (Cambridge, UK: Cambridge University Press, 1992).

Nuttall, Jenni, *Troilus and Criseyde: A Reader's Guide* (Cambridge, UK: Cambridge University Press, 2012).

Patterson, Lee, "Troilus and Criseyde and the Subject of History," in *Chaucer and the Subject of History* (Madison, WI: University of Wisconsin Press, 1991): 84–164.

Pugh, Tison, and Smith Marzec, Marcia, ed., *Men and Masculinities in Chaucer's* Troilus and Criseyde (Woodbridge, UK: D. S. Brewer, 2008).

Schultz, James A., *Courtly Love, The Courtliness, and the History of Sexuality* (Chicago and London: University of Chicago Press, 2006).

Shoaf, R. A., ed., *Chaucer's* Troilus and Criseyde: *Subjit to alle poesye: Essays in Criticism* (Binghamton, NY: Medieval and Renaissance Texts and Studies, 1992).

Strohm, Paul, *Social Chaucer* (Cambridge, MA; London: Harvard University Press, 1989).

Vitto, Cindy L., and Smith Marzec, Marcia, ed., *New Perspectives on Criseyde* (Asheville, NC: Pegasus Press, 2004).

Windeatt, Barry, *Troilus and Crisyede,* Oxford Guides to Chaucer (Oxford: Clarendon Press, 1992).

Troilus and Criseyde

BOOK I

Of Troilus'[1] double sorrow I shall tell—[2]
Troilus, son of Priam, Troy's chief lord—
In loving, how that knight's adventures fell
From woe to weal, then back into discord.
Before we part, I'll show all that occurred.
Tisiphone,[3] I ask you, help me to indite   *a Fury in classical myth, but*
These woeful verses, weeping as I write.   *here treated as Chaucer's muse*

I call to you, you goddess of torment,
You cruel Fury, sorrowing in pain,
Aid me as the mournful instrument   10
Who helps such lovers as I can complain.
For it sits well—this truth must be plain—
A woeful soul should have a dreary mate,
And heavy minds should heavy tales relate.

For I who serve Love's servants[4] must admit
I dare not love for my unlikeliness,
But pray for love, though death should come with it,
So dark I am, and helpless, I confess.
Yet if this tale brings gladness, nonetheless,
To any lover, and his cause avail,   20
Give Love the thanks, and mine be the travail.

---

1. Chaucer sometimes makes the name two syllables (*TROY-lus*), sometimes three
(*TROY-a-lus*).

2. This and the following seven stanzas (through line 56) do not appear in
Boccaccio, who writes a much different introduction to his own ladylove, saying
she is his muse.

3. *Ti-SIF-o-nee*. In *Il Filostrato*, Boccaccio invokes his lady as his muse, so this
address to Tisiphone and the narrator's pose as one who has no lady himself are
Chaucer's additions.

4. Here Chaucer echoes the traditional description of the Catholic pope as *servus
servorum Dei*, the servant of the servants of God. That lovers belonged to the
religion of Cupid, the god of love, was a poetic convention of Chaucer's day.

And now, you lovers bathed in happiness,[5]
If you've one drop of pity in your veins,
Remember all the times of heaviness
You suffered through, and others' cruel pains.
Recall the doubts you felt in love's campaigns:
How Love at times has chosen to displease you,
Or other times has seemed too quick to ease you.

And pray for those who languish in the case
Of Troilus, as you afterward will hear,   30
That Love may grant them heaven and his grace.
Then pray for me, as well, to God so dear,
To give me power to show in some form here
Such pain and woe as Love's true servants bear
In Troilus' sorry lot and doleful care.

And pray alike for those who have despaired—
Those loving souls who never will go free—
And those as well who falsely were aspersed
By wicked tongues wagged by some he or she;
Pray God may give them for His charity   40
An early exit from this worldly race,
Who've lost all hope of winning love and grace.

Next, pray for lovers who are now at ease
That God may grant their love will not decay,
And send them might their ladies so to please
That Love gains power and pleasure in that way.
As I hope too to win what grace I may,
I pray for them who Love's true servants be—
And write their woes, and live in charity,

And offer them approval and compassion   50
As if I were their own good brother dear.
But listen to me now with good attention,
As I pass straight on to my subject here,
In which you will the double sorrows hear

_____

5. This and the next three stanzas recall the part of the Catholic Mass in which
the celebrant asks the congregation to pray for various people or causes.

Of Troilus—though his love was not denied—
And how Criseyde[6] spurned him ere she died.

It's widely known the angry Greeks, Troy's bane,
Took arms and with a thousand warships went
To break that city through a long campaign.
For near ten years they fought there as they spent   60
Their wrath in diverse ways with one intent:
To win revenge for Helen's late abduction;
They spared no pains to punish that seduction.[7]

It so fell out that living at that time
Was Calchas,[8] lord of great authority,
Troy's greatest seer, a prophet and divine
Whose knowledge was so deeply laid that he
Knew Troy would be destroyed by fate's decree.
He learned this from his god, whom men named thus:
Lord Phoebus, or Apollo Delphicus.   *i.e., of Delphi*

When Calchas knew this through his calculations,
And when his lord Apollo had revealed
The Greeks should bring such force against his nation
That they would drive the Trojans from the field,
He sought a way to quit the town concealed.
His divinations showed in every way
That Troy must fall, whatever men might say.

And so he slipped outside Troy's walls unknown—
As was his purpose, this foreknowing seer—
And to the Greek encampment, quite alone,   80
He made his way. The men there made him cheer.
They rushed to do him honor, held him dear,
For they hoped such a cunning man could say
In each new trial where their advantage lay.

---

6. Chaucer's pronunciation: *Cra-SAY-da*.

7. Helen of Troy, the wife of Menelaus of Sparta, brother of King Agamemnon, the chief of the Greek expedition. Her elopement with Paris, a Trojan prince, brought on the Trojan War.

8. *KAL-kus*. In the *Iliad*, Calchas is a Greek, but Chaucer and Boccaccio follow a medieval tradition making him a Trojan.

The noise rose up when this was apprehended.
Throughout all Troy the news was widely spread:
Their prophet had turned traitor and befriended
The men of Greece. Then furious Trojans said
That they would soon avenge the faith he'd shed,
Proclaiming he and all his kin at once   90
Deserved no less than burning, skin and bones.

Now Calchas left behind him when he fled,
Unknowing of his false and wicked deed,
His widowed daughter, who was cast in dread,
And fearful for her very life indeed.
She hardly knew what course would serve her need,
Left as she was sequestered and afraid,
Without a friend whom she could ask for aid.[9]

Criseyde was this ill-placed lady's name.[10]
If I may judge, in all the town of Troy   100
She was the fairest woman known to fame.
So angel-like she looked, to all men's joy,
She seemed a thing immortal, unalloyed,
As if she were a creature from above
Sent down in scorn our nature to reprove.

All day this lady heard what people said—
Her father's shame, his treason to the town—
Well nigh beside herself for woe and dread
In a silken widow's habit long and brown,[11]
She came before Prince Hector[12] and knelt down,   110
And with a piteous voice and sobs and tears
Excused herself and told the prince her fears.

---

9. While Chaucer makes a point of Criseyde's isolation, his own text mentions she is befriended by her uncle Pandarus and her three nieces, named in Book 2, line 816.

10. Boccaccio's name for her. Earlier texts had called her Briseida.

11. Criseyde's brown habit is Chaucer's idea, perhaps required by the rhyme. Boccaccio merely says her dress was *dolente,* or sorrowful. In line 170 and later her mourning clothes are black.

12. Troy's greatest hero. Oldest son of Hecuba and King Priam and therefore Troilus' full brother. A notably good man in all accounts of the Trojan War.

This Hector was a man of gentle mind.
He saw that she was sorrowfully beset,
And how she was a creature fair and fine.
To cheer her, he made little of the threat
But said, "Now may your father's treason yet
Meet with misfortune, but you yourself with joy.
Dwell here with us, as you may wish, in Troy.

"What honor men may give or that they gave you   120
While your father lived among us here,
You shall have, and men to guard your life too,
As far as I can make my wishes clear."
She thanked him with a modest, lowly cheer
(And would have thanked him more if he had let her)
And took her leave for home, his grateful debtor.

There, she maintained the least establishment
That fit her honor—less she could not hold—
And while she lived in Troy, opinion went,
She kept her house so that to young and old   130
She was beloved, and good of her was told.
But whether she had children or had not
I never read, and so I tell you naught.[13]

Meanwhile, things fell as things fall out in war
Between the Trojans and the Greeks full oft.
Sometimes the Trojan army's pains were sore,
But then the Greeks would find them far from soft,
Those men of Troy. Thus fortune reared aloft
And then plunged down both armies on her wheel,[14]
As is her way, while they went raging still.   140

But how the town at last came to destruction[15]
It doesn't suit my purpose here to tell
For that would raise a needless, long obstruction
Within my tale—and waste your time as well.

---

13. A strange passage. Boccaccio and Benoît both state that Criseyde was childless.
14. Dame Fortune's turning wheel is a constant medieval theme.
15. This stanza does not appear in Boccaccio.

You'll find the full account of how Troy fell
In Homer and Dares and Dictys[16] written down.
Let those who can, read there about the town.

Yet though the Greek invaders shut them in,
Besieged the walls and ranged the plains about,
The Trojans kept their customs as they'd been;   150
To honor their old gods they were devout.
And foremost in their care, without a doubt,
They kept a holy relic called Palladium,[17]
Revered above their others, all and some.

And so it happened at the pleasant time
Of April, when the fields are softly spread
With new green leaves, the mark of lusty Prime,   *spring*
And sweetly smelling flowers of white and red,
In sundry ways the Trojans, as I've read,
Kept their observance as they'd always done,   160
And held their solemn feast of the Palladium.

Thus to the temple, clad in all their best
The people went in crowds as well they might
To hear Palladium's service with the rest,
Namely many a handsome, lusty knight
And many a lady fresh and maiden bright,
All well arrayed from great ones to the least
In keeping with the season and the feast.

Among the other folk there came Criseyde,
Wearing widow's black, but nonetheless,   170

---

16. The *Iliad*, of course, stops short of the fall of Troy. Dares Phrygius (*DAR-eez*) and Dictys Cretensis (*DIC-tees*) were purportedly present during the Trojan campaign and wrote firsthand histories of the war. While no one today regards them as authoritative, their accounts, translated into Latin in the fifth or sixth century, were taken seriously and often cited during the Middle Ages.

17. As long as Troy held the Palladium, a wooden statue associated with Athena, the city could not be taken. Diomedes and Odysseus later carried it off to open the way to the final Greek victory. Chaucer isn't entirely clear on this matter, speaking in line 164 almost as if the Palladium were Athena herself.

As surely as our letters start with *A,*[18]
She was the foremost beauty in the press.
She gladdened every heart above the rest.
For she was praised as others seldom are:
No blackness might obscure so bright a star

As Criseyde was, and so said everyone
Who saw her shining, black robed, in her place;
And yet she stood there humbly and alone
Behind the others in a little space
Beside the door as if she feared disgrace.   180
But though her dress was plain, she bore an air
As gentle and assured as any there.

This Troilus, as his custom was no doubt,
Led his troop of young knights up and down
Through that large temple, looking all about,
Beholding all the women of the town,
Now here, now there, for he was not yet bound
To any lady there, to spoil his rest,
But free to praise or fault as he thought best.

And as he walked, the prince was quite aware   190
If any knight or squire as they came nigh
Began to sigh, or pause and closely stare
At any woman as he passed nearby.
If so, the prince would smile and hold it vain,
And tell the man, "God knows, she sleeps full soft
For love of you, while you lie turning oft!

"I have been told, by God, from the beginning,
Of lovers and your foolish superstition,
How earnestly you drive yourselves in winning
Your loves, yet hold them in suspicion,   200
And when the prey is lost, woe and perdition!

---

18. Pronounced "ah," as in modern German. This reference may serve in part as
a compliment to Queen Anne of Bohemia, whom Richard II married in 1382,
about the time Chaucer was working on *Troilus and Criseyde.* It does not appear
in Boccaccio.

No fool like you can see beyond his nose
Or learn to rule himself from others' woes!"

And with those words the prince raised up his brow
As if he thought, "Now, that was wisely said!"
At which the god of love began to scowl.
He felt despised. And as his anger spread
He showed his bow was still a thing to dread.
He shot and hit the prince, and not by luck—
No peacock lives that Cupid cannot pluck.   210

Unseeing world! O uninformed intention!
How many cursed effects flow from displays
Of vanity and overblown pretension.
The proud are caught; the coxcomb always pays.
This Troilus had climbed up the stair a way,
And little thought that he would ever sink—
But every day upends what such fools think.

See proud Bayard[19] begin to buck and skip   *traditional name for horses*
Out of the way, when pricked on by his feed,
Until he has a lash of the long whip.   220
Then he must think: "Though I prance in the lead,
First in the traces, fat and sleek indeed,
Yet I am but a horse, and horses' law
I must endure and with my fellows draw."

So fared it with this fierce and noble knight.
Though he was son to a most worthy king
And thought that nothing earthly had the might,
Against his will, to make his proud heart sting,
A chance look left his heart a flaming thing,
So he who had gone so proud and far above   230
Became at once the most enslaved to love.

And therefore take example of this man
You wise ones, proud and worthy though you be,

---

19. *BY-ard.* Well-bred horses were expected to be proud and willful. This Bayard reference and the following six stanzas (through line 266) do not appear in Boccaccio.

Scorn earthly love, for as you see it can
Enthrall your hearts and never set them free,
For it has been and it will ever be
That Love is he who everything can bind.
No living man can rise above his kind!

All stories show this true, and it is yet;
For I believe each one among you knows,   240
As we may read, no men had greater wit
Than those most deeply snared in lovers' throes.
The strongest have succumbed as learning shows,
The worthiest and greatest of degree.
This was and will be too,[20] as men shall see.

And truly it sits well that it is so.
The wisest men have loved and love has pleased them,
And those who suffered in love's deepest woe
Have felt its comfort most when love has eased them.
For love may warm cruel hearts and so appease them,   250
And worthy folk grow worthier of fame
Because love makes them dread all vice and shame.

And since love is so mighty and profound
And such a thing of virtue in its kind,
Do not refuse it. Let yourself be bound,
For anyone he wishes, Love can bind.
That branch is best that bows before the wind
While others break, and so I say take heed
And gladly follow Love, so fit to lead.

But now to tell you plainly as I planned   260
Of this king's son whose tale I have begun
I'll leave all other matters if I can.
(I mean to sift him fully ere I'm done;
His coldest cares and every joy he won,
And all his works I'll set out here, I vow.
That was my tale. Let me resume it now.)

---

20. This phrase echoes the "*Gloria Patri*," or "Glory Be," a well-known prayer used in Catholic rituals.

Within the temple as he went lighthearted,
This Troilus, mid the ladies all about,
On this one first then that his glances darted,
Ladies of the city, or without.   270
But then it chanced that piercing through the rout,
His eye shot in so far until it dropped,
Upon Criseyde's form, and there it stopped.

He suddenly was struck as by a spell.[21]
He watched her, but aslant, as one who spies.
"O God," he thought, "Where could this marvel dwell,
So fair a lady, such a goodly prize?"
With that his heart began to spread and rise.
He sighed, yet softly, lest his friends might hear,
But then took up again his mocking cheer.   280

Criseyde overtopped most ladies there,[22]
But she was made so finely, formed so true—
Just as a woman should be—that nowhere
Was anyone less mannish to the view.
Her modest, graceful movements promised too
That in her men might find all that was best:
As honor, high estate, and nobleness.

Now Troilus like the rest was firmly caught;
He relished both her movements and her cheer,
Which seemed a little haughty as she shot   290
A sidelong glance his way, discreet but clear,
As if to say, "What? May I not stand here?"
But then her aspect grew a bit more light.
He thought he'd never seen so fair a sight.

And with her glance, in him began to race[23]
So great desire and such a warm affection
His stricken, inmost heart soon made a place
For that fine face, a fixed and deep impression.[24]

---

21. This stanza does not appear in Boccaccio.

22. Boccaccio says she was tall.

23. This stanza does not appear in Boccaccio.

24. A common observation: the image of the loved one is imprinted in the lover's heart.

He'd looked her up and down, an indiscretion;
Now he was glad to let his horns retract,[25]   300
Scarce knowing where to turn or how to act.

Lo, how the man who thought himself so cunning,
And scorned all those who breathed love's pain in sighs,
Was unaware the love that he was shunning
Lived in those subtle glances of her eyes.
Now suddenly he felt as one who dies.
Her glances quelled the spirit in his heart.
Ah, blest be Love and his transforming art!

She, the one in black, whom Troilus now
Esteemed above them all, he *must* behold.   310
Yet what hunger held him there or how
He felt could not be shown or much less told;
So from afar, as if he still were bold,
He gazed at other things as in the past,
But every look returned to her at last.

Later, not yet knowing all his plight,
He left the temple, musing as he went—
Regretting that he had ever made light
Of loving folk. He feared that this event
Might cast his scorn back on him. What he meant,   320
Lest those should know who followed at his side,
He kept within as something he must hide.

And going from the temple as he'd started
He made his way directly to his palace.
Though pierced by that transfixing look she'd darted,
He made himself act cheerful nonetheless
And shaped his looks and speaking for the best,
Deriding Love's sad servants all the while
To hide himself behind his former style.

He said, "Lord, how you live among the blest,[26]   330
You lovers! For the wisest of you yet

25. The comparison is to a snail that meets some obstacle.
26. This and the following three stanzas do not appear in Boccaccio.

Who serves Love most attentively and best,
Wins harm as soon as profit for his sweat.
God knows you get full payment for your debt!
Not good for good, but scorn for all you pay.
In faith, your order's ruled the proper way!27

"You pass your lives amid uncertainties
Except in some small matters (two or three),
For nothing asks more effort than to please,
Which is your creed, as all you must agree.   340
Still, that is not the worst it seems to me.
But if I named the worst thing, I believe,
Though I said right, you all would be aggrieved.

"But take just this: what lovers may eschew
Or what perform, and with the best intention,
Full often your proud dear will misconstrue—
Condemn it as a hateful intervention.
And yet if she on any vain pretension
Is angry, you must bear a talking to.
Who wouldn't care to live in love like you?"   350

In spite of this when he could see his time
He stopped such talk—for speaking was a strain—
As Love began his feathers so to lime28
That even to his folks he scarce could feign
That other matters pressed his busy brain.
So woebegone he was, so lost and daunted,
He left them free to wander where they wanted.

And then within his chamber all alone,
He sat himself down close beside his bed,
And there began to sigh and twist and groan,   360
As thoughts of his new lady filled his head.
And though he sat awake, his spirit bred
Her image from the temple as of late.
He called back every look to contemplate.

---

27. Troilus is comparing lovers' rules with the rules of a religious order.
28. Chaucer is thinking here of birdlime, a sticky paste once commonly smeared on branches to ensnare small birds.

And so he made a mirror of his mind
And there he saw her figure in its beams,
And told himself how bright her semblance shined
And how his fortune flourished, as he deemed,
To love so good a lady; for it seemed
That if he served her well he might win grace,   370
Or else at least assume a servant's place.

Imagining that no travail or pain
Might be too much to bear for such a one,
Prince Troilus felt no anxiousness or shame.
For even if found out, he thought he'd won
All other lovers' praise for what he'd done.
His love just underway, he argued so,
Full unaware his course was shaped for woe.

He thought how this affair should be pursued,
And first he felt a need for secrecy:[29]   380
He'd keep his feelings hid. He'd leave no clue
That any living soul would ever see
(Unless their seeing might advance his plea).
He knew full well that love too widely known
Yields bitter fruit although sweet seeds are sown.

And more than all of this, the young prince thought
What he should say and what he should hold in
So he might win the lady's love he sought.
In hopes a song might help him to begin,
He voiced aloud the ache he felt within,   390
As with good will he gave his full assent
To love Criseyde well, and not repent.

Now of his song not just the broadest sense,[30]
(As written by my author, Lollius),[31]

---

29. Secrecy was a standard requirement of courtly love. The model lover gave no outward sign of love for fear of damaging his lady's reputation.

30. This stanza does not appear in Boccaccio.

31. Chaucer derived his story from Boccaccio and a few less important sources but here he pretends it came from "Lollius," a nonexistent writer whose name is probably based on a misunderstanding of one of Horace's Epistles.

But all, save what our tongues make different,
I dare to tell you here—what Troilus
Said as he sang. His every word was just
As I shall write it now. Who would it hear
Look one verse down, and there it will appear.

           Canticus Troili[32]   *Troilus' Song*

"If no love is, O God, what pains me so?   400
And if love is, O say, what might it be?
If love is good, then what has caused my woe?
If it is not, I swear I cannot see
Why every torment and adversity
That comes of love is pleasant, as I think;
For still I thirst for more the more I drink.

"And if it is my pleasure so to burn,
Whence come my sorry wailing and my plaints?
If harm is sweet, to whom then can I turn?
I don't know why, unwearied, I should faint.   410
O living death, sweet harm, and soft constraint,
How can you multiply yourselves in me,
Except that I consent that this may be?

"And if I do consent, why then, what right
Have I to grudge? Lo, tossed thus to and fro,
I strive to steer my boat through starless night
Amid the sea, compelled by winds that blow
Contrary to me now, and evermore.
Alas, what is this wondrous malady?
Afire with cold, cold fire is killing me."   420

And to the god of love the prince complained
With piteous voice, "O lord, now all yours is
My spirit, as you've rightfully ordained.
I thank you, lord, for bringing me to this.
But if she's god or woman, by my bliss,

---

32. Although Chaucer did not reproduce the original form, the next three stanzas
are based on Petrarch's sonnet *In Vita* 132, the first use of an Italian sonnet in
English. This song does not appear in Boccaccio.

I know not, she whom you would make me serve.
Yet I will be her man and never swerve.

"You shine forth in her eyes with power and might
As from a place that suits your dignity.
Wherefore, my lord, if I can serve you right   430
And please you, why, I pray be kind to me,
For all my royal estate I offer free
Into her hand, and with a humble cheer,
To be her man for life and hold her dear."

The fires of love and longing would not spare him.
They scorned his blood (God keep them from my breast!).
Indeed, their licking flames would not forbear him
For all his noble virtues and prowess.
Love held him as a servant in distress,
Burned him so hot and often, ever new,   440
That sixty times a day he lost his hue.

So greatly, day by day, his constant thought,
For love of her, grew quicker and increased,
That every other charge he set at naught.
Therefore in hopes his painful fire would cease,
He strove to see her face and be at peace.
For ease he sought out her for whom he yearned,
But the nearer he approached the more he burned.

The closest to the fire the hottest is—
This all men know by every kind of test.   450
But whether he was near or far from bliss,
By night or day, wherever he might rest,
His heart, the seeing eye within his breast,
Stayed fixed on her, more fair and more compelling
Than Polyxena was or regal Helen.[33]

Throughout the day an hour never passed
He didn't stop a thousand times to say:

---

33. Helen was often considered the greatest beauty of the ancient world. Polyxena (*Pol-ex-EE-na*), Troilus' youngest sister, was sacrificed by the Greeks to appease Achilles' spirit after the war. In some versions of the story she was with Troilus when he was ambushed and killed by Achilles.

"Good lady, whom I serve until the last,
As best I can, Criseyde, hear me pray:
Your pity ere I die, as die I may,   460
My dearest heart! My health depends on you:
My life is lost unless you love me too!"

All his former, lesser fears were fled,
Both of the city's siege and his salvation.
His hot desire no good inventions bred
But arguments to serve his one fixation:
That she would bring an end to his frustration
And let him be her man, for it was sure
She was his life. He'd die without her cure.

The sharp attacks of arms and men of proof   470
That Hector bore, his brothers at his side,
Came as before but left the prince unmoved,
And yet he was, wherever men might ride,
The very best, and fittest to abide
Where peril was, assuming such travail
That anyone would wonder at the tale.

It wasn't all his hatred for the Greeks
Nor yet the rescue of his threatened town
That stirred his rage and valor to their peaks.
To one great purpose only he was bound: 480
To win Criseyde's love through his renown.
From day to day in arms the prince so sped,
Not death itself could cause the Greeks more dread.

From this time forth love took away his sleep
And made his meals his foe; then too, his sorrow
Was multiplied so all within the keep
Saw paleness in his hue each night and morrow.
Therefore, a false complaint he sought to borrow—
Some other sickness—lest all men should know
It was the fire of love that burned him so.   490

He said a fever made him fare amiss.
Now how it was in truth I cannot say;
Perhaps Criseyde never heard of this

Or feigned that she had not—yet either way,
I know full well that not once, come what may,
Did it appear she cared at all for aught
The young man felt or anything he thought.

Ah, then this Troilus weltered in such woe
That he was nearly mad. His daily dread
Was this: that she might love some other so   500
She wouldn't spare a thought for how he sped.
That wrung him so he felt his whole heart bled,
And yet he dared not tell her of his pain.
No, not if all the world were his to gain.

But when he had a moment free of care,
Thus to himself he often would complain:
"O fool," he'd say, "now you are in love's snare,
Who used to scoff and ridicule its pain.
Now you are caught. Now gnaw upon your chain!
You reprehended lovers and dismissed   510
The thing that you yourself cannot resist.

"And now what will those lovers say of you,
If this is known and you're not there to hear?
They'll laugh and say, 'Just see what he's come to,
That clever man who thought he needn't fear
And only looked at us to mock and jeer.
Ah, now, thank God, he's thrust into the dance
Of those whom Love is slowest to advance.'

"Meanwhile, O woeful Troilus, God so would,
Since you must love (for love's your destiny),   520
That you have set your heart on one who should
Know all your woe yet never hear your plea—
So cold indeed, for all your love, that she,
Is hard as frost beneath the winter moon,
While you, like snow in fire, are soon consumed.

"Would God that I were anchored in the port
Of death—to which my sorrows soon shall lead—
For that would bring me solace of a sort:
Then I'd be free from further pain indeed.

But if my hurt is known and men take heed,   530
I shall be put to scorn a thousand times
More than those fools whom poets mock in rhymes.

"O god of love and she for whom I plain,
You never held another man so fast.
O pity me, dear heart; help me refrain
From death. I swear until my time is passed,
I'll love you more than life unto the last.
Now with some friendly look restore me, dear;
Yea, though you never give me further cheer."

These words he spoke and others like them too   540
And called her name aloud in his complaint,
As if to tell the lady how he rued
Until his weeping made him nearly faint.
But all for naught. She never heard his plaint.
And knowing that his love could not be told
Increased his private woes a thousandfold.

Now while he wailed alone inside his room,
A wellborn passing friend, one Pandarus by name,[34]
Unnoticed, heard him weeping for his doom
And grieved to find his friend so lost to shame.   550
"What?" he said. "This wailing is to blame.
Mercy, God! Say, Troilus, what you mean.
Has fighting with the Greeks worn you so lean?

"Or are there secrets tucked within your conscience
That make you go in dread of some perdition,
Regretting sins, repenting your offense,
Afraid you have not shown enough contrition?
God save our Greek besiegers and their mission
If they can lay our jollity to rest
And bring our lusty lads to holiness!"   560

---

34. *PAN-dar-us.* In the *Iliad* Homer names Pandarus as a Lydian supporting
Troy who breaks a truce by shooting an arrow at Menelaus. It was Boccaccio who
developed his character as a panderer, or go-between.

He jested in this way to serve his purpose.[35]
He hoped his words would irritate his friend,
So wrath might push his woes beneath the surface
And give his slackened courage time to mend.
But yet he knew wherever men contend
There never was a man of more prowess
Or one who strove so hard to be the best.

"What now," said Troilus, "tell me what misfortune
Has brought you here to see me so obsessed,
With nothing but rejection for my portion?   570
For love of God, man! Go, and let me rest.
Go, or see me die of my distress.
You yourself will suffer if you stay.
Leave me at once. There is no more to say.[36]

"But if you think that I am sick for dread,
That isn't so, so put it from your thought.
Another matter rages in my head,
A thing far worse than all the Greeks have wrought,
A woe to cause my death, sad and distraught.
But though I will not say why I'm distressed,   580
Don't grudge at that. I hide it for the best."

Pandarus, though, was grieving for the youth
And often cried, "Alas, what can this be?
Now, friend," he said, "if ever love or truth
Has been or is between us, you and me,
Don't use me with such heartless cruelty,
And hide from me, your friend, so great a woe.
I'm Pandarus, my lord, or don't you know?

"I'll partner you in pain, prince, if I may.
But if I can't bring comfort to your plight,   590
A friend should have the privilege, truth to say,
To join his friend in woe as in delight.
Through anything that happens, wrong or right,

---

35. This stanza does not appear in Boccaccio.

36. It is typical of Chaucer's humor that there *is* more to say, as the next stanza immediately demonstrates.

I'll never cease to love you, by my bliss.
Don't hide your grief, but tell me what it is."

Then this sorry Troilus gave a sigh
And said, "God grant my choice is for the best—
To tell you all—you asked and I'll comply,
Although the heart should burst inside my breast,
But nothing you can do will give me rest.   600
So just to show I trust you as you see,
Now listen, friend, to how it goes with me.

"Love, against whom he who struggles most
Prevails the least, as everyone agrees,
Has driven me against despair's hard coast
And now destroys my heart, which cannot flee.
Yet though I grieve, desire still burns in me
So that to die would seem a greater joy
Than king it over all of Greece and Troy.

"So let this much content you, my good friend,   610
What I have said explains my care and woe;
But now by God, whatever may impend,
Sir, hide it well so no one else will know.
Great harm might follow if my feelings show
And others learn my grief. Go with success,
And let me die, unknown, of my distress."

"Now how have you, unnatural and wrong,
Hid this from me, you fool?" Lord Pandarus said.
"It could be that the girl for whom you long,
Is one I know and I may see you sped."   620
"A wondrous thing!" the prince cried. "On my head,
You're never wise yourself in such affairs.
The devil knows how you can help my cares!"

"Just listen to me now," said Pandarus.
"I've played the fool. It happens, even so,
That one who falls himself into excess
Can tell a friend some things that he should know.
Yea, I myself have seen a blind man go
Where others fell who looked with both their eyes.
A fool may be a guide to those more wise.   630

"A whetstone is no carving instrument[37]
And yet it serves to sharpen carving knives.
So those attempts of mine that were misspent,
Eschew them, lord. For that's how learning thrives.
Thus I, a fool, can help you to be wise.
If you heed me you'll go discreet and wary,
Your wisest course defined by its contrary!

"For how could something sweet be understood
By him who never tasted bitterness?
Nor can a man be truly glad or good   640
Who never suffered sorrow or distress.
Put white by black and shame by worthiness:
Each sets the other off, and that's the way
We come to know the world, as wise men say.

"Since thus from two contraries comes one lore,
I, who have in love so often strayed,
And grieved myself, am able all the more
To counsel you, however you're waylaid.
Don't fear that you'll be evilly repaid.
I simply hope to help your lordship bear   650
Your heavy charge so you may feel less care.

"I know the very words apply to me
A nymph once wrote and sent your brother, Paris—
A shepherdess whose name was Oënone.[38]
She wrote to tell him of her heaviness.
You may have seen her letter, sir, I guess?"
"Never," answered Troilus, "I must say."
"Then hark," Pandarus said; "it went this way:[39]

"*Phoebus, who first founded medicine,*
Knew well the cause of every person's care,   660
Its remedy and all the herbs therein,
Yet to himself his learning proved full bare

---

37. This and the following four stanzas do not appear in Boccaccio.

38. *Ee-NOAN-ee.* A nymph Paris deserted for Helen of Troy.

39. The stanza that follows is based on a passage from *Heroides* 5, where Ovid tells Oënone's story.

Once love had tightly bound him in its snare.
For King Admetus'[40] *daughter he so yearned*
That all his craft went useless, while he burned.'[41]

"Now I say, lord, that I have smarted too.
I love one best. For that I've suffered sore;
And yet perhaps, I've good advice for you
(Though not myself—don't fault me on that score).
I have no cause, as I know well, to soar   670
As does a hawk when she is pleased to play,
But yet you may be helped by what I say.

"And on one other thing you may depend:
That come what may, though I should die in pain,
I won't betray your trust for any end.
Upon my honor! Nor shall I restrain
Your ardent love. If Helen were her name—
Your brother's wife herself—and if I knew,
Be who she might, I'd never hinder you.[42]

"So trust me, lord—you'll find my friendship sure—   680
And tell me flatly what has gone amiss.
Say what caused this woe that you endure.
Don't fear me; my intention, by my bliss,
Is not to call you foolish or remiss
(At least not now), for no one can retrieve
One lost in love until he wants to leave.

"I know that both these things are equal vices:[43]
To mistrust all or show trust everywhere.
And I know too the middle course is wisest,
For when you trust in someone you declare   690
There's truth in you as well. Therefore, forbear

---

40. *Ad-MEE-tus.*

41. Apollo fell in love with the daughter of King Admetus in Thessaly and became a shepherd to be near her. Jesus cited the proverb about the physician who cannot heal himself in Luke 4:23.

42. Boccaccio doesn't include this reference to Helen.

43. This and the next stanza do not appear in Boccaccio.

This wrongful silence. Speak, for it may ease you
To tell your woe. . . . So tell it, if it please you.

"Wisdom says: 'It's woe to go alone
For if you fall there's none to help you rise.'[44]
So since you have a friend, say why you groan.
It's not the way, for certain, to your prize
To disregard the teaching of the wise—
Lamenting like Niobe,[45] stricken queen,
Whose marble tears, men say, can still be seen.   700

"Let be your weeping and your dreariness,
And let us lessen woe with other speech.
So may the hurts you suffer now grow less.
Don't add to grief more woe that you must seek
As do those fools who make their trials more bleak
By eking out the pain of each new sore.
They never even try to seek a cure.

"Men say, 'It is a wretch's consolation[46]
To have another being share his pain.'
My lord, let's share each other's situation.   710
Let both of us love sadly and complain.
For my part, such great sorrow fills my brain
That certainly no further lack of grace
May sit upon me. Why? There is no space!

"God knows you cannot think so ill of me
To fear I'd steal your lady by some guile.
You know full well the one I love, indeed.
I've loved her hotly, for no little while.
Now, since you know I don't say this through wile,
And since I am your friend and not your foe,   720
Confide in me, for all *my* pains you know."

Young Troilus all this while had held his tongue.
He lay unmoved, as still as dead men do.

---

44. Based on Ecclesiastes 4:10.

45. *Ni-O-be.* In *Metamorphoses* 6, Niobe is transformed into a weeping statue after her children are killed by Apollo.

46. This stanza does not appear in Boccaccio.

But now he heaved a sigh and up he lunged,
As if Pandarus' words had been his cue,
And rolled his eyes as pain gripped him anew,
So Pandarus feared his friend had caught a fit
And might go mad or even die of it.

"Awake!" Pandarus cried then, brisk and sharp.[47]
"What! Do you slumber with your wits decayed?   730
Or are you like an ass before the harp?
He hears some clamor when the strings are played,
But in his mind no melody is made
To fill his head and glad his heart for he
Is dulled by his own bestiality."

With that his friend's exhorting speeches ended.
But Troilus wouldn't answer to the prod,
For telling all was not what he intended.
No one should know for whom he longed, by God!
For it's been said: "Men often make a rod   740
With which the fools themselves are later maimed
In different ways, as wise men have proclaimed."

He didn't mean to tell his counsel here.
What touches love should stay inside one's mind,
For love itself will make one's love appear
Without a constant watch to hide its signs.
And one may prosper who seems disinclined
To what he really wants with all his will.
Or that's what Troilus thought, for good or ill.

But nonetheless he heard Pandarus cry,   750
"Awake!" and sighed aloud and wondrous sore,
And said, "Though I lie still, you'll find that I
Am hardly deaf. Peace, now. Cry out no more.
I've heard your lordship's wisdom and your lore,
But let me rest and weep my sorry plight.
In my case all your proverbs have no might.

_____

47. This and the following seventeen stanzas (through line 854) do not appear in Boccaccio.

"There is no cure that you can work on me,
For I will not be cured. I mean to die.
Why tell me of your queen, this Niobe?
I won't hear such examples, old and dry."   760
"Indeed," Pandarus said, "I'll tell you why:
No one but fools delight to sit and wail,
Nor seek a better ending for their tale.

"I know, of course, your reason isn't clear,
But tell me, what if I knew who she were—
The one for whom you moan and suffer here—
Might I then explain your woe to her,
Since you yourself don't dare and will not stir?
Could I implore her, lord, to pity you?"
"Indeed not!" Troilus said. "As God is true!"   770

"Though I should be as earnest," asked his friend,
"As if my own life hung upon the scale?"
"No, no, my brother," Troilus said again.
"And why? Because I know your suit would fail."
"You do?" "Ah, yes I do, and know it well.
No matter, lord, what you might do or say:
A wretch like I . . . she'll never look my way."

Pandarus said, "Alas, how can this be,
That you've despaired and with so little cause?
How can she live and never hear a plea?   780
Why should you think of nothing but your flaws?
No woman is so cold she never thaws.
Don't put all hope of help beyond your reach,
For no one knows what things to come may teach.

"I grant it's true that you've endured a grief,
As sharp as that of Tityus[48] in hell,
Whose stomach is devoured without relief
By birds called vultures, as the old books tell;
But I can't simply leave you here to dwell
In this opinion, though it's so absurd: 790
That you've a woe too hurtful to be cured!

---

48. *TIE-tee-us.* Mythical giant punished this way for attempting to rape the goddess Artemis.

"Won't you, sir, despite your coward heart,
Despite your ire and foolish willfulness
And hopeless fear, tell me what makes you smart?
Why can't you help yourself in your distress?
Just tell me why you suffer such duress.
You lie here, wretch, as if you'll never stir.
What woman could approve of such a cur?

"What could she think, say, even of your death—
If you die thus—not knowing why it is,   800
But that for fear you yielded up your breath
In terror of these Greeks and their prowess?
What comfort can you hope to have from this?
She'll say, and all the town, the very stones:
'The wretch is dead; the devil take his bones!'

"Now you may skulk alone and weep and kneel . . .
But love a woman so she knows it not!
Say, how can she requite the love you feel—
Unknown, unseen, unkissed, and so unsought?
Lo, many a man's love has been dearly bought: 810
Say twenty years pursuing some hard miss
And still he's never yet received a kiss.

"And what of that? Why, must he then despair,
Or give up hope because he goes in pain,
Or kill himself, although the lady's fair?
Why, no! But rather rouse himself again
To serve his heart's dear queen and let her reign
And think it is a grace to stand and serve,
A thousand times beyond all he deserves."

These final words made Troilus pay him heed.   820
He thought at last what folly he went in here,
For what Pandarus said was true indeed.
To kill himself would never help him win her,
But blacken him, a coward and a sinner.
How could Criseyde know why he was slain?
God knows he'd shown her nothing of his pain!

And with that thought he breathed a deep-fetched sigh
And said, "Alas, alas! What should I do?"

To which Pandarus answered, "If you like,
You'd best explain to me what troubles you.   830
You have my word. Unless you find it true—
If I don't help before much time has passed—
May I be pulled apart and hung at last!"[49]

"That's what you say," said Troilus. "But, alas,
God knows it may not happen sooner so.
It will be hard to make these troubles pass
For I have found that Fortune is my foe.
Not all the men on earth who ride or go
Can stand against Dame Fortune's turning wheel:
For free or serf, she orders all we feel."   840

Pandarus said, "Ah, Fortune is to blame
Because you're grieving! Now at last I see!
Why, don't you know that Fortune is the same
To every sort of man in his degree?
And this should comfort mortals such as we:
That as her joys must surely pass away
Her woes will too, however sharp today.

"For if her wheel should stop and fail to turn,
Fortune herself would cease anon, you see.
Now, since her progress never can adjourn,   850
Why won't her very mutability
Bring you at last to where you long to be?
Perhaps with her next turn your luck will spring.
Perhaps you'll find that you have cause to sing!

"And therefore do you know what I beseech?
Give over woe and gazing at the ground.
For he who would have healing from his leech   *doctor*
Must let the one who treats him see his wound.
To Cerberus[50] in hell may I be bound—
If my own sister caused you all this sorrow,   860
I'd see to it that she was yours tomorrow!

---

49. This recalls the medieval punishment of being drawn and quartered.
50. *SER-ber-is.* Hellhound that patrols the far side of the River Styx.

"Look up, I say, and tell me who she is.
Speak, so I may go about your need.
Someone I know? By my love, tell me this
So I can help you better, lord, to speed."
Lo, now the prince's veins began to bleed,
For he was hit. He grew all red with shame.
"Aha!" Pandarus said. "We start the game!"

And with that word he gave his friend a shake,
And said, "Tell me her name, you thief! Now tell!"   870
But Troilus, simple lad, began to quake
As though men tried to thrust him into hell,
And said, "Alas, she holds me in her spell—
My sweetest foe. . . . Criseyde, lord!" he cried.
And with that word the poor boy almost died.

When Pandarus heard him speak despite his shame,
Lord, he was glad! He said, "My friend so dear,
Now you may thrive, by heaven, in Jove's name,
Love has bestowed you well, so now take cheer!
For name and wit and manners, never fear,   880
She has enough. Yea, she is noble too.
And is she fair? I leave that up to you!

"There's not a woman who's more generous
With her estate or friendlier of speech.
No one displays a greater graciousness.
At doing well. None has less need to seek
The wisest course. Criseyde is unique
In honor too, as that applies to her.
Her heart would make a king seem but a cur.

"And therefore be of comfort, heaven knows,[51]   890
My prince and lord, the first and cardinal part
Of noble life and honor, calm repose,
Is peace within oneself—a settled heart—
And yours should be content. Great good may start

---

51. This stanza does not appear in Boccaccio. Chaucer draws on ideas from Seneca
and Boethius

From loving well and in a worthy place;
Don't call it chance, my lord. You love by grace.

"And also think—and with the thought be glad—
That since the lady's virtuous in all,
It follows that some pity may be had
Among the rest when she learns you're her thrall.   900
But never, lord, no matter what befall,
Require her to betray her worthy name.
For virtue cannot share one soul with shame.

"It pleases me, indeed, that I was born[52]
To see you fixed in such a worthy place!
For by my truth, my lord, I would have sworn
You never would achieve so fair a grace.
Do you know why? You once said Love was base,
And laughed at him and scoffed at all his rules.
'Saint Idiot,' you called him, 'lord of fools'!   910

"How often have you made your silly japes,
And said Love's loyal servants, every one,
Are from their birth but chuckleheaded apes;
For some would take their tearful meals alone
And lie abed and utter bogus groans.
Others (you said) were struck with love's white fever   *love's pallor*
And prayed to God they never should recover.

"And some of them, as you have often said,
Complained of cold, as if love chilled them oft.
While others feigned at other times instead,   920
They woke all night, although they slept full soft;
And thus they thought to lift their love aloft,
But nonetheless went under at the last.
That's what you said. The jokes flew thick and fast.

"And you said too that for the greater part
These showy lovers spoke of love in general
Because they thought it was a safer art—

_____

52. This and the following eight stanzas (through line 966) do not appear in
Boccaccio.

For fear of failure—to make love to all.
Now I can joke myself at your own fall.
But truthfully, my lord, though I might die,   930
I see your love can hardly be a lie.

"So beat your breast before the god above.
Say, 'Mercy, lord, for now I must repent,
If I misspoke. Now I'm myself in love.'
Say that with all your heart and good intent."
Troilus cried: "Great Lord, I do consent
And pray your mercy, that you will forgive.
I'll joke no more on lovers while I live."

"Well prayed," Pandarus said, "and now I trust
That you will find the god's just wrath appeased;   940
And since you've wept as Love requires you must,
And said such things, he surely should be pleased.
Perhaps he will relent and see you eased.
Consider! She who raises all this woe
Has equal power to comfort you, you know.

"For soil that bears the wickedest of weeds
Bears wholesome herbs as well, and just as oft.
Beside the foulest nettles where they breed,
The rose spreads sweetly swelling, smooth and soft.
Above the valley, hills rear high aloft.   950
The dark of night gives way unto the morrow,
And joy treads shortly on the heels of sorrow.

"Now look that you go easy in your bridle,
And for the best submit to what may tide,
Or else our hopes and labors will be idle.
He hastens best who wisely can abide.
Go diligent and true but undescried.
Be glad and free; persist in your attentions,
And all is well. Remember your intentions.

"For he whose love is scattered every place   960
Is nowhere whole, as some wise men have said.
What wonder if he never merits grace?
You know, my lord, how love may spring and fade

It's as if one who planted herbs essayed
To pull them up next day. Would they survive?
No wonder no such love can ever thrive!

"And since the god has urged you to resort
To such a place as fits your worthiness,
Stand fast! You've rowed into your proper port.
And if you suffer any heaviness,   970
Hope for the best. Unless your dreariness
Or too-great haste should spoil our labor here,
I trust the end you long for will appear.

"And do you know why I am less afraid
To undertake this matter with my niece?
I've heard, my lord, the wisest men have said
No man or woman, from the best to least,
Was ever yet exempt from love's caprice.
They love some god or else they love their kind;
So we may find a way into her mind.   980

"And speaking of Criseyde, now, in special,
Recalling all her beauty and her youth,
She shouldn't limit love to things celestial
(At least not yet), although she might forsooth.
No, it would suit her better now, in truth,
To love a worthy knight, a man of price,
And if she won't, why, I say that's a vice.

"Wherefore I am, and will be, ever ready
To do my best to serve you in this way.
To please you both I hope that I prove steady   990
In this affair, while you two, as you may,
Must keep your counsel close in such a way
That no one else will any wiser be.
So we will thrive—in gladness, all we three.

"And, by my truth, my lord, there comes to me[53]
A new idea of you to swell my wit.
I'll tell you what it is if you will see:

---

53. This and the following stanza do not appear in Boccaccio.

I think since Love, for reasons he saw fit,
Converted you, your wickedness to quit,
You'll be the stoutest pillar, I believe,   1000
Of all his church. Ah, how his foes will grieve!

"And why? I'm sure you've seen these learned clerks
That err the most against a given law,
But then renounce their former wicked works
Through God's great grace, that has such power to draw—
Those are the folk who most hold God in awe.
They have the strongest faith, I understand,
And can all further errors best withstand."

When Troilus heard how his good friend assented
To help him gain Criseyde, as he said,   1010
His woe drew back and left him less tormented
But love waxed hotter in him, as he pledged
With sober face, although his hopes were fed:
"Now, blissful Venus, help me ere I die,
To make Pandarus grateful by and by.

"And yet, dear friend, how shall my woe be less
Till this is done? Then too, please tell me this:
How will you speak of me and my distress
So she's not angered—I dread that, I confess—
And will not hear the love that I profess?   1020
All this I fear, and also that for shame
She will not let her uncle speak my name."

Pandarus said, "You might as well take care[54]
To keep the man from falling from the moon!
Lord, I despise the timid way you fare.
Just think of all that you'll be doing soon!
For God's love, lord, grant me a little boon:
Let me alone. I'll see to all the rest."
Troilus answered, "Just as you think best.

"But hear another word. Sir, I would hate   1030
For you yourself to think the worst of me:

---

54. This stanza does not appear in Boccaccio.

I promise you that I will never prate
Against her honor, preaching villainy.
I'd rather die, by all the powers that be,
Than she should think me false or that I would
Urge her to any course that's less than good."

Pandarus laughed and answered with good cheer:
"With me as your pledge? That's what all lovers say.
I wouldn't care if she stood by to hear
Your every word! Farewell, for I'm away.   1040
Adieu! Be glad! God speed us in this game,
We two! Give me love's labor and conceits,
And for my work may you enjoy the sweets!"

Then Troilus fell right down upon his knees
And took Pandarus closely in his arms.
He said, "Now I defy the wretched Greeks,
And yet may God defend us from their harms.
And if my life may last mid their alarms,
I swear I'll make a number of them sting!
But I should not go boasting of such things.   1050

"And now, my friend, there's little more to say,[55]
But wisely think: you are the only key.
My life, my death, are in your hands today."
Pandarus said, "Well placed, as you will see."
"God pay you," Troilus said. "Do this for me:
Commend to her warmly. By my hand,
I'm hers and live or die at her command."

Pandarus then, who was most keen to serve
His bosom friend, told Troilus in reply,
"Farewell, my lord. Your thanks will be deserved.   1060
You have my word a good outcome is nigh."
And then he went off thinking by the by
How he might best beseech the lady's grace
And what might be the proper time and place.

---

55. This stanza does not appear in Boccaccio.

For no wise person with a house to build[56]
Runs at the site all eager to begin,
But waits until his urge has somewhat chilled,
And stakes the lines he means to build within.
From first to last he's thinking of the end.
All this Pandarus pondered in his heart   1070
And cast his work full wisely from the start.

Now Troilus didn't lie there longer sighing
But mounted up upon his dappled bay,
And in the field he played the raging lion:
Woe to all the Greeks he met that day!
And in the town his manners and array
Were so well seen and got him such a grace
Each Trojan looked with love upon his face.

For he became more friendly and more bright,
The gentlest and also the most free,   1080
The foremost, greatest, noblest Trojan knight
That was in all his time or that could be.
Dead were all his jokes and cruelty,
His haughty bearing and disdainful face.
As each vice left, a virtue took its place.

Now let us spare this Troilus for a bit,
Faring like a man who's hurt and sore,
Whose former wounds, unhealed, are aching yet,
Attended to in part, but needing more.
A willing patient, he must wait his cure;   1090
Another man's advice must mend his state,
While he himself bears up beneath his fate.

Explicit liber primus[57]

---

56. This and the following three stanzas do not appear in Boccaccio.
57. Here ends the first book.

BOOK 2

Incipit prohemium secundi libri[1]

Beyond these harsh black waters as we sail,[2]
Wind, O wind! The weather starts to clear,
For in this sea our boat has such travail—
My wit, that is—that I can scarcely steer.[3]
By *sea* I mean these troubles that you hear,
The dark despair that Troilus went in.
But now we see the day of hope begin.

O lady, be my muse, Clio by name;   *the muse of history*
From this point on, I pray, assist my heart
To rhyme this book till I complete the same.   10
With you to help, I need no other art.
You lovers, now forgive me for your part:
It's not my own inventions that I cite
But English drawn from Latin[4] that I write.

Wherefore I'll not have either thanks or blame
For all this work, but pray you'll by and by,
Forgive me if the words you read are lame,
For as my master says, why, so must I.
Though I may speak of love unfeelingly,
No wonder that, for this cannot be news: 20
No blind man is a subtle judge of hues.

You know as well the forms of speech may change
Within a thousand years. Words come and go.

---

1. Here begins the prologue to the second book.
2. This and the following 38 stanzas (through line 273) do not appear in Boccaccio.
3. The opening lines are based on Dante, *Purgatorio*, I, 1–3.
4. Chaucer is maintaining the fiction that Lollius, not Boccaccio, is his chief source.

What once was common now seems quaint and strange,
Or so we think; and yet men once spoke so
And sped in love as well as we, you know.
To win a woman's love at sundry times
In sundry lands, took different arts and rhymes.

And should it happen here in any wise
That there be any lover in this place   30
Who hears what now my story will devise—
How Troilus came to win his lady's grace—
And thinks, "Why, this would never serve *my* case!"
Or wonders at his speech or some odd guise,
I can't help that, nor will I be surprised.

Not every man who makes his way to Rome
Keeps to one path or works the selfsame way.
And in some lands he'd be a true coxcomb
Who wooed his love as men do here today,
That is, in outward actions and array   40
Or how he calls on her or pleads his cause.
As men have said, "Each country has its laws."

Why, scarcely in this place can there be three
Who said or did the same in love affairs.
For one man's purpose, this may turn the key,
But not another's. Yet all gets said, I swear.
Some carve in wood, some stone, as you're aware,
As suits each case. But now as I began
I'll follow my good author, if I can.

Explicit prohemium secundi libri[5]

Incipit liber secundus.[6]

In May, that mother of the gladdest season,   50
When fresh new flowers of blue and white and red
Spring up again, that winter had imprisoned,
And balms breathe forth, perfuming every mead,

---

5. Here ends the prologue to the second book.
6. Here the second book begins.

When Phoebus' grateful, warming beams are spread
Right in the Bull—why here is what occurred,   *the constellation Taurus*
As I shall sing. The day was May the third.[7]

Pandarus, now, for all his knowing speech,
Had felt himself Love's arrows, sharp and keen.
Just then despite his eagerness to preach,
His own love turned his color sickly green.   60
His own affliction flared in him, I mean.
He went to bed in woe to dream and yearn,
But half the night he twisted, tossed, and turned.

The swallow Procne,[8] with her doleful lay,
When morning came bewailed her fate again,
Lamenting her lost form; yet Pandarus stayed
Abed, now halfway out of sleep, and now back in,
Until so near she chittered her small din—
How Tereus lusted for her sister's sake—
That with her noise he rose up wide awake.   70

Then he began to call and dress and rise,
Thinking of the errand to be done
For Troilus and his loving enterprise.
His calculations showed him that the moon,
Stood well for business, so he went full soon
Forth to his niece's palace, close beside him.
May Janus,[9] god of entrances, now guide him!

He soon arrived before his niece's place,
"Where can I find your mistress now?" he said;
They told him, and he walked inside a space   80
And found three ladies, Criseyde at their head,
Within a stone-paved parlor, all well sped.

---

7. Chaucer includes specific references to May 3 in "The Knight's Tale" and "The Nun's Priest's Tale" in *The Canterbury Tales*. The date seems to have meant something special to him. No one knows what.

8. *PRAK-ne.* Procne was married to King Tereus (*TER-ee-us*) of Thrace, who raped her sister, Philomela. After the two women cooked Tereus' son Itys and fed him to his father, Procne became a swallow and Philomela a nightingale.

9. *JAY-nus.* Roman god of doorways and beginnings—hence *January*.

They listened as a maiden read the story
How Thebes was once besieged in all its glory.[10]

Pandarus said, "My dear, God guard you yet,
Your book as well, and all of you by rights!"
"Uncle," Criseyde answered him, "well met."
And rising up, she grasped his hand full tight
And drew it close and said, "Three times last night
I dreamed of you; I pray that foretells good,"						90
And sat him on a bench near where they stood.

"Yea, Niece, you shall fare well, and better too,
This very year," the man proclaimed, "God send.
But I am sorry if I hindered you
From hearing this, a book that all commend.
For God's love tell me, what does it portend?
Is it of love? Say, can it mend my cheer?"
"O no," she said. "Your mistress is not here."

That made them laugh, and then she said as well,
"This is the tale of Thebes my maiden reads;						100
Just now we heard of how King Laius fell
Through his own son, Prince Oedipus,[11] indeed.
But here red letters[12] show a new account proceeds.
The book contains a bishop's tale as well:
Amphiaraus'.[13] He tumbled down to hell.

---

10. This is the tale of Oedipus' sons Eteocles and Polynices, who were supposed to share kingship in Thebes but killed each other in a civil war instead, leaving their uncle Creon on the throne. Chaucer probably knew the story from the *Thebaid* of Publius Statius (first century AD), though a twelfth-century French translation was also available, and sometimes his version here seems closer to the French one. The communal reading party illustrates a custom of medieval and classical times. Chaucer's own works would often have been read aloud the same way.

11. *EE-da-pus*. He attacked and killed his father Laius (*LAY-us*) on the road, not knowing who he was.

12. Red letters—rubrics—were used to mark important points or new beginnings in medieval manuscripts.

13. *Am-phee-a-RAY-us*. A priest-king of Argos, whom Zeus caused to be swallowed by the earth before he could be killed by his enemies.

Pandarus said, "All this I know myself—
The siege of Thebes and all the Thebans' care—
I've read the books that tell it, one through twelve;[14]
But let that be, and tell me how you fare.
Remove your veil[15] and show your fair face bare.   110
Put down your book, rise, dance with me today,
And let us do our best to honor May!"

"God forbid!" she said. "What, are you mad?
Is that a widow's life, so God you save?
By God, you fill my very heart with dread!
You are so wild! It seems, my lord, you rave.
I'm far better suited for some cave
Where I could sit and read saints' pious lives.
Let maidens dance . . . and maybe younger wives."

"As ever I may thrive," Pandarus said,   120
"I could tell a thing to make you play."
"Well, Uncle," said Criseyde, "go ahead
For God's own love. What, are the Greeks away?
My fear of them grows stronger every day."
"No, no," he said, "whatever else ensues,
My tale is five times greater than such news."

"Yea, Holy God," she said, "what thing is that?
What, better than five such? It must be less.
Ah, not for all this world could I say what
That thing could be—some jape of yours?—confess!   130
Unless you choose to tell me what it is,
I'll never guess. I swear my wit's too lean.
By God, I cannot think what you may mean."

"I vow," Pandarus said, "that not from me,
Will you find out, no matter what you do."
"Why so, my uncle? Why indeed?" said she.
"By God," he said, "I tell you if you knew
No lady would be half as proud as you,

---

14. Statius' epic poem is divided into twelve books.
15. A pleated neck cloth, part of her widow's dress.

Not here and not in all the town of Troy,
And that's no jape, as I have hope of joy."   140

Then she began to wonder more and more
A thousandfold, and cast down both her eyes;
For not from birth in all her life before
Had learning anything seemed such a prize.
At last she said to him, but with a sigh:
"Alas, my uncle, I will not pry or tease you
Nor ask again, for fear I may displease you."

Then after this with many more glad words
And friendly tales, and with a merry cheer,
Of this and that they spoke, of things they'd heard,   150
Sounding many themes, both far and near,
As such friends do, who hold each other dear,
Till she asked after Hector, who, heaven knows,
Had been the Trojans' wall against their foes.

"He does full well, thank God," Pandarus said,
"But on one arm he has a little scratch;
And Troilus fares as well, upon my head—
So wise and worthy, Hector's nearest match—
In whom all virtues grow with such dispatch,
As perfect honor and all gentleness,   .   160
Wisdom, bounty, truth, and worthiness."

"In good faith, Uncle," she said, "it pleases me
They both are well. God love and keep them too.
For truly it's a proper dignity,
That a king's son so much in arms may do
And yet for all his force be kind and true;
For power, moral virtue, and command
Are seldom found together in one man."

"In good faith, that is so," Pandarus said,
"King Priam has indeed a pair of sons[16]—   170
For Troilus, Niece, is equally well bred—
That certainly, although my life were done,

---

16. Traditionally he had fifty sons in all, most with different mothers.

Are quite as void of vice as anyone.
No one can match those two beneath the sun
Or rival all the mighty deeds they've done.

"Of Hector, though, I hardly need to tell.
In all this world there is no better knight.
He tops them all and bears his worth right well.
His virtues are still greater than his might.
He shines in every knowing worthy's sight.   180
But Troilus is the same, unless I err.
God help me if I know of such a pair!"

"By God," she said, "of Hector that is true,
And I believe the same is so of Troilus;
For, doubtless, all men praise what he can do.
In arms each day he works to shelter us.
In town, though, he's a gentle man, and thus
In every part of Troy his name is raised
By those from whom I most would value praise."

"You surely speak the truth," Pandarus said.   190
"Just yesterday, who'd ever been with him
Might well have watched the raging prince with dread:
No thicker swarm of bees could ever skim
And flee a place than Greek troops fled from him.
Throughout the field, in every warrior's ear
There was no cry but 'Troilus is here!'

"Now here, now there, he hunted them so fast
There was but Grecian blood—and Troilus.
Now he hurt these, now those he overpassed;
Everywhere he went it fell out thus: 200
He was their death, but shield and life to us,
So all that day no Greek could make a stand
While Troilus' bloody sword was in his hand.

"And yet he is the mildest, kindest man
Of great estate I've seen in all my life;
And where he likes, he's welcoming, not grand,
To those he thinks are worthiest to thrive."
With that, Pandarus, bustling and alive,

Began to take his leave with "Now I'll go."
"No," said Criseyde, "don't you leave me so. 210

"What ails you to grow weary, and so soon,
Of women, sir? We all will be aggrieved.
Sit down, by God, I have a private tune
To try upon your ear before you leave."
Now everyone within a little throw
Who heard her speaking thus withdrew some way
And left those two to say what they would say.

When she brought her accounting to an end,
Of her estate and of its governance,
Pandarus said, "I've no more time to spend, 220
But I still say, 'Rise up and let us dance!'
Now toss your widow's habit to mischance!
Why should you sit here draped in black and sad,
When there is such adventure to be had?"

"Ah, nicely urged, for love of God," said she.
"But won't you tell me what you mean by this?"
"No, that would take too long just now," said he,
"And I'm afraid that I would be remiss
If I should speak and you take me amiss.
It's better now to hold my poor tongue still 230
Than speak a truth contrary to your will.

"For Niece, by our good goddess, wise Minerva,[17]
And Jupiter, who makes the thunder roar,
And by dear, blissful Venus, whom I serve,
You are the one of all upon this shore
(Except my mistresses), who heretofore
I've loved the best and fear the most to grieve.
You know that's true yourself, as I believe."

"Surely, Uncle," she said, "mercy, now!
I've found you my good friend forever yet. 240
I owe no other man, as I allow,

17. The Roman goddess of wisdom, generally equated with the Greek goddess Athena.

As I owe you, nor can I pay the debt.
So with the grace of God, my course is set:
I never will offend you through my fault.
Or if I have, say how, and it will halt.

"But for the love of God, sir, I beseech you,
As you are he whom I most love and trust,
Give over all this riddling speech, do,
And tell me what you mean. My lord, you must!"
Her uncle kissed her cheek and answered thus: 250
"Gladly, lady, and my niece right dear!
But take it for the best, what you may hear."

With that she looked again toward the floor.
Pandarus cleared his throat and coughed a mite
And said, "My niece, I tell you, evermore,
Although a kind of carping men delight
To complicate their tales with arts and sleights,
For all of that their constant aim, you'll find
Is to advance some point they have in mind.

"But since the end is every story's strength   260
And since what I must say is for the good,
Why should I paint or draw it out at length
To such a friend? No, God forbid I should!"[18]
And with that word he watched her where she stood,
And said, while peering closely in her face,
"May such a prize as you win every grace!"

But he thought thus: "If I now make my tale
Difficult or roundabout in style,
I'll never win her favor or prevail.
She'll only think I'm practicing some wile,   270
For tender wits fear that they'll be beguiled
When anything confuses them a bit.
I'll make my words right plain, to match her wit."

He watched his niece intently while he thought,
And she could see that he beheld her so.

18. In spite of what he says here, Pandarus' speech is conspicuously windy and indirect.

She said, "My lord, why are your looks so fraught?
You've seen my face full often, as I know."
"And yet I'll know it better ere I go,"
He said, "for I was weighing if you'll be
Rewarded as I hope. Lo, now we'll see.   280

"To everyone alive some lucky chance
Comes late or soon, supposing he can seize it,
But if he only looks at it askance
When it's at hand, though he can plainly see it,
It's not by chance or fortune that he flees it.
It comes of sloth and wretched idleness.
And we may blame the man himself, I guess.

"Good fortune, pretty niece, has come to you,
And light to grasp, if you will only take it.
Now for the love of God, and for mine too,   290
Pray snatch it up before some hazard slakes it!
But why adorn my tale or longer make it?
Give me your hand. No one, however placed—
If you consent—has been more highly graced.

"And since I speak for good, as you have found,
And as I've often told you here before,
And since I love your honor and renown
As much as any creature's, no one's more,
By all the oaths to you I ever swore,
If you think I speak out of turn, or lie,   300
I'll never see your face again, nor try.

"Don't be aghast or quake, my dear. Whereto?
Don't let some unknown fear disturb your hue.
The worst is past. There's little more to do.
And though my tale now springs upon you new,
Yet trust in me. You'll always find me true.[19]
If this were something I thought dangerous,
I never would have come before you thus."

"Good Uncle, for God's love, hear me I pray,"
She said. "Come, sir! Now tell me what it is!   310

---

19. These five consecutive rhymes echo Chaucer's.

For I am both aghast at what you say
And longing too to reach the end of this.
Now, whether it goes well or goes amiss,
Say on, say on, don't leave me in this fear."
"And so I will," he said. "Just listen, dear.

"Now, my niece, the king's most favored son
(So kind, so wise, so worthy, fresh, and free),
Who strives for good as well as anyone—
Troilus, I mean—loves you so abjectly
Unless you help, he'll die, as I can see.   320
Lo, that is all. No need to amplify.[20]
Do what you please to make him live or die.

"But if you let him die, know I'll go too.[21]
You have my promise, for I cannot lie.
I'll cut my throat before I'll be untrue."
With that a flood of tears burst from his eye,
And then he said, "If you will see us die,
Both guiltless, then you've caught two pretty fish!
No gain to you. . . . Yet kill us if you wish.

"Alas, for he who is my lord most dear,   330
That faithful man, that noble, gentle knight,
Desiring nothing but your friendly cheer—
He dies already though he goes upright.
He presses on with all his will and might
Just to be slain, should fortune nod that way.
Alas God made you beautiful, I say!

"If it be that you're so cruel, indeed,
You care as little for the prince's death
(Who is so true and good, as we agreed)
As for some scurvy rascal or some wretch . . .   340
If you are thus, your beauty will not stretch
To make amends for such a cruel act.
Advice is always best before the fact.

---

20. This is followed by sixty-four lines of amplification.
21. This and the next twelve stanzas (through line 413) do not appear in Boccaccio.

"Woe to the finest gem that has no virtue!²²
Woe to the herb that offers no one good!
To beauty without pity, woe is due,
That tramples others under when it would.
In you great beauty flowers as it should,
But if no pity dwells inside your heart,
I'm sorry you are living for my part!   350

"Now you must never think I mean some fraud,
For I would rather you and I and he
Were hanged before I'd be his lordship's bawd—
Yea, hanged on high for everyone to see.
I am your uncle. Shame would light on me
As well as you if I should acquiesce,
And help him soil your name and make it less.

"Now, understand; I don't request you here
To bind yourself to him by some great oath,
But only that you make him better cheer   360
Than you have done before and be less loath,
And so preserve his life and comfort both.
That's all and some, the scope of our intent,
So help me God, Niece. Nothing else is meant.

"Lo, this request is well advised, my dear.
There's not a thing against it, heaven knows.
For there is nothing worse in this to fear
Than men might wonder why he comes and goes.
To that I could make answer if I chose:
No one but a born fool would contend   370
That he was any more than just your friend.

"What? Who would think that every man he sees
Inside a shrine is there to eat the gods?
Consider too how well he can appease
And rule himself so everyone applauds—
So where he goes he meets with smiles and nods.

---

22. Many gemstones were thought to have some useful application, for instance,
causing wounds to stop bleeding (bloodstone) or easing heartburn (hematite).

Know this as well: he'll visit you so seldom.
You needn't fear though all the town beheld him.

"Such love of friends is common in this town,
And wrapped in that same mantle as you go,   380
By God, where my salvation may be found,
As I have said, no one would need to know.
And thus, my niece, to salve the prince's woe,
Let your pride be sweetened just a bit,
So he won't die with you to blame for it."

Criseyde, as he discoursed in this wise,
Thought: "Now I shall discover what this is."
"Uncle," she said, "say, what would you advise?
What is your will that I should do in this?"
"Well asked," he answered. "You'd not go amiss   390
To love him for the love he shows to you,
For love for love is every lover's due.

"Think too how age consumes with every hour
A part of beauty in the both of you.
And so I say before you feel its power,
Go love. Once old, no new love will ensue.
This saying holds a useful lesson too:
'It's late to treasure beauty when it's passed,
And age will daunt the proudest heart at last.'

"The king's own fool will often call aloud,   400
When any woman holds herself too high:
'Now may your life be long as you are proud—
Till crows' feet grow beside each precious eye—
And may you have a mirror then to pry
And see your face grow old with each tomorrow!'
I couldn't wish you any greater sorrow."

With this he stopped and bowed his saddened head,
And bitterly the lady wept anon,
And said, "Alas, now why am I not dead?
For in this world all faith is fled and gone.   410
Tell me what some stranger might have done

To me, when he I thought my dearest friend
Bids me to love, who should his niece defend?

"Alas! Alas! I would have trusted thus:
That if by evil chance despite my plight
I loved the fierce Achilles or your Troilus—
Or Hector, yea, or any other knight—
You'd sternly work it so by speech or sleight
That this should stop, and hold your niece in scorn.
False world instead, where everything's forsworn!   420

"And is this then the feast of joy you meant?[23]
Is this your will? Is this my blissful case?
Is this the very meat of your behest?
Was all your painted fable said—alas!—
To such an end? O Pallas, may this pass!   *Pallas Athena*
Dear goddess, please protect me from on high,
For I am so astonished I may die."

With that she sighed as if she couldn't speak.
"What? Can this go so ill?" Pandarus said.
"By God, I'll leave and not return this week!   430
I won't be mistrusted, by my head.
I see that you don't care if we lie dead
Or what we feel! Alas, how can this be!
But may he live, whatever comes to me.

"O cruel god, O Mars with your despite!   *Roman god of war*
O Furies out of hell, on you I cry!
I'll never leave this house by day or night,
If I meant any harm or villainy!
But since my lord and I must surely die,
I here confess me with my final breath,   440
For wickedly you've done us both to death.

"And since it pleases you to see me dead,
By Neptune, who is god of all the seas,
From this day forth I never shall eat bread

---

23. This and the following eleven stanzas (through line 504) do not appear in Boccaccio.

Until my heart's last blood drains out of me,
For certainly I'll die as soon as he."
With that he started up upon his way,
Until she caught his hem and made him stay.

Criseyde, now, was well nigh slain with fear.
(There was no more fretful lady in the town.)[24]   450
So when these bitter words fell on her ear
And when she saw her uncle's earnest frown,
His plan took on a more appealing sound,
And thinking that his loss could hurt her sore,
She began to rue the words she spoke before.

This was her thought: "Misfortune may fall thick
In love affairs and cases of that sort,
As men are apt for every cruel trick.
Should Uncle kill himself here in my court
And in my presence, what will that import?   460
What men would think of it I cannot say.
And so I have a subtle game to play."

And with a doleful sigh she said three times,
"Ah, Lord, Lord, Lord! This is a sorry chance.
My state's uncertain since my father's crimes,
And Uncle's life may hang upon my stance;
But nonetheless, and with God's governance,
I'll find a way. My honor I shall keep
And his life too"—with that, she ceased to weep.

"Of two bad things," she said, "we choose the less,   470
And I would rather show this prince good cheer—
With honor—than my uncle's life oppress.
You say you have no secret purpose here?"
"O no," he said, "as you're my niece, my dear."
"Well then," she said, "I'll carry out my part,
Against my will, and overrule my heart.

"But I will not deceive him or pretend
To love a man where I cannot nor should.

---

24. All through this encounter between Pandarus and Criseyde, Chaucer heightens
Criseyde's fearfulness. Boccaccio has her behave far more coolly.

But short of that I'll serve you in your ends—
My honor safe—and treat him as he would.   480
Nothing he may ask will be withstood
Unless I fear it may do harm to me;
Then 'Stop the cause and stop the malady.'

"Here, Uncle, I must make a protestation
That if you draw me deeper in, or try,
That certainly for anyone's salvation,
Yours or his, although you both should die,
And though the world should hate me by and by,
I'll give no further favor than you've heard."
"Granted," Pandarus said, "upon my word."   490

"But may I trust you now, my dear," said he,
"That in this thing as you have told me here,
You'll do my will as you have promised me?"
"Yea, doubtless," she replied, "my uncle dear."
"Nor will I have," he said, "more cause to fear
Or need to lecture you in this affair?"
"Why no," she said, "and now let's leave it there."

Next, they fell to other gladsome talk.
"Good Uncle," said Criseyde, speaking low,
"By God above who made us for his flock,   500
Tell me how you learned the prince's woe.
Does no one know but you?" He answered, "No."
"And can he speak of love?" she asked. "I pray,
Tell me, so I'll know what I should say."

Then Pandarus smiled a little smile
And said, "My dear, in truth, now I shall tell.²⁵
The other day, passed just a little while,
Within the palace garden, by a well,
We walked a half a day as it befell,
Speaking of a clever stratagem   510
To practice on the Greeks and baffle them.

_____

25. Pandarus' story here conflicts with Book 1 (lines 547–95), where he implies he doesn't know what's troubling Troilus.

"Soon after, we began to leap about
And practice with our lances, thus and so,
Until at last he said he would sleep out;
And on the grass he stretched himself right low.
Now I still stood and wandered to and fro,
Until I heard, as I walked there alone,
How he began most woefully to groan.

"I stalked up softly, just a bit behind,
And surely it's the truth—what I shall say—   520
As well as I can call it to my mind,
The prince complained to Love and spoke this way:
'Have mercy, lord, upon me if you may,
Although I once rebelled, now that's all spent.
Now, *mea culpa*,[26] lord, for I repent!

"'O god, that at thy worthy disposition
Directs the fates and lives by just purveyance
Of all of us—dear lord, my low confession
Accept with grace and send me such a penance
As you may wish; but from despair's black trance,   530
That thrusts itself between my soul and thee
Be thou my shield, through thy benignity.

"'For surely, lord, she wounded me so sore,
Who stood in black and shot me with her eyes,
That now my heart is sounded to its core.
Through this I know that I shall shortly die,
And what is worse, I must love silently.
You know how coals grow hotter, glowing red,
When covered up with ashes, pale and dead.'

"With that he smote his head upon the ground,   540
And then he muttered, though I don't know what.
And I, still softly, began to circle round,
Approached again as if I had heard naught.
This way I came at length back to the spot,
And said, 'Wake up, my lord, you sleep too long!
I see by this love hardly does you wrong.

---

26. "Through my fault." Words used to acknowledge one's sins in the Catholic
Latin Mass.

"'You're sleeping here as if you'd never wake.
Who ever saw so indolent a man?'
'Yea, friend,' he said. 'Go let your own head ache
For love, and let me live free as I can.'   550
And though his pains had turned him pale and wan,
He made himself put on a countenance
As if he led a company in dance.

"Things went like this until the other day;
It fell that I came roaming all alone
Into his room, and found him where he lay
Upon his bed and venting such a groan
As I had never heard, but why he moaned
I never knew, for just as I was coming in
He swiftly stilled his heavyhearted din.   560

"He stopped, but I still felt a mild suspicion,
Drew nearer still, and found he wept right sore.
As our wise God may grant me my salvation,
I never pitied any person more,
For no invention, remedy, or lore
Could help me keep his coming death at bay.
Yea, even now I weep for him, I say.

"And, God knows well that not since I was born
Did I so lecture anyone, or try.
I never was to secrecy so sworn   570
Before he'd say who turned his life awry.
But now to tell you all his doleful cry,
Or all the bitter words I heard full soon,
Command me not, unless you'd see me swoon.

"So just to save his life—for that alone,
And for no harm to you—I made my plea,
And so, as God has made us for his own,
Amend your cheer; give life to him . . . and me.
Now I have bared my heart to you, you see,
And since you surely know I mean no sin,   580
Oblige me! There's no bad intent herein.

"I pray to God success will be your fee,
That captured such a one without a net!

Dear, be as wise as you are fair to see,
And then within the ring the ruby's set.
No pair was ever better suited yet
As he when wholly yours and you when his.
God grant us that we live to see such bliss!"

"No, I'll not speak of that," she said. "Ha, ha!
So help me God, you'll spoil our bargain now!"   590
"O mercy, dearest Niece, forgive my flaw,
I spoke for naught but good, my dear, I vow—
By Mars and that steel helmet on his brow.
Don't be angry, Niece, as I may live."
"O, very well," she answered, "I forgive."

With that he took his leave and went away,
And, Lord, he fared as glad as anyone.
Criseyde roused herself. She didn't stay,
But went straight to her private room anon,
And sat her down as still as any stone,   600
And every word began to turn and wind,
As what he said came back into her mind.

She grew a bit astonished in her thought.[27]
This was so new! Yet on reflection she,
Revolving all, decided there was naught
Of peril, leastways not that she could see.
A man might love a woman—love was free—
And love until he thought his heart would freeze,
And she not love him back, unless she pleased.

But as she sat alone and thinking thus,   610
She heard a noisy hubub start without,
And men cried in the street, "See, Troilus.
He's put the Greeks to flight and all their rout!"
And then she heard her own men start to shout:
"Ah, let us see! Now swing the gates aside.
He'll pass this way and we can see him ride!

27. This and the following twenty stanzas (through line 749) do not appear in Boccaccio.

"There is no other way for him to go.
The Dardan gates nearby have been unchained."   *the chief gates of Troy*
He came with his retainers, high and low.
Two files of armored men passed down the lane.   620
It seemed a day when Troilus' fortune reigned,
But fortune is no more than what must be.
What happens here obeys necessity.

Troilus sat astride his dark bay steed,
All armed except his head, and richly too.
His horse's many wounds began to bleed,
As he rode forward softly with his crew;
But such a knightly vision, such a view!
For surely, sitting proudly in his saddle,
He looked as fine as Mars, the god of battle.   630

He seemed a peerless man of arms and knight
As they could see, and one of high prowess,
For he had both the body and the might
To make a fighter, and with these hardiness.
To see him in his knightly gear and dress,
So fresh, so young, so vigorous and swift—
The vision that he made was heaven's gift.

His helm was hacked in twenty different places,
And hung behind him from a woven strap.
His shield bore marks of angry swords and maces.   640
There many a broken arrow had been trapped
That pierced both horn and hide before it snapped.   *two layers of his shield*
And always people cried, "Here comes our joy—
Beside his brother, the holder up of Troy!"

He turned a little red for modesty
When he heard people crying out this way.
His manner was a noble sight to see—
How soberly he blushed and looked away.
Criseyde watched him earnestly that day,
And let his looks fill her with soft emotion,   650
"As if," she thought, "I'd drunk a lover's potion."

Then with these loving thoughts she blushed all red
As she reflected thus: "And is this he

My uncle swore might soon be lying dead,
Without some sign of loving grace from me?"
That prospect so abashed her heart that she
Withdrew her head, pulled it back in full fast,
While he and all his men were riding past.

She started then to scan and coyly sound
Within her thought, his excellent prowess,   660
And his high rank, and also his renown,
His wit, his shape, and all his gentleness.
And best by far was that his deep distress
Was all for her. She thought it would be hell
To murder such a man if he meant well.

But now some envious heart may jangle thus:
"This was a sudden love! How, by my creed,
Could she so lightly turn to Troilus
Right from the time she saw him first indeed?"
May anyone who says that never speed!   670
For everything we know must start somewhere
Before we see the rest of the affair.

And I don't say that she so suddenly
Gave him her love, but she began to deign
To like him first, and I have told you why.
And after that, his manhood and his pain
Made love within her heart unwind its skein,
So that with time and service love awoke.
He got her love, but not all at one stroke.

And also blissful Venus, well arrayed,[28]   680
Reposed within her seventh house aglow,
Well disposed, her signs most fitly laid
To help this earnest Troilus in his woe.
And truth to tell she hardly was a foe
To all his hopes. From his nativity
God knows she often helped him busily.

---

28. The planet Venus was well disposed to help Troilus at this time and was also
in an advantageous position when he was born, so the goddess seemed ready to
favor him.

But let us turn from Troilus for a throw,
Who rode away, and look, now that he's passed,
At how Criseyde hung her head full low
There where she sat alone, a bit downcast, 690
Pondering what she'd have to do at last
If her uncle wouldn't cease his stir,
But kept on pressing Troilus on her.

And, Lord! How she debated in her thought
All the things that I've already told.
What course was best for her and what was not
She pleated in her mind with many folds.
At times her heart grew warm, at others cold.
A part of what she thought I'll tell you now
As fully as my author will allow. 700

She thought it good she knew how Troilus looked.
She'd seen him now and knew his gentleness.
She said, "Although this thing cannot be brooked—
To grant him love—yet for his worthiness,
It would be joy and honor, I confess,
To join with such a lord in honesty
For my welfare and his, if that might be.

"Then too, I know that he is my king's son,
And since it seems I give him such delight,
If I grant him less sight of me, or none, 710
Perhaps he'll come to hold me in despite.
What could that do but worsen my sad plight?
Would I be wise to buy this prince's hate,
Or bend a bit and better my estate?

"In everything there is a proper measure,
For though a man may outlaw drunkenness,
He can't forbid that every other creature
Go drinkless for all time, or so I guess.
Since it was I who caused the man distress,
His hurt's not something I should now despise, 720
Especially as he loves me in good wise.

"And then I know, and have known for some time,
His traits are good, as no one here denies.
Nor does he boast; no, that would be a crime.
He's far too wise to practice such a vice.
And I will never grant him such a prize
That he can boast about me honestly.
No, he will never win that much from me!

"Then what's to lose? The worst that I can see
Is that men might discover whom he loves.   730
But what dishonor would that bring to me?
Can I stop him from loving? Lord above!
As I have seen and also heard thereof,
Men who love women never ask their leave.
(Nor do they ask to quit us, I believe.)

"I think then too of how his wide acclaim
Could win the best in all this noble town
To be his love, if she could save her name,
For he's the worthiest hero to be found—
Save Hector, who remains the most renowned—   740
And yet his life is mine to spill or cure.
That's how love works, or how his does, I'm sure.

"Nor can I wonder much that he loves me,
For I know well myself, so help me God
(Though here's a thought I must let no one see),
I am the greatest beauty, that's no fraud,
And loveliest of women now abroad,
And so men say in all the town of Troy.
What wonder then if I am this man's joy?

"And I am my own woman, well at ease—   750
Thank God for that—concerning my estate.
I'm free to graze wherever I may please,
No fear of other ties or harsh debate.
No husband now can say to me, 'Checkmate!'
Though husbands all are full of jealousy,
Or masterful, or wed to novelty.   *philandering*

"What shall I do? Why live as I have done?
Shall I not love if that would please me best?

I know, by God, that I am not a nun.
And if I choose to set my heart at rest   760
Upon this knight, why, he's the worthiest,
And he will guard my honor and my name.
By all that's right, now how can that be shame?"

But just as when the sun appears most bright
In March, then shows the world a shifting face
As wind-borne clouds scud swiftly in their flight
To cover his bright beams from place to place,
A cloudy notion sailed across her soul apace.
It darkened all her wishful thoughts full well
And made her falter so she almost fell.   770

That thought was this: "Alas, since I am free,
Should I now love and put in jeopardy
My own self-government, my liberty?
Can such a foolish state appeal to me?
I look at other lovers here and see
Their dreadful joy, their sharp constraints, their pain.
No woman has more reason to complain.

"Love brings us all the stormiest of lives
(Such are his gifts) that ever were begun.
Mistrust or other trouble always thrives.   780
In love some cloud must overcast each sun.
Each woman does what those before have done.
When sorrow strikes she sits and weeps and thinks.
She's punished thus: her self-made woe she drinks.

"And then, bad, wicked tongues will never rest.
They must speak harm. And men are so untrue!
The moment that we cease to please them best,
So ceases love—they're chasing someone new!
The harm once done is done, though we may rue.
Although they scourge themselves for love at first,   790
The ends of sharp beginnings may be cursed.

"How oftentimes, indeed, has it been seen
That women come to grief through some man's treason.
I cannot say what good such love has been

Or where it goes when it's no more in season.
No one knows at all, and with good reason:
No lost love ever stubbed a person's toes.
No, that which rose from naught to nothing goes.

"How busy too, if I love, must I be
To fend off those who feed on lovers' dreams—   800
Divert them so they find no harm in me—
For though no hurt is done, yet they will deem
All love is wrong, however right it seems.
And who can stifle every wicked tongue,
Or stop the sound of bells when they've been rung?"

But after that her mind began to clear,
For "He who never undertakes a thing,"
She said, "will fail no matter where he steer."
But then another thought would make her sting,
Then hope would sleep, and up her fears would swing—   810
Now hot, now cold. Still veering either way,
She left her room, for now she meant to play.

And down the stairs anon the lady went,[29]
Into the garden with her nieces three.
Now up, now down, their time was nicely spent—
Flexippe, Tharbe, Antigone,[30] and she—
In pretty play that was a joy to see,
With others of her women, a great rout,
To trail them through the garden round about.

The grounds were large and fenced along each way   820
And shaded well with blossoms everywhere,
The benches new, walks strewn with sand and clay.
Thus arm in arm they went without a care
Until Antigone, so young and fair

---

29. This and the following eighteen stanzas (through line 938) do not appear in Boccaccio.

30. *Flex-IP-ee, THAR-bee, An-TIG-o-nee.* Chaucer seems to have made up the first two names. Antigone was a daughter of King Oedipus, so that name is probably borrowed from the stories surrounding Thebes. Statius' *Thebaid* was Chaucer's chief source for these.

Began to brightly sing a Trojan song
So it was bliss to hear her in that throng.

       Cantus Antigone   Antigone's song

"*O Love, to whom I have been and shall be*
A humble subject, true in my intent,
As best I can I offer, as you see,
My heart's desire, Lord, for your proper rent,   830
For up to now your grace had never sent
So glad a cause as I have for my life.
Through you I live in joy and out of strife.

"*You, blissful god, have left me so well placed,*
In love I mean, that no one who's alive
Could ever, Lord, invent a better grace.
For I, and with no jealousy or strife,
Love one who labors hard to see me thrive.
He serves me well, unwearied, always true,
No living man could give less cause for rue.   840

Because he is the well of worthiness—
The ground of truth, the glass of excellence,
An Apollo for his wit, a stone of steadiness,
The root of virtue, pleasure's residence—
Through him all sorrow's banished from my sense.
I know I love him best, as he does me;
Lord, may he thrive wherever he may be.

"*Whom should I thank but you, the god of love,*
For all the bliss that I now bathe in here?
I thank you that I love, great god above.   850
This life is right for me. I hold it dear.
You've banished vice so no sin can appear.
Love bends my heart toward honesty and good.
Now more and more I want just what I should.

"*Whoever says that loving well is wrong*
Or thralldom, though he says it from distress,
His wits are neither generous nor strong,
Or he's unable, through his bitterness,

To love himself; for all such folks, I guess,
Who carp at Love must nothing of him know.   860
They speak of him but never bent his bow.[31]

"What is it to the sun in all his might
That earthly men of dim and feeble eyes
May not endure to look into his light?
Is love the worse if wretches are unwise?
No good's worthwhile that can't withstand their cries.
No, only those who wear a head of glass[32]
Must shrink from stones until all threats have passed.

"But I with all my heart and all my might,
As I have said, will love while I shall last   870
My own dear heart, my worthy, loving knight,
On whom my heart is now affixed so fast,
And his on me. Our love will never pass.
I dreaded once to feel my love begin,
But now I know no peril lurks therein."

And with that word her song came to its end,
And as it did, "Now Niece," Criseyde said,
"Who made this song of yours, so fitly penned?"
Antigone answered briskly on that head:
"Surely, Madam, she was finely bred,   880
One of the highest state in all of Troy.
She leads her loving life with pride and joy."

"It seems so by her song," Criseyde said.
And as she spoke she uttered one more sigh
And asked, "Are lovers really so well sped?
As happy as their songs proclaim on high?"
"They are," said fresh Antigone, "and why?
Not all the folk who are or were alive
Can tell the joy of love, although they strive.

---

31. Recalling a proverb concerning Robin Hood. Many people talk of him who never bent his bow.

32. Apparently based on a saying like the idiom "people who live in glass houses shouldn't throw stones."

"For do you think that every wretched sot   890
Knows love's full bliss? Why, no indeed!
They think that they're in love because they're hot.
Away! Such folk know nothing, by my creed!
Ask no one but a saint—those you may heed—
If things are fair in heaven. Saints can tell.
Fiends know no more than all is foul in hell."

Criseyde answered nothing on that theme,
But said, "Lo, night will be upon us fast."
Yet every word of lovers' bliss it seemed
She printed in her heart before it passed,   900
For love now made her feel much less aghast
Than at the first. It sank into her heart
And made the ground more ready for Love's dart.

The day's proud honor, and the heavens' eye,
The foe of night (all this I call the sun)
Was westering fast, and sank as if to die,
As one who has his daily courses run.
Then white things in the world grew dim and dun
For lack of light, and stars shone far and wide
As Criseyde and her women went inside.   910

And when the lady chose to go to rest
The others there withdrew just as they ought,
She said that now to sleep would suit her best.
Her women dressed her room as they'd been taught,
And when the house grew still she lay and thought
Of all things that had happened and their lore.
But I need not rehearse what's gone before.

A nightingale upon a cedar tree
Under the wall where her bedchamber lay
Sang out beneath the moonlight, flowing free,   920
Perhaps intending in his birdlike way
A song of love that made her fresh and gay.
She listened to him singing from his keep
Until at last she drifted off to sleep.

Sleeping, though, she fell into a vision:
An eagle with white feathers, white as bone,

Clawed beneath her breast a deep incision.
He plucked away her heart, and having done,
He thrust in his own strange heart anon.
She felt no hint of fear, no kind of smart.   930
As he flew forth and left her heart for heart.

But let her sleep as we return our tale
To Troilus, as he rode toward the palace.
Away from all the tumult in his trail,
He sat now in his royal room at last.
He'd sent away some messengers as he passed,
For Pandarus, whom they sought for everywhere,
And found at last, and swiftly brought him there.

This Pandarus came leaping in at once,
And speaking thus: "Say, who is suffering yet   940
From Grecian swords and well-slung flying stones,
But Troilus, who's still heated and upset."
He joked a bit and said, "Lord, see you sweat!
Now rise and let us sup and take our ease."
Troilus answered briefly: "As you please."

With all the seemly haste they could put on,[33]
They hurried from their supper into bed;
Dismissed their men full soon to see them gone,
And where they pleased the freed retainers sped.
But Troilus, who felt his whole heart bled   950
For grief until he heard the last detail,
Said, "Tell me, friend, now shall I laugh or wail?"

Pandarus said, "Lie still and let me sleep!
Content yourself. It's as you'd have it be.
Choose for yourself if you will dance or leap.
In plainer words, if you will credit me,
Sir, my niece looks well upon your plea.
She'll love you best, by God and by my truth,
Unless you now grow slack, you idle youth!

"For this is how your great work was begun: 960
I dogged her until earlier today

---

33. This and the next two stanzas do not appear in Boccaccio.

Her love and friendship finally was won.
Because of me her faith is pledged your way.
Your sorrow's lame in one foot now, I say!"
But why should I tell things already old?
All that you heard before, now Pandarus told.

You know how flowers that spend the cold of night
Closed and stooping as their stalks bend low
Redress themselves beneath the sun's new light
And spread their blooms by nature in each row;   970
The prince cast up a joyous look just so.
He sat up then and said, "O Venus, dear,
Your might, your grace are great. I praise them here!"

And to Pandarus he held up both his hands
And said, "I give you, lord, all that I have!
For I am whole! All broken are my bands!
A thousand Troys, if Troy were what I craved—
One piled upon another, God me save—
Could not please me as much. Lo, here's my heart.
It's swelling so for joy it bursts apart!   980

"But, Lord, what shall I do? How shall I last?
And when shall I behold my dearest she?
How can I make the dull time quickly pass
Before you speak to her again for me?
Now you may say, 'Abide! Abide!' But he
Who's hanging by his neck, sir, must complain.
He cannot hang at ease for all his pain."

"Easy, easy now! For love of God,"
Pandarus said, "each part must bide its time.
For certain we must wait while night's abroad;   990
But surely as you're here I say that I'm
(God willing) bound to speak to her at prime;   *around 9 a.m.*
And so, my lord, indulge me as I ask,
Or give some other man your precious task.

"For God may witness I have ever yet
Been quick to serve, and now until this night
I've not misled you, but with all my wit

Done as you wished, and shall with all my might.
Do as I say now, lord, and tread aright.
If not, then you're the cause of your own care,   1000
And I won't bear the blame for how you fare.

"I know that you are wiser far than I,
A thousandfold, but still, if I were you,
So help me God, I know what I would try.
With my own hand I'd write her something true—
A letter, lord—and write it so she knew
I fared amiss, and ask her to take heed.
Now help yourself, for sloth won't fit your need.

"And I myself will carry it to her,[34]
And when you know that I am with your dear,   1010
Mount up astride a noble courser, sir,
With all your will and dressed in your best gear.
Ride by as if you merely wandered near.
You'll find us, if I carry off the feat,
Before a window, looking on the street.

"Then if you wish, lord, send us up a greeting—
But look at me, not her, as you advance.
And on your life make this encounter fleeting.
Don't stay too long. God stave off that mischance!
Ride on your way. Observe good governance.   1020
We'll speak of you in fine round terms, I know.
When you are gone, we'll cause your ears to glow!

"Touching your letter, you are wise enough.
I know you won't write down from some great height
With arguments that she will find too tough,
Nor as some scribe or artful man would write.
But blur it with your tears to please her sight,
And if you write some tender word to soften her,
Use it once, or twice at most, not oftener.

"For, lo, the greatest harper now alive   1030
Who sounded the best note upon his harp

_____

34. This and the following four stanzas do not appear in Boccaccio.

That ever was, if he with fingers five
Touched just one string or on one warble carped,
Then, though his nails were pointed oh, so sharp,
Everyone who listened would grow bored
To hear him harp forever on one cord.

"Nor should you lump discordant things together—
For instance, mix such terms as doctors name
With terms of love. A smooth discourse is better,
An even style where things are all the same.   1040
If someone showed a scaly fish's frame
With ass's feet and headed like an ape,
He would paint wrong, unless he meant a jape."

This counsel seemed quite fitting to the other,
But as a worried lover, he said this:
"Alas, alas, Pandarus, my dear brother,
I'm something loath to write her, by my bliss,
For ignorance may make me say amiss,
Or she may never read it for despite.
Then I would die, resist death though I might."   1050

Pandarus answered, "Fie, sir, if you please,
Do as I say, and then let me be gone;
For by that Lord who formed both West and East,
I hope to bring an answer back anon
From her own hand. If that can't draw you on,
Let be. I pity anyone alive
Who must beat down your will to help you thrive."

Said Troilus, "Then by God, sir, I assent!
Just as you say, I'll get up now and write;
And I pray blissful God with good intent,   1060
Our projects and my letter have the might
To speed full well. Minerva, goddess white,
Give me wit to write it, bolster me!"
With that, he sat and wrote as you shall see.

He said she was his lady, he her thrall,[35]
His dear heart's life, his love, his sorrow's leech,   *physician*

---

35. Chaucer summarizes the letter. Boccaccio gives it in full.

His bliss and such like titles, one and all,
That lovers use to wheedle and beseech,
And humbly, as it were, in his own speech,
He began to commend himself unto her grace—   1070
To tell you how would take up too much space.

And after this her sufferance he prayed,
Not to be angry. His folly made him try
To send her this appeal that he had made.
Love forced him to intrude, or else he'd die!
And piteously for mercy next he cried,
And after that he said (and lied full flat)
He wasn't valued much, and not worth that.

He hoped she would excuse his lack of art—
His skill was small, and fear now laid him low—   1080
He grieved at his own vileness from his heart,
And then at last began to tell his woe.
But that was ceaseless—it would always flow.
He said he'd love her always, no one better,
Then scanned the sheet and folded up the letter.

And with his salty tears he bathed at last
The ruby in his signet, which he pressed
Upon the sealing wax with one deft pass.
And then a thousand times before he'd rest
He kissed the letter, clutched it to his breast,   1090
And said, "O letter, a blissful destiny
Awaits you now. My lady shall you see!"

Pandarus took the letter up betimes
That morning as he left to see his niece.
He swore to her that it was now past prime   *after 9 a.m.*
And, joking, said, "My heart can find no peace,
It is so fresh, although its pains won't cease.
I can never sleep in May, you know;
I feel such lusty grief, such jolly woe."

When Criseyde heard her uncle speak this way,   1100
Timorous, yet desiring much to hear
Why he had come, she said to him in play:

"Now tell me by your faith, my uncle dear,
What lucky gust of wind has brought you here?
Explain this 'jolly woe' you feel, perchance.
How do your wishes fare in Love's great dance?"

"By God," he said, "I always hop behind!"
She laughed at that as if her heart would burst.
Pandarus said, "Yea, may you always find
Joy in my woes, but listen to me first.   1110
A man has come to town who is well versed
On all the Greeks, a spy with news to tell.
I'll pass his tidings on to you as well.

"Come into the garden. There you'll hear
A long account of what's been said in town."
Then arm in arm they went with pleasant cheer
Beneath her room into the palace grounds,
And when they'd entered in so far the sound
Of what he said could not be overheard,
He held out Troilus' letter with these words: 1120

"Lo, he that is all wholly yours, you see,
Commends himself full lowly to your grace,
And he has sent this letter here by me.
Consider it when you have time and space.
Return some goodly answer in its place,
Or, as I trust in God, I tell you plain,
He may not live much longer in his pain."

Full of dread, Criseyde stood stock-still
But took it not, and all her humble cheer
Transformed itself as she said, "Note or bill,   *letter*
For love of God, that speaks as you speak here,
Bring not to me; and also, Uncle dear,
Take warmer care for my good fame, I pray,
Than his desires! That's all I have to say.

"But tell me now if his request is fit,
And don't hold back from love of him or waver.
Just say what's true, lord. How can I submit,
Given my estate, which you should save, sir,

To read his words and plaints or show him favor,
When that would bring me harm and make me grieve?   1140
No! Take it back, by all that you believe!"

Pandarus now began to stare at her.
He said, "This is by far the greatest wonder
That I have ever seen. A wicked slur!
Let me be stricken dead by heaven's thunder
If for Troy—the town and all its plunder—
I would any letter bring or take
That meant you harm! What wild complaints you make!

"You act as if—I tell you all and some—
Concerning him whose sole hope is to serve,   1150
You don't care at all what he becomes
Or if his life decay or be preserved.
But take this as you must and I deserve.
He took the letter up and held her fast
And thrust it down her bosom at last.[36]

"Now," he said, "just throw it down anon,[37]
So folk may see and stare at both of us."
She said, "I'll let that wait till I'm alone,"
And then began to smile, and said, "I pray,
What words to him you wish, sir, you'll purvey,   1160
For I won't write to him though you're irate."
"No? Then I will," he said, ". . . if you dictate."

Therewith she laughed and said, "Let's go to dine."
And he began to joke as in the past,
And said, "My niece, I have so great a pain
For love that every other day I fast!"
And with such droll remarks and gay bombast,
He made her laugh so hard that by and by
She feared she'd split her sides and surely die.

And later when she came into the hall,   1170
"Now, sir," she said, "we'll go dine anon."

---

36. Chaucer's invention. In Boccaccio, Criseyde herself briskly slips the letter into the bosom of her dress.

37. This and the following stanza do not appear in Boccaccio.

She called out to her women, one and all,
And went into her room, which lay beyond.
Among the things she did there, this was one:
She took out Troilus' letter and acceded:
She found a private moment there to read it.

She conned it word by word and line by line
And thought that Troilus wrote just as he should,
Then put it up and went away to dine
Where Pandarus in a brown study stood.   1180
Before he saw her, she grasped him by the hood
And said, "Ha, now I've caught you unaware!"
"You have," he said. "Do anything you dare."

And then they washed and sat them down to eat,[38]
And after noon full slyly Pandarus
Drew closer to the window on the street,
And said, "Niece, who refashioned thus
That other house that stands across from us?"
"Which house?" she said, and looked along his gaze.
She knew it well, and all the owner's ways.   1190

They talked a while of small things by the way,
Together at the window now, alone.
When Pandarus saw his chance, he had his say.
(Her servants all were off upon their own.)
"Now tell me, Niece," he said, "what have I sown?
How do you like the letter that you got?
Does he know much of love? For I know not."

On hearing this, her face grew rosy red.
She hummed a bit, and said, "I think he does."
"Requite him well, by God," Pandarus said.   1200
"I'll sew it up myself, as I am just."[39]
He raised his hands and knelt down in the dust:

---

38. This and the following eighteen stanzas (through line 1316) do not appear
in Boccaccio, who takes up some of the space by quoting Criseyde's whole letter,
which is far more forward than the summary Chaucer offers here.

39. In the absence of envelopes, letters could be stitched shut as well as sealed
with sealing wax.

"Niece," he said, "my offer isn't rich,
But give me what you write to fold and stitch."

"Yes, I could write to him, I think," she said,
"But truly I don't know what I should say."
"Come," said Pandarus, "now upon my head,
At least you'll send some gracious thanks his way,
For his good will, and save him one more day.
Niece, for love of me, as you are fair,   1210
Now don't refuse to hear your uncle's prayer."

"By God," she said, "God grant that this is well.
God knows I've never written such a letter,
Or any other kind as you can tell,"
And to a study where she could think better
She went to do the task her uncle set her.
She softened her disdain—but just a bit—
And sat her down to write as she thought fit.

To tell the briefest way is my intent
Of what she wrote, from what I understand.   1220
She thanked him for the courtesy he meant,
But she would never lead on any man.
No more would she embroil herself in bands
Of love. But as a sister, for his ease,
She would do his will and try to please.

She closed it then and went to Pandarus
Where he still sat and looked into the street.
And sitting down nearby to show her trust
On a gold-embroidered cushion trim and neat,
She softly said, "My lord, without deceit,   1230
I never had a harder thing to do
Than write this letter you constrained me to."

She handed him the letter, and he said,
"God knows a thing reluctantly begun
May often end in good. Now, Niece, we're sped.
He should be glad that you're not lightly won—
He should, by God and also by the sun—
Because, as all men say, 'Impressions light
Are lightly lost and readily take flight.'

"But you have played the tyrant near too long,   1240
Your heart was hard to scratch, for you're so proud.
Stop now, or you'll be trapped in doing wrong;
Of course you may *pretend* you're still unbowed.
But hurry now and grant the joy you vowed.
Believe me, wait too long to tell him yes,
And he may hate you in his great distress."

Just as they were talking of this then,
Lo, Troilus, at the entrance to their lane,
Came riding with his entourage of ten.
Softly toward Criseyde's house they reined,   1250
Where those two sat. It seemed the prince again
Was going palace-ward. Pandarus cried,
"See, Niece, who's riding here, and just outside!

"Don't draw back (he sees us, I suppose);
He may conclude that you despise his suit."
"No, no," she said, and colored, red as rose.
Then Troilus stopped to give her his salute.
With fearful looks and changing hues and mute,
He gazed in their direction, but not long,
Then nodded to his friend and passed along.   1260

God knows if he sat on his horse aright
Or made a handsome sight that signal day!
God knows if he looked like a manly knight!
Why should I linger on his fine array?
Criseyde saw it all and thought it gay.
To tell it short, she relished all she saw—
His person, cheer, behavior, gear, and all.

His goodly manner, and his gentleness,
She liked so well that not since she was born,
Had she so pitied anyone's distress.   1270
She rued that she had made him so forlorn.
I hope to God that she has felt a thorn
She shall not pull out within a week.
Indeed, God send such thorns to all who seek!⁴⁰

---

40. A small reminder of Chaucer's pose as a narrator unsuccessful in love himself.

Pandarus saw all this as he stood by.
The iron was hot, and so he chose to smite.
He said, "Now Niece, I pray you heartily,
I'd like to hear your answer if I might:
Say this same knight should die for someone's sight,
Not for his guilt, but for her cruelty.   1280
Would that be good?" "O, no indeed!" said she.

"By God," he said, "you're right to answer thus.
You feel now for yourself I didn't lie.
Lo, there he goes!" She answered, "So he does!"
"Well, then," he said, "as I have told you thrice,
Let be your shame and don't be overnice,
But speak with him to ease his anguished heart.
No holding back should cause you both to smart."

But love affairs are not that easy, surely.
Considering all, she said, it could not be.   1290
There might be talk. Besides, it was too early
To grant the prince so great a liberty.
Plainly what she ought to do, said she,
Was love him, but in secret if she might—
Rewarding him with nothing but her sight.

Pandarus thought, "She won't be that severe
If I can help it. This foolish resolution
Shall not remain in place for two full years."[41]
But why go on where nothing new was done?
He must defer to Criseyde's conclusion, . . .   1300
At least for now. So at the close of day,
As all was well, he rose and took his way,

And on his road toward the palace sped
And in his joy he felt his spirit dance.
Troilus he found alone and in his bed.
He lay, as lovers do, wrapped in a trance,
Caught now in hope and now in dread by chance.
Pandarus, just as he was coming in,
Sang out, as if to say, "Guess where I've been?"

_____

41. Two years was a common period for mourning husbands.

And then he said, "Who lies in bed so soon,   1310
All buried thus?" "It's I, my friend," said he.
"Who, Troilus? No! As I revere the moon,"
Pandarus said, "You must rise up and see
A charm someone has sent to you by me,
A charm that's meant to cure your sad complaint.
But help yourself, my lord, and be less faint."

"Yea, through the might of God!" Prince Troilus said.
His good friend Pandarus handed him the letter
Saying, "God has shown us favor, on my head!
Call for a light and read all that she said here!"   1320
Then Troilus' feeling heart beat worse or better
As he took up the message there and read
Just as her words built up his hope or dread.

But finally he took it for the best—
What she had written—for something he beheld,
On which he thought his yearning heart might rest.
Her words were guarded, though, not clearly spelled,
And so upon the welcome parts he dwelled.
Between his hopes and what his friend professed,
His awful woe indeed grew somewhat less.   1330

As any one of us can always see,[42]
The more the wood or coal, the more the fire,
Just so as hopes increase of what may be,
The more these swell, the more they swell desire.
A twig becomes an oak tall as a spire;
And so this little bill for which he yearned
Fed his desire, the fire with which he burned.

And thus it was that always, day and night,—
His hope awake—he yearned for more and more.
In view of this, as strongly as he might,   1340
He followed his friend's counsel as before
And wrote to her (in mortal pain, he swore).
He wouldn't let his suit grow cool or end,
But sent more letters daily by his friend.

———————————

42. This stanza does not appear in Boccaccio.

And he did other things of lesser weight,[43]
Like any lover of the selfsame caste.
And as a gambler's dice foretell his fate,
So he was glad, or else proclaimed, "Alas!"
Each trick of fortune turned his mood full fast.
Depending on each answer that he had,   1350
His days were sad and slow or quick and glad.

But meanwhile he resorted to Pandarus[44]
And sadly grieved before him and complained
And asked his friend for counsel in his trust.
Pandarus, who could see his numbing pain,
Felt he might die for pity of such strain.
So busily with all his heart he cast
For ways to quiet Troilus' woe at last.

He said, "My lord, my friend and brother dear,
God knows how your disease has saddened me,   1360
But you'll escape from all this sorry cheer.
In just two days I promise you'll be free.
I swear I'll make it so, as you will see.
I'll bring you, lord, into a certain place
Where you yourself may pray to her for grace.

"And certainly—although you may not know—
As those who are best versed in love will say,
One thing that can encourage love to grow
Is for a man to have a chance to pray
And show his woes somewhere out of the way.   1370
For it may wake some rue in her, I guess,
To hear and see you, guiltless, in distress.

"Perhaps you think, 'Ah well, it may be so
That Nature's force will cause her to begin
To take a bit of pity on my woe,
But then her pride will say, "He mustn't win!"
She'll listen to her haughty heart within.

---

43. This stanza does not appear in Boccaccio.

44. Here and in the next five stanzas, Chaucer relates what Pandarus said to
Troilus. In Boccaccio, Pandarus beleaguers Criseyde instead.

So, though she bends, she's held fast by her roots,
And what will happen then to my poor suit?'

"But think again. You know the sturdy oak,   1380
Which men may hack full often for the nonce,
When it receives the final felling stroke,
In one great swoop it comes down all at once.
And rocks fall just as hard, or great millstones;
For heavy things crash down more fast and straight,
When they descend, than things of lesser weight.

"A reed that bows itself before each blast
Full lightly when the wind gives out will rise.
An oak stays down when it is felled at last.
But why go on much further in this wise?   1390
Men all rejoice when some great enterprise
Is well achieved and now stands out of doubt,
And most when it was hard to bring about.

"But, Troilus, tell me, say that you were pressed,[45]
Answer this question, if you will, for me:
Which of your brothers do you love the best
In your heart's truest depths and privacy?"
"Assuredly, Deiphobus,"[46] said he.
"Well," said Pandarus, "before twelve hours from now
He'll cause you ease, although he won't know how.   1400

"Now let me go arrange things as I may,"
He said, and went to find Deiphobus,
Who was his lord and friend in every way.
He loved no one as well, excepting Troilus.
To keep this short, I'll tell what happened thus:
Pandarus said, "I pray you, lord, to be
Friend to a cause that closely touches me."

"I will," he said. "For certainly you know
I'll do all that I can, for God knows too,

---

45. The Deiphobus episode from here to the end of Book 2 does not appear in Boccaccio.
46. *Dey-IF-a-bus*. Priam and Hecuba's third son, after Hector and Paris.

There's not another man that I love so   1410
But Troilus, my brother. And now, what must I do?
Ever since my birth, I swear to you,
I never have, nor shall, as I suppose,
Favored any measure you oppose."

Pandarus gave him thanks, and then he said,
"Lo, sir, there is a lady in this town,
My niece Criseyde, who has grown dismayed,
For wicked men conspire to put her down
And wrongfully acquire her goods and grounds.
And so I pray you, sir, to turn the tide.   1420
Lord, be our friend in this, uphold our side."

Deiphobus answered, "Say now, isn't this—
The one you cite as if she were unknown—
Criseyde my good friend?" He answered, "Yes."
"Then, lord, you have no need to take that tone.
In fact, say nothing more. I freely own
My spurs and spear will guard her, rest assured.
I'd say so if her foes stood near and heard.

"But tell me how—for you must know their plot—
I can help her fully as may be."   1430
Pandarus said, "If you would hear my thought,
Perhaps—and this would honor her and me—
You might require tomorrow, lord, that she
Come here herself to tell you what's at stake.
Yea, that would make her adversaries quake!

"If I can ask a greater favor too,
And charge you with a heavier travail,
Sir, have some of your good brothers here with you,
For that might help her rightful cause prevail.
And then I'm sure that she can never fail   1440
To prosper, whom a lord like you defends
Along with the support of other friends."

Said Deiphobus, who was always drawn by nature
To give all good and honor his consent:
"It shall be done, Pandarus, and I'm sure,

I'll bring in yet more help, with your assent.
What would you say if I found Helen bent
Our way in this? I think that would be good
For she leads Paris anywhere she would.

"Now Hector, who's my greater lord and brother . . .   1450
We hardly need persuade him to our ends,
For I have heard him, one time and another,
Recall Criseyde, and such praise expend
That he could say no more for any friend.
We needn't plead; we'll have his help for free.
No, he'll be just as we would have him be.

"And you yourself go speak to Troilus
On my behalf, and pray he'll come to dine."
"All shall be done, good sir," answered Pandarus.
He took his leave and never stopped to grind,[47]   1460
But to his niece's house, straight as a line,
He came as she was rising from her meal
And sat him down and spoke as I'll reveal:

He said, "O holy God, I have run so!
Lo, my niece, can you not see me sweat?
I fear you don't appreciate me, though.
Do you know Polyphetes[48] now is set
To plead in court for all that he can get
Attacking you? His charges are arranged."
"O no!" she answered, and her color changed.   1470

"Why does he go about harassing me
And doing wrong? Say, what can I do more?
Still, I'd not care for such a one as he
But for Aeneas, sir, and Antenor.
They've been his friends in suits like this before.
Yet for God's love, indeed, my uncle dear
Let's give him what he wants when he appears.

---

47. That is, he never stopped to carry out any other task, like grinding grain.

48. *Pol-uh-FEE-tees.* Chaucer's invention, and very probably Pandarus is making up Polyphetes' current plans for a lawsuit.

"As you must know I have enough for us."
"No," said Pandarus, "it cannot be so.
For I have just now seen Deiphobus,   1480
And Hector and some other lords I know,
And I have made each one of them his foe,
So, as I thrive, that man will never win
No matter what, so let the wretch begin."

As they considered what was best to do,
Deiphobus, of his own courtesy
Came there to ask, for he was good and true,
If she would come and join his company
At dinner. She thought it prudent to agree.
Full graciously she promised to obey,   1490
And so he said his thanks and went his way.

When this was finished, Pandarus rose anon;
In brief, he went as straight as any rule
To Troilus, who was sitting still as stone.
He outlined all he'd done, as if in school—
How he had made Deiphobus his tool—
And said, "Now we must finish what's begun.
If you do well tomorrow, all is won!

"Now speak, now pray, now piteously complain.
Don't be put off by sloth or dread or shame.   1500
Sometimes a man must demonstrate his pain.
Believe me, she'll take pity on the same.
Your suit itself will save you,[49] in God's name.
But lo, I see you fear more now, not less.
I know what you're afraid of, or can guess.

"You must think thus: 'How can I do all this?
For by my cheer the others will espy
The love of her that makes me go amiss.
I'd rather keep my love unknown and die.'
But don't think that, and don't sit here and sigh;   1510
For I've made up a cunning sort of trick
To have them think they know why you are sick.

---

49. Chaucer says, "Thow shalt be saved bi thi feyth," a profane echo of Luke
8:48 and 18:42.

"Go there tonight. Go soon, for that's my plan;
And let the people think you mean to play
And drive away your sickness if you can—
Because you do look poorly, truth to say—
Then get to bed as if you meant to stay,
And say you can no longer stand at all
And lie there to await what will befall.

"Say that your fever always starts to flare   1520
About that time and lasts all through the night.
Just play your part; there's nothing you must spare,
For you are sick enough by love's cruel might.
Go now. Farewell! If Venus sees you right—
For that's my hope—and if your will is firm,
All Criseyde offered, she'll confirm!"

Troilus said, "Surely there's no need
To counsel me to act sick and to feign,
For I am more than sick enough, indeed—
So sick I'm nearly dying of the pain."   1530
Pandarus said, "Let that help you complain;
Then you'll have so much less to counterfeit.
They'll think you're feverish when they see you sweat.

"Lie close inside your blind, my lord, and I
Will drive the deer you seek up to your bower."
He took his leave right softly, looking sly,
And Troilus, too, set out within the hour.
He'd never had so little cause to lower.
He gave his friend's new plan complete assent,
And straightway to his brother's house he went.   1540

What need is there to tell you all the cheer
Deiphobus provided for his brother,
Or how the prince fell sick while he was there,
Or how they piled him up in heaps of covers,
Provided one diversion or another?
But nothing helped. He stuck close to the guise
You just now heard his clever friend devise.

But yet before the prince took to his bed
Deiphobus enlisted him that night

To back Criseyde in the fight ahead.   1550
God knows he said that he'd uphold her right!
He'd be her firmest friend, use all his might.
They didn't need to urge on such a one—
No more than ask a crazy man to run.

The morrow came and drew on to mealtime,
The hour when lovely Helen, once a queen,   *of Sparta*
Had pledged to come, about an hour past prime,[50]   *i.e., 10 a.m.*
To Deiphobus, to whom she'd always been
His loving sister, his familiar kin.
To dine with him that day was why she went,   1560
But God knew—Pandarus as well—much more was meant.

Criseyde joined them there, all innocent,
Antigone and Tarbe, who was her sister, too.
But I won't be prolix if you consent;
By God, I'll hasten on to something new—
Right to the point, not one word more than due:
Why all these people came and each one's station.
So let us pass right by their salutations.

Deiphobus did the company great honor
And fed them dainties; each one had his pick.   1570
But evermore he called out like a mourner,
"Alas, my brother Troilus is taken sick
And lies abed." His heavy sighs came thick.
But then he brightened, pained himself to cheer
His other guests and show he held them dear.

Helen, too, lamented Troilus' fever
So forcefully that it was sad to hear.
Then all the others, hoping to relieve her,
Became physicians, saying, "Never fear;
Just try this cure," or "This charm has no peer."   1580
But there was one who, though she didn't speak,
Thought, "I'm the finest cure that they could seek."

From pitying Troilus then they turned to praise him—
As people will when someone has begun—

---

50. People commonly ate a full meal around ten in the morning.

To magnify his noble deeds and raise him:
A paragon on high, beyond the sun.
"He is . . . ," "He can . . . ," "No other, no, not one . . ."
Pandarus then, whatever they affirmed,
Made sure their praise was thoroughly confirmed.

Criseyde heard these tributes for her part,   1590
And noted every word and set it by.
Restrained outside, but laughing in her heart—
How could a woman not be gratified
To move a knight like him to live or die?
But I'll pass on. You've more things to attend,
And all I tell must lead toward my end.

The time had come to push back from the board,
And all of them stood up, just as they ought,
And spoke of this and that, of one accord.
Till Pandarus stepped in to steer their thought.   1600
"Deiphobus," he said, "will you say aught . . .
If it's your will, I pray you, take the lead . . .
Say somewhat of Criseyde's urgent need."

Helen, who held Criseyde by the hand,
Was first to speak and said, "Why yes, at once."
The look she gave her friend was mild and bland.
She said, "May Jove rebuke him for the nonce
Who does you harm, and wreak a mighty vengeance;
For he'll gain only bitterness and rue
If I and all your friends now side with you."   1610

"Explain the case," Deiphobus said then
To Pandarus. "You, lord, know it well."
"My lords and ladies, pray let me begin.
Why drag this out?" he said. "Here's what befell."
He rang out the whole process like a bell—
Gave Polyphetes such a part in it
That it would make an honest person spit.

Then each one spoke more strongly than the other
Cursing Polyphetes in this way:
"I'd hang that man if he were my own brother!"   1620

"And hang he shall. We've doomed him here today!"
But why hold up my story, as I say?
They all proclaimed Criseyde in the right
And vowed to help her any way they might.

"Pandarus," said Helen, "tell us if you will;
Does my great lord and brother know of this—
Hector, I mean—or Troilus, though he's ill?"
"He does," he said, "but let's not be remiss;
Since Troilus is nearby, upon my bliss,   1630
She might herself, if all of you so chose,
Tell him of this affair before she goes.

"For he will take her troubles more to heart
Once he can see how ladylike she is.
So by your leave, I'll look in for my part
And let you know, before I'm even missed,
If he's asleep, or wants to hear of this."
He went inside and said in Troilus' ear,
"Lie there and die on what I've brought you here."[51]

Troilus roused himself and smiled at this.
Pandarus never paused but made his way   1640
Back to the queen and Prince Deiphobus,
And said, "To move as quickly as we may
With little crowding, send Criseyde in, I say.
The prince assents, though he's still sick I fear,
Yet while he can endure it, he will hear.

"But you know well his chamber is quite small.
A little group of folks can make it warm,
And I won't be responsible at all
If all of us crowd in and do him harm
Or bring him some discomfort or alarm.   1650
Or should she wait? What course should we pursue?
Advise me if you know what we should do.

---

51. Chaucer's language is even more obscure. He has Pandarus say, "God have thy soul, I have brought thy [funeral] bier," probably intending at least two sexual innuendos: he's brought Troilus something to lie upon (Criseyde) and something to die upon. In Chaucer as in Shakespeare, "to die" can refer to sexual climax.

"For me, I say as far as I can know
That no one should be there except those two,
Unless I go, for I can in one throw
Explain the case—as she can't—through and through.
And then she can petition him and sue
For his protection. And then to leave is best,
Before we tire him out or break his rest.

"Now just because she is a stranger here,   1660
He'll pain himself for her, if not for you.
There's something else as well for you to hear,
Apart from this—I think it's time you knew—
It's for the city's good, yet known to few."
So they, not understanding all he meant,
Agreed with him and in to Troilus went.[52]

Helen, in her soft and goodly wise,
Made the prince a show of women's play.
She said, "Now certainly you must arise,
My handsome brother. Yea, be well I pray!"   1670
She put her arm around him as a stay,
Employing all her wit to bring him ease
As best she could, a loving, kindly tease.

And then she said, "Now we beseech you,
My brother—Prince Deiphobus and I,
For love of God (and so does Pandarus too)—
To be a friend and trusty lord on high
To Criseyde here, who, as affairs now lie,
Receives great wrong, as Pandarus soon will show.
For he can tell you much more than I know."   1680

This Pandarus began to file his tongue,
To air the case again and make it plain.
When all was said and he'd set out her wrong,
The prince replied, "When I am up again,

---

52. Chaucer appears to be inconsistent on how many people actually visit Troilus. Pandarus says only he and Criseyde should go in, but then they all do, though Pandarus soon draws Helen and Deiphobus away with his news of "something else."

I pledge to work with all my might and main—
God has my word—to help her for the nonce."
"God give you health!" Queen Helen said at once.

Pandarus said, "Now then, is it your will
That she may say goodbye before she goes?"
"She may," he said, "or God would take it ill.   1690
I'll see her if she wishes, heaven knows."
And then Pandarus said, "If I may close—
Deiphobus and Helen, good and dear—
I have a new concern for you, I fear.

"I need the benefit of your advice."
And near the bed he found, as if by chance,
A copy of a letter for their eyes
That Hector sent to ask him in advance
If such a one should die for some mischance
(I don't know who), and looking stern and grim   1700
He asked the two of them to counsel him.

Deiphobus shook the letter from its folds
All earnestly, and Helen, too, the queen;
And roaming out they took it to behold
Down a stair, out to a patch of green,
And read it well for all that they could glean.
They conned it there an hour at least, indeed,
Pacing back and forth to parse and read.

Now let them read, and let's turn back again
To Pandarus, who was not slow to spy   1710
That all was well, and when that much was plain
He went into the palace hall nearby
And said, "Now may God save you all on high!
Come, Criseyde, for the queen by rights
Is waiting for you now with both young knights.

"Rise up and bring your niece Antigone,
Or whom you like. It cannot matter much.
The fewer folk, the better. Come with me
To thank them for their aid and show you're touched—
The three of them—and after you approach   1720

Look for your time to leave them. That is best,
And leave the sick Prince Troilus to his rest."

All innocent of what Pandarus meant,
Criseyde said, "Let's go then, Uncle dear,"
And arm in arm along with him she went,
Arranging on the way her words and cheer;
Pandarus told the others, quite austere,
"Now for God's love, ladies, let me pray
Just stay here as you are. Don't go away.

"Be quiet, though, for those who are within.   1730
You know that one is sick. God grant he mend!"
But privately he said, "Now we begin,
Go gently, Niece. Take care you don't offend.
By God, who gave us souls and is our friend,
And by two crowns[53] I hope will never wane,
Don't kill this man, to whom you've brought such pain!

"Fie on the devil! Remember who he is
And how he's lying here. Come up anon!
Delay will only waste your time and his,
As both of you will say when you are one.   1740
Besides, for now you know there can be none
Who thinks you are a pair. Come, see this done!
While folks are fooled, lo, all that time is won!

"In teetering, pursuing, and delays,
You give yourself away so people see.
And later though you long for merry days,
You daren't have them. Why? For she and she
Spoke such a word, and thus looked he and he!
O loss of time! I cannot bear such grief.
Come then, my niece, and bring him some relief!"   1750

But now to you, you lovers who are here,
Wasn't Troilus in a pretty place?
He lay inside and heard them whisper there
And thought, "O Lord, right now begins my race:

_____

53. Possibly love and hope; Chaucer's meaning is unclear.

Die now, or win some comfort in a space!"
This was his chance, the first time he could pray
His lady's love. My God, what would he say?

Explicit secundus liber.[54]

---

54. Here ends the second book.

BOOK 3

Incipit prohemium tercii libri[1]

O holy, blissful light whose beams shine clear,[2]
Adorning the third sphere of heaven fair;
O sun's beloved, Jove's bright daughter dear,
Delightful Love, so good, so debonair,
Who opens gentle hearts, abiding there;
O truest cause of health and wholesome pleasure,
Thy goodness merits praise beyond all measure.

In heaven, hell, and earth and briny sea[3]
Thy might rules all, if I discern aright,
As man and beast and bird and fish and tree   10
Feel thy eternal sway from that great height.
God loves the world and love will never slight.
Thus in our world no loveless thing may live
Or last without the worthiness you give.

You first moved Jove toward those glad effects[4]
Through which all things on earth may live and be,
And made him amorous, eager to perfect
Mere mortal things; and as you pleased, we see,
He thrived or failed in love by your decree
As in a thousand forms you guided him   20
To love some earthly creature at your whim.

---

1. Here the prologue to the third book begins.

2. The prologue addresses Venus, sometimes as a goddess, sometimes as a planet residing in the third sphere of the medieval heavens. Boccaccio's much shorter invocation at this point is addressed like the opening of his poem to his own lady.

3. This and the following thirty-two stanzas (through line 238) do not appear in Boccaccio. Like Troilus' song below (lines 1744–71), Chaucer's proem here is based on a poem set down by Boethius in his *Consolation of Philosophy*.

4. That is, love and sexuality.

You soothe fierce Mars and so appease his ire[5]
And cause each heart you wish to swell with good.
You make fond lovers whom you set afire
Flee vices and dishonor as they should
To live in love and freedom as you would.
And high or low, whatever lovers do,
If they succeed, they owe success to you.

You keep our realms and households in accord,
Promoting faithful friendship as we see.   30
You know those reasons, seeming untoward,
Why this one's drawn to that one—he or she—
When no one else can guess how it may be
That she loves him or why his love's so hot,
No more than why this fish, not that, is caught.

Your laws hold sway across the universe
(I know quite well, for lovers tutored me),
So any who resist them come off worse.
And thus, bright lady, by thy nobility,
And care for faithful lovers serving thee   40
(Whose clerk I am), now teach me how to write
Some of their joy who flourish in thy sight.

Enter my naked heart, infuse in me
The power to show thy jocund kindliness.
I call upon thy voice, Calliope,   *the muse of epic poetry*
For I have need. You see my great distress.
How can I write of Troilus' happiness
So Venus may be praised by all who read?
God send such joy to lovers in their need!

      Explicit prohemium tercii libri[6]

      Incipit liber tercius[7]

All this while, Prince Troilus lay abed   50
Going through his plans, what he would say.

---

5. Venus was not just Mars' complement; she was his lover.
6. Here the preface to the third book ends.
7. Here the third book begins.

He thought, "I'll tell her this, or this instead;
I'll see she knows my love for her today.
This word I'll surely use. I'll look this way.
I can't forget myself for any reason."
God grant he work his purpose in good season.

But, Lord, then how his heart began to pound
On hearing her come in. Just hear him pant!
Pandarus then, who led her by her gown,
Drew back the curtains of the bed aslant   60
And said, "Good health to all the sick, God grant!
Now look who's come to see you, if you please!
Lo, here she is, the cause of your disease!"

At that the prince began almost to cry.
"Ah, ah," he said, but said it pitifully.
"How sad I am, God knows alone on high.
Who's standing there? For I'm too sick to see."[8]
"Sir," said Criseyde, "Pandarus is, and me."
"You, sweetheart? Alas, that I can't rise
To honor you and kneel before your eyes."   70

As he struggled up, Criseyde bent
And laid her soft hands gently on his chest.
"No, for God's love," she said, "sir, be content.
Kneel to me? Surely, lord, you jest.
I've come here with two matters to address:
To thank you for your notice and to ask
For your protection, which I pray will last."

This Troilus, when he heard his lady pray
For his regard, felt half alive, half dead.
Abashed, he couldn't find a thing to say—   80
No, not if men should smite away his head.
But, Lord, how hot and swiftly he blushed red!
All that he planned to say to her that day
Flew from his head and flitted quite away.

Criseyde saw it all, and well enough,
For she was wise and moved by his distress,

_____

8. So much for Troilus' plans to "speak of love" (Book 2, line 503).

Although he couldn't make himself be rough
Or bold or falsely fawning in address.
Yet when his shame and bafflement grew less,
He spoke. I'll try to tell you what he said   90
As it appears in those old books I read.

In a shrinking voice inspired by quaking dread,
A voice that shook, and trembling for fear,
Discomfited—for now his face went red,
Then pale—unto Criseyde there, his dear,
With downcast looks and humble, careworn cheer,
He spoke two opening words, a fitting start:
"Mercy, mercy have on me, sweetheart!"

He stopped a while, and when he next could speak,
"God knows, my lady, I am yours," he said.   100
"As far as I know how, my dear, I seek
To be all yours, God save my soul from dread.
I will be so—in sorrow—till I'm dead.
My lady, I don't dare complain to you
But suffer just as much as if you knew.

"This much for now, dear flower of womanhood,
I must make clear, and if you are displeased
I'll kill myself—for such a death were good—
And quickly too, in hopes you may be eased
If death to me would see your wrath appeased.   110
Now that you've heard this much, my dear one, I
Don't care, I promise you, how soon I die."

To see his sorrow—no man's could burn hotter—
Would have caused a heart of stone to rue.
Pandarus wept as if he'd turn to water
And nudged and urged his pretty niece anew,
And said, "How sorrows rain on hearts so true!
For love of God, now, end this grievous show
Or kill us both at once before you go."

"I? What?" she said. "By God without dispute,   120
Sir, I don't know what you would have me say."
"Indeed?" said he. "That you will grant his suit.

Great God! You mustn't let him die today."
"Then let him tell me in the plainest way,
Where this will end and what is his intent.
I hardly know," she said, "what all is meant."

"You're asking what I mean, O dearest prize?"
Said Troilus. "O my lady, fresh and free,
That you would turn the clear beams of your eyes
My way sometimes, look as a friend on me,   130
Then kindly grant that I may be the he—
Without a trace of villainy or crime—
Who serves you as you wish at any time.

"Let me be your first and foremost stay
With all my wit and all my diligence,
And give me any comfort that you may
Beneath your rule; and if I give offense
Then bid me die for disobedience.
Dear, do me honor; hold me in your power.   140
Command me anything at any hour.

"And I will be your own, humble and true,
In secrecy, and patient in my pain;
And evermore, dear one, I'll look anew
For ways to serve you, counting each my gain;
And with good heart I'll answer to your rein—
Your every wish—no matter how I smart.
Lo, that is what I mean for us, sweetheart!"

Pandarus said, "Yea, here's a hard request!
One that any lady would deny!
And now, my niece, by mighty Jove's behest,   150
Were I a god, I'd surely see you die
For hearing how this man holds nothing high
Except your honor, and how he's like to perish
If you won't give yourself to him to cherish."

With that Criseyde eyed the prince once more,
Now at her ease, indeed, quite debonair.
She stood a while in silent thought before
She said a word, then spoke with all due care:

"If my honor's safe, well then, I dare—
But only on such terms as he disclosed—   160
Accept the loving service he's proposed.

"Beseeching him for all God's love that he
Would in good heart, eschewing any ill,
As I mean well, mean well himself by me.
My honor, sirs, with all his care and skill
He must keep safe. Then if I can I will
Do him some gladness. No, I won't hold back.
Now, sir, be well. I've offered what you lack.

"But nonetheless I warn you here," said she,
"King's son as you may be, I tell you this,   170
That you will never have full sovereignty
To make me do a misdeed, by my bliss.
I won't forebear, if you should go amiss,
To punish you. But while you truly serve,
I'll cherish you as well as you deserve.

"In short, dear one and my most worthy knight,
Be glad, and shape your mournful heart to pleasure.
And I shall truly, dear, with all my might,
Turn bitter thoughts to sweet in equal measure.
If I am she, the one whom you would treasure,   180
For every woe you've felt you'll have a bliss."
She took him in her tender arms to kiss.

Pandarus knelt and cast his tearful eye
To heaven above, his hands held high in prayer.
"Immortal god," he said, "that cannot die—
Cupid, I mean—you may rejoice, I swear,
And, Venus, you may sing a merry air!
Bells untouched, both here and through the town,
In faith, here is a deed to make them sound!

"But ho! Let's have no more of this just now.   190
The others will be coming back anon,
They must have read that letter. Hush! I vow
I hear them coming! Criseyde, you for one
And Troilus when you rise and get you gone,

Come to me at my house on my cue.
I'll arrange it all to solace you.

"There you'll ease your hearts and be beguiled.
And then we'll see which one of you is best
At loving talk"—and here he laughed and smiled.
"Then each of you may bare your inmost breast."   200
Said Troilus, "How much longer must I rest
Before this thing is done?" His friend replied,
"Until you're well enough to walk and ride."

By then the lady Helen and Deiphobus
Had mounted up, right to the stairs' head,
And, Lord! So sorely sighed and moaned Prince Troilus!
To fool them now, he acted halfway dead.
Pandarus said, "Ach, leave him to his bed,
And let us take our leave here of you three.
Leave them to speak, my niece, and come with me."   210

She bid them all goodbye full gracefully—
As well she could—and they were most polite
And saw her off with pleasant gallantry
And spoke as well of her as any might,
Commending her despite her sorry plight—
Her governance, her carriage, and good cheer—
They praised her so it was a joy to hear.

Now let her make her way home as she can,
While we go back to Troilus once again.
He quickly took the letter up to scan   220
That Deiphobus and Helen had brought in,
But of the two of them, his noble kin,
He freed himself by saying it was best
To let him sleep, and after talk take rest.

Helen kissed him and left him lying so,
Deiphobus went too. When they retired,
Pandarus came as fast as he could go
Straight to Troilus. Both their hearts were fired.
They lay there on a pallet, far from tired—
He and Troilus—as with a merry cheer,   230
They talked all night and held each other dear.

When everyone was gone except those two
And all the doors were shut and fastened close,
To tell it just as short as I can do,
Soon as he might this Pandarus arose,
And sat upon the bed outside the clothes,
And so began to speak with sober cheer
To Troilus, his good friend, as you will hear:

"My most beloved lord and brother dear,
God knows, and you, it troubled me full sore   240
To see you pale and languishing this year
For love, which made your woe grow more and more;
So I, with all my might and all my lore,
Have ever done such things as I thought best
To see you filled with joy and less distressed.

"My lord, I've brought affairs to such a state
So now, through me, you're standing in the way
To fare right well. But I won't boast or prate.
Do you know why? I'm half ashamed to say.
For you I have begun and mean to play   250
A game I'd not attempt for any other
Although he were a thousand times my brother.

"That is to say, for you I have become,
Half in game, half earnest, such a means,
As makes good women unto men succumb.
To put it short, I'm now a go-between.
For you I've made my niece, whose life is clean,
So trusting of your gentle lordship's honor
That you're now free to do your will upon her.

"But God, who sees all things, will say for me   260
That not for my own good did I do aught,
But just to ease your mind and set you free
When you were close to dying, as I thought.
But now, good brother, treat her as you ought.
Keep her free from blame and condemnation.
Use discretion. Guard her reputation.

"For you must know till now the lady's name
Among the people has been reverenced,

For no man ever born, I swear, can claim
That she's been guilty of the least offense.   270
And woe to me, who caused this to commence,
If she remains to me my darling niece
And I become a traitor to her peace.

"And were it known that I through my design[9]
Instilled in her a willful inclination
To do your bidding and be wholly thine,
I'd have to bear the whole world's condemnation.
For acting as a traitor to my station
Through such a deed—the worst that could be done.
She'd be lost, and not a tittle won.   280

"And so, before I take another stride,
I must beseech you, aid us in this way:
Be discreet, let caution be your guide.
That is, make sure you never shall betray
Us two. Don't grudge at me, I pray.
Again, be secret in this high affair.
You know I'm right to bid you go with care.

"Just think what woe has come to folk ere now[10]
Through boasting of a conquest, as men say;
And what misfortunes rise, as you'll allow,   290
From loose and wicked talking every day.
That's why these old clerks pass on as they may
This proverb, speaking mostly to the young:
'The best advice in life is, "Hold your tongue!"'

"And if I didn't mean to keep this short—
This speech, that is—I swear I could relate
A thousand dreary stories of one sort:
How women were lost through fools who boast and prate.
I'm sure you know the proverbs I could state
Against that vice—to win one's love and blab—   300
Even if there's truth in what you gab.

---

9. This stanza does not appear in Boccaccio.

10. This and the following five stanzas (through line 329) do not appear in Boccaccio.

"O tongue, alas, how often heretofore
Have you made lovely ladies bright of hue
Say 'Wellaway, my life has wrung me sore!'
And many a maiden's grief to spring anew,
Though most of what you say is quite untrue.
Love boasts are mostly lies—pure, unrelieved—
And bragging lovers should never be believed.

"A braggart and a liar, sir, are one—
As thus: suppose a woman grants to me   310
Her love and says all other loves she'll shun,
And I am sworn to hold this secretly,
And yet I tell it all to two or three.
I prove myself a braggart, as you heard,
And liar, too, who will not keep my word.

"Now look if all these men are not to blame
(Such as I mean—what shall I call them, what?),
Who boast about their ladies, and by name,
Who never yet were promised this or that,
Who were no more their friends than my old hat!   320
It's not a wonder then, but merely just,
That women are afraid to deal with us.

"I don't say this mistrusting you, I vow,
Nor any such, just dolts and all their kin
Who cause most of the harm we suffer now
Through foolishness as much as outright sin,
For I know well what wise men do herein
No woman dreads if she be well advised.
The harm fools do gives warning to the wise.

"But to my purpose, beloved brother dear: 330
Keep all these things that I have said in mind.
Conceal your love! And now be of good cheer,
For when it's time I will be true, you'll find.
I'll guide your doings, sir, of every kind
So that, God knows, whatever will transpire
Shall be in full accord with your desire.

"For as I know, you mean well, through and through;
That's why, my lord, I dare take up your cause.

And you're aware of what she granted you—
We've but to set the charter and the laws.   340
Good night to you, for sleep now bids us pause.
Pray this for me, since you are now well placed:
God send *me* joy in love or death in haste."

Now who might tell the joy or half of it
That entered Troilus' loving soul to dwell?
Pandarus was his man, their causes knit.
The former woe that made his sore heart swell
Drew back as joy began to make him well.
And all the sorrow of each heartfelt sigh
Flew off at once wherever such things fly.   350

And just as every frozen hedge and wood,
So dead and dry when winter winds held sway,
Breaks out in green when May proclaims it should,
And lusty lads and lasses yearn to play—
Right in the selfsame manner, truth to say,
His shriveled heart grew big and filled with joy.
There never was a gladder man in Troy.

And looking at Pandarus there just so
Full soberly, yet friend-like, so to say,
He said, "In April, just a month ago,   360
As well you know if you recall the day,
You found me sunk in woe and in death's way.
And you did all you could to pry and press
And learn from me the cause of my distress.

"You know how long, lord, I refused to tell you—
You, the man on whom I most rely—
Although no danger made me so repel you,
As I well knew. So tell me, by the bye,
Since I was loath to let *you* guess, or try,
How could I now tell others what you know   370
When telling you yourself made me quake so?

"But nonetheless, I swear, and without fear,
By God who rules this world of ours, I say,

If I'm untrue may Achilles[11] with his spear
Cleave my heart, and rip my life away.
As I'm a man, I never will betray
This secret. No, I neither would or could
For all this world that God has made so good.

"I'd rather die and end my sorry days,
As I think now, in prison in the stocks.   380
In wretched filth and vermin I would stay,
Trussed up by Agamemnon,[12] put to mock;
And this in all the temples where men flock
Throughout the town, by every god, I'll swear.
And you may hear me pledge my honor there.

"You have done so much for me, my lord,
Much more indeed than I can now repay,
Even if to give you your reward
I died a thousand thousand times a day.
But yet I vow I'll serve you if I may   390
As your bound slave, whatever you may do,
Until my life is ended, serving you.

"But here, with all my heart, lord, I must pray
You never think that I'm so deeply flawed
That I would call you false in any way.
You helped me, sir, for feelings I applaud.
I'd never think you did it as a bawd.
I'm not that mad, though I may be untaught.
God knows, I swear, that's never what I thought!

"Now, he that works for gold, as I profess,   400
In such a matter, name him what you please;
But what you did, sir, call that gentleness,
Compassion, love, and trust at all degrees.
Divide it so. In matters such as these,
As all men know, we need discrimination.
Things may seem alike, yet differ in causation.

---

11. Achilles will eventually kill Troilus. This reference to him does not appear
in Boccaccio.
12. *Ag-a-MEM-non.* High king over the Greek army.

"And so you'll know I don't think you're untrue—
That what you've done is bad when it is not—
I'll win my sister Polyxena[13] for you,
Or Cassandra[14] or Helen or any of the lot,   410
However fair of shape or widely sought.
Choose any one you want, and you will see.
She's yours, my lord. Just leave it up to me.

"But since you've given me such welcome aid
To save my life and for no hope of gain
For God's good love, those offers that you made,
Perform them, sir! You see my need is plain.
Then high or low I never will disdain
To do your bidding any way I can.
And now good night and let us sleep a span."   420

Thus each man thought that he was well repaid.
The world could not improve on what he'd earned.
Next morning when the two were both arrayed
They went their way, to other business turned.
And Troilus, although hot as fire he burned
For sharp desire and hope of further pleasures,
Did not forget to take all proper measures,

But ruled himself in the most manly way,[15]

---

13. *Pol-ex-CEN-a*. Troilus' youngest sister. A wise virgin, she attracted Achilles, whose ghost later demanded she be killed (as she was) to appease his spirit. Ovid's sympathetic portrait of her death guaranteed her a high reputation throughout the Middle Ages, so Troilus' offer here would seem almost sacrilegious to its original hearers.

14. Another famously virtuous sister of Troilus. When she rejected Apollo's advances, he cursed her, making her able to foretell the future, but ensuring no one would believe what she said. When Troy fell, she was raped by the lesser Ajax and then carried back to Mycenae by Agamemnon as his concubine. There, Agamemnon's wife, Clytemnestra, and her lover, Aegisthus, murdered her. Boccaccio's Troilus doesn't include Cassandra in his offer to Pandarus.

15. This and the following 112 stanzas (through line 1309) do not appear in Boccaccio, who gives a much different version of the affair. Boccaccio's Criseyde plans her meeting with Troilus on her own behalf, and it takes place in her house, not Pandarus'. She makes no bones about the purpose of their tryst, coming herself to lead Troilus to her bed and teasing him when it is time to remove her shift and let him see her naked.

Repressing each rash deed or careless look,
So not a soul then living, truth to say,   430
Could have known or guessed, by any crook,
How he felt, with what desire he shook.
Drawn up within himself, as in a cloud,
He kept his secret hidden from the crowd.

Throughout the time ahead of which I tell
This was his life. By day, with all his might,
He worked in Mars' high service, always well—
That is, he went in arms, a famous knight—
But for the greater part—each long, slow night—
He thought of things to do, however hard,   440
For his dear love, to keep her good regard.

But I can't swear, though he was now well placed,
That his night thoughts were not a bit diseased.
Indeed, he tossed in bed or sometimes paced,
Feeling some great lack to give him ease.
But in such cases men aren't always pleased,
For all I know, no more than he was then.
I've heard that lovers say so now and again.

But it is certain, returning to my tale,
That all along, as I have read of it,   450
He saw his love at times to good avail.
She spoke to him whenever she saw fit;
Then they would shape their plans with all their wit
Full warily to answer to their need
As vigilance allowed them to proceed.

Yet all their talk was circumspect and brief.
They both were always watching out of fear
Lest anyone should bring their love to grief—
Come close enough to see or overhear.
They couldn't think of anything more dear   460
Than Cupid would provide a time and place
So they could speak more fully by his grace.

But in the little that they spoke of aught,
His loving spirit always took such heed,

It seemed to her he knew just what she thought
Without a word, and so she had no need
To tell him what to do or how to speed.
This made her think that love, though it came late,
Let joy into her heart, unlocked its gate.

And so of this affair to tell it all,   470
So well his workings pleased her, made her fast,
That soon he had his ladylove in thrall.
For twenty thousand times from first to last
She thanked the Lord above for what had passed.
So well he strove to serve her and abet her
That no one in the world could suit her better.

She found him wise and so discreet in all,
So secret, loving, eager to obey,
That soon she came to see him as a wall,
A shield to keep displeasure far away.   480
In giving her his governance, I say,
He was so wise that she grew less afraid
(So far as it was safe to let fear fade).

Pandarus, too, to stoke the lovers' fire
Was ever keen and always diligent.
To ease his friend was his foremost desire.
He shuttled to and fro and was content
To bear such letters as the lovers sent.
No man has ever served a close friend so
Or done his work much better that I know.   490

But now some thoughtless reader may demand
That every word or sound or look or cheer
Of Troilus should be set down here at hand,
Each jot pertaining to his lady dear.
Ah, that would be too much for you to hear.
For who would tell at length—say that he might—
The smallest loving deeds of such a knight?

In truth, I've never heard that done till now,
And no one wants to do it that I've seen;
And if I wished, I couldn't, you'll allow.   500
So many fervent letters went between

Those two that just the words they wrote would clean
Fill half this book. My author left them out.
It's better that I do the same, no doubt.

More to the point, indeed, the case stood thus:
They lived just then in quiet unity,
These two—Criseyde and her loving Troilus—
In such concord as you have heard from me
(But meeting far less often than might be,
And never able to say all they desired).   510
Now I'll go on to tell what next transpired.

Pandarus all along did what he might
To bring about the end I speak of here—
To convey somehow into his house by night,
Troilus and the niece he held so dear,
Where they would have the leisure to make clear
Their mutual love and bring it to conclusion
And entertain each other in seclusion.

He planned it all with fine deliberation,
Had everything thought out that might avail,   520
Forecast events and worked by calculation,
Ignoring every cost or hard travail.
If they would come, he'd see to each detail.
No one would get wind of them or see.
He made full sure that that could never be.

No telltale breeze would broadcast his design
To any magpie, snoop, or chatter-brain.
No, things went well, for all the world was blind
In this affair, yea, every Jack and Jane.
The boards were cut to hoist aloft and frame.[16]   530
We lack for nothing neither sweet or sour
But that the lady now should name the hour.

And Troilus, who knew all of this by heart—
Knew it all and waited for that day—
Had made some preparations on his part,
Devised a scheme and told men what to say.

_____

16. Carrying out the plot is compared to raising a house.

They'd claim if someone saw he was away
While setting sly Pandarus' scheme in motion,
He visited a temple, doing his devotion.

He must, they'd say, keep vigil there all night   540
Waiting for the god Apollo's word,
To see the sacred laurel shake aright[17]
As the god's soft, rustling answer stirred
To date the Greek's departure and be heard.
Thus, no one should disturb him as he prayed
But pray themselves for great Apollo's aid.

There's little now remaining to be done.
Pandarus rose and, to tell the matter right,
Soon after the next changing of the moon,
When all the world was dark for several nights,   550
And heavy clouds showed rainstorms left and right,
He went out early on to see his niece.
And tell her what? You know that, every piece.

Arriving there, he set himself to play
As was his wont, and joke of his affairs,
Then with an oath he turned from that to say
She'd not escape this time or put on airs
Or make him plead with her from here to there;
No, no, by God, he said, despite her whims
That very night she'd come and sup with him.   560

Criseyde laughed and offered an excuse:
"How can I, sir? Alas, it's raining so!"
"Let be," he said, "I'm not at all amused.
This shall be done! You must be there, you know."
And she agreed at last that she would go;
If not, he softly whispered in her ear,
He'd never see her more or hold her dear.

Soon after, though, she asked him quietly
If his friend, Prince Troilus, would be there.

---

17. The laurel was Apollo's sacred tree, and his prophecies were sometimes
conveyed by its whispering leaves.

He said, "He's left the town. How could he be?   570
But yet suppose he would, why, what's to fear?
You still could freely come, and with good cheer.
Before some meddler saw him there and told,
I swear to you I'd die a thousandfold."

My author wasn't ready to declare
What she thought to hear him speaking so—
Saying her absent friend could not be there—
Or if she thought he spoke the truth or no.
She promised once again that she would go,
Agreeing as his niece, and fearing naught,   580
She'd come to him for supper as he sought.

But nonetheless she thought good to beseech,
Though she might visit him with little fear,
He'd keep her safe from foolish people's speech,
Who dream of scandalous things that never were,
Advised him to think well who would be there,
And said, "My uncle, know you have my trust;
Protect me. I'll obey you as I must."

He swore he would by all Troy's stocks and stones   *i.e., all Troy's idols*
And all the gods that in the heavens dwell.   590
If not, he'd suffer wholly, soul and bones,
In Pluto's realm to lie as deep in hell   *god of the underworld*
As Tantalus[18]—what more is there to tell?
Things settled, he rose up and went his way,
And she was at his house by close of day.

She brought a little troop of her own men,
Antigone, her niece, fared there as well,
And others of her women, nine or ten.
And who was glad? I hardly need to tell.
Troilus saw it all as it befell,   600

---

18. *TAN-ta-lus.* He fed his son, Pelops, to the gods and was punished in Tartarus, the deepest part of hell, doomed to stand beneath a tree that drew back whenever he tried to reach its fruit in a pool of water that receded whenever he bent to drink.

From a window in a secret room,[19]
Locked away since midnight in the gloom,

Unknown to any person but Pandarus.
But to the point! Criseyde soon arrived
With joyous greetings and a friendly fuss.
Her uncle embraced her closely. He'd contrived
That at this supper, none would be deprived.
When it was time they softly sat them down.
My Lord! No finer dainties could be found.

And after supper all of them arose   610
At ease and well. Their hearts were fresh and gay.
And lucky was the man who could propose
A pleasing game or make her laugh some way.
He sang; she played. He chattered like a jay.
But at the last, as every good thing ends.
She asked his leave to go home with her friends.

O Fortune, skillful servant of the Fates!
Divine influence from the heavens high!
Under God, you rule us in all straits.
We cannot read your courses though we try.   620
Her honest plan to leave him went awry.
The gods' will not Criseyde's ruled that day.
She wished to go, but she was forced to stay.

The sickle moon in Cancer, slim and pale,   *a region of the zodiac*
With Jupiter and Saturn there as well,[20]
Caused such a rain from heaven now to hail,
That every woman quailed, the truth to tell.
They feared that smoking rain as they feared hell.
Pandarus, laughed and called on common sense:
"Now is no time for ladies to go hence!   630

"But, my good niece, if ever I might please you
In any way, I pray that you will now

---

19. Chaucer calls the room a "stewe"—a heated chamber or bathroom, but also from the mid-fourteenth century a brothel.
20. The astronomical conjunction Chaucer describes took place in June of 1385.

Accept my shelter here; that's but your due.
Yea, stay with me tonight, for, lo, I vow
My house is yours—and dry, you must allow!
Yea, by my truth, and don't take this in game,
Your going now would cause me needless shame."

Criseyde was as wise as anyone
In half the world and listened to his prayer.
The streets were flooded; still the rain came on.   640
"I'd rather be inside than wet out there,"
She thought. "Agreeing with a friendly air
Is better than to grouch and yet remain.
For now's no time to stir abroad, that's plain."

"I will," she said, "my loving uncle dear.
Because you wish it, sir, it shall be so.
I'm glad indeed to stay with you in here.
I only said in jest that I would go."
"Now surely, Niece," he said, "I'm pleased to know,
In jest or not, you'll stop here either way.   650
I'm passing glad to think that you will stay."

So all was well, and then began aright
Another round of joy and festive play.
Pandarus, though, thought if he only might,
He would have sent the bulk of them away.
He said, "We've had a mighty rain today!
Such weather's meant for sleeping, on my head.
That's my advice, good people. Let's to bed!

"Now do you know, my niece, where you will lie?
Not far from my own chamber, if you deign.   660
From there you won't—should you be wondering why—
Hear all this din of thunderclaps and rain,
I'll put you in a closet I maintain.
And I will in the bigger room alone
Be guardian of your women, every one,

"For in this middle chamber that you see
Shall all your household women rest full soft.
And over there, I say, is where you'll be;

If you sleep well tonight, come to me oft
And never care what weather is aloft.   670
Let's have some wine, my dear, and when you please
We'll lie down in our beds and take our ease."

There is no more of this, but on that cue,
The nightcap drunk and curtains drawn anon,
The company with nothing more to do
Out of Criseyde's room were quickly gone.
Meanwhile the slashing rain outside rained on
With howling winds no sturdy walls could smother.
The folks inside could hardly hear each other.

Pandarus, then, her uncle, as he ought,   680
With her familiar women ranged about,
Brought her to bed and left her in that spot.
Bowing low, he showed the women out,
He said, "Outside your door this little rout
Of women will be sleeping, one and all.
If you have need of some of them, just call."

So when Criseyde in her couch was laid
And all her women duly sent away,
All took their beds, and that is where they stayed,
With no one left to skip about or play;   690
For they'd been told to lie still as they may.
Ill luck to anyone who stirred abroad,
Disrupting others sleeping there, by God!

Pandarus, though, had mastered every move
Of that old dance, and every point therein.   *love affairs*
Finding no more roadblocks to remove,
He thought it time his night's work should begin.
He went to Troilus' cell and pulled the pin.
And silently he went in, smooth and pat,
Where Troilus lay awake, and down he sat.   700

And shortly, not to beat around the bush,
He whispered to his friend there with a hiss,
"Now you must give the wheel another push,
For you're well on your way to heaven's bliss."

"May Dame Venus send me grace in this,"
Said Troilus. "I never had such need before,
Nor ever felt a fearfulness so sore."

Pandarus said, "Don't be afraid. Now come.
These doings shall be just as you desire.
As I may thrive, by God, I'll make them hum.   710
Or toss the curdled gruel into the fire."   *give up the game*
"May blissful Venus lead where I aspire,"
Said Troilus. "For I'm her lovesick minion here
And hope to serve her better, year by year.

"And if I bore, O Venus, full of mirth,
Signs of Saturn or of warlike Mars   *malign planets*
Or you were rendered weaker at my birth,   *by nearness to the sun*
Implore your father, Jove, to mend my stars
By his great grace, so I may have some cause
For gladness. I pray by him you loved full sore—   720
Adonis, who was savaged by the boar.[21]

"O Jove, for Europa's love, whom thou did rape,
The girl you stole away in bullish form,
Thy help! And thou, red Mars in bloody cape,
For love of Venus, fend off any harm.
And Phoebus, whose Daphne twisted in alarm
Beneath the bark, turned laurel in her fear,
For that nymph's love, lord, aid my venture here.[22]

And Mercury for love of Herse[23] as well
For which Athena was with Aglauros wroth,   730

---

21. Venus loved Adonis, a mortal youth (in many versions of the story) who was killed by a wild boar.

22. Jove enticed Europa in the form of a bull and carried her off across the sea. Mars loved Venus, though she was married to the god Vulcan. Phoebus Apollo pursued the nymph Daphne until she had her father, a river god in Ovid, turn her into a laurel tree to escape his advances.

23. *HER-see*. In Ovid's version of the story, Mercury loved Herse and bribed her sister Aglauros (*Ag-LAUR-os*) to carry a message to her (as Pandarus carries messages to Criseyde). The dispute between Aglauros and Athena comes from another story Chaucer mixes in.

Now help! And thou, Diana, I beseech.
Favor my undertaking, goddess, by thy troth.
And fatal sisters,[24] who before my cloth
Was woven for me all the yarn had spun,
Approve the bold adventure I've begun."

Pandarus said, "You wretched mouse's heart!
Are you so afraid that she will bite?
Wrap up in this fur cloak and do your part;
I'm the one who bears the blame tonight.
Be still, though, as I work another mite."   740
He softly opened up a hidden door
And led his friend to his long wished-for shore.

The stern wind now so loud began to rail
That no one there could hear another sound,
And those outside the room, so goes my tale,
Slept deeply in their blankets all around.
Pandarus, went ahead, grave and profound,
And closed the outer door without delay
Against Criseyde's women where they lay.[25]

As he came back again, all still and sly,   750
His niece awoke and asked, "Who's come in here?"
"Lie back, dear niece," he said. "It's only I,
Don't be alarmed; there's nothing you should fear."
And coming close, he whispered in her ear,
"Say nothing now, for God's love, I beseech!
Let none outside rise up and hear our speech."

"How came you here," she asked, "by secret lore?
Say how you managed this unknown to all."

---

24. The three Fates—Clotho, who spun the thread of life; Lachesis, who measured it off; and Atropos, who cut it short at the end—controlled the thread from which everyone's life was woven.

25. These arrangements are far from clear, but Troilus seems to have been hidden in a small room (perhaps a bathroom) adjoining the bedroom in which Criseyde sleeps alone. Pandarus has another room of his own, perhaps adjoining the bathroom on the other side, while both his and Criseyde's rooms look out to a central area where her serving women are sleeping.

"Just over there," he said, "I have a hidden door."
Criseyde said, "My women . . . let me call."   760
"No! God forbid that such a thing befall,"
Pandarus said. "For then we would be caught,
And they might think some things they never ought.

"It isn't good to wake a sleeping hound,
Nor give rise to speculations base.
Your women all are sleeping, I'll be bound.
They wouldn't wake if men should mine the place.   *undermine, as in*
They'll sleep until the sun begins his race.   *siege warfare*
Now, when I say what I am here to say,
Unnoticed, as I came, I'll go away.[26]   770

"My niece," he said, "I know you understand,
As sure as every living woman should,
That one who holds a lover in her hand
And calls him her dear sweetheart as he would,
Yet blears his eye and wears a double hood,   *engages in trickery*
That is, she loves another all the while,
She shames herself by her deceit and guile.

"But here's the reason that I say all this:
You know yourself, as well as any can,
That now your love entirely granted is   780
To Troilus, the most worthy knight and man
In all the world. Think how your promise ran:
Unless he wronged you by some grievous sin,
You'd not revoke the love you held him in.

"Now it stands thus, that since I left before,
This Troilus, to make all these things quite plain,
Through a passage and a private door[27]

---

26. Of course, he has no intention of going away.

27. Pandarus says Troilus came through a "goter" or "by a pryve." Both references
are unclear, but they suggest Troilus has come in through a sewer passage into
the "stewe" where he is waiting. "Stewe" carries associations with bathrooms and
brothels, both of which cast a seamy light on the whole affair. But at the same time
the whole story is Pandarus' invention. We already know that Troilus has been
waiting in the house since the previous midnight (line 602).

Has come into my house despite the rain,
Unknown to anyone in our domain,
Except myself, as sure as I'd have joy.   790
I swear it's so by Priam, King of Troy.

"And he's come here in such distress and pain
That if his brain's not now gone quite amiss,
He will be mad enough, and soon, that's plain,
Unless God helps him. And, Niece, the cause is this:
He lately found out from a friend of his
You love Orestes,[28] someone from your past.
Now Troilus swears this night will be his last."

Criseyde listened, saying not a word,
But as he spoke she felt her heart grow cold.   800
The charge itself, of course, was quite absurd.
She said, "No matter who it was that told
Such tales, my dearest heart should never hold
Me so false. Such stories, though they're wrong,
Can do such harm! O God, I've lived too long!

"Orestes! What? And false to my love Troilus?
I know him not, God help me so!" said she.
"Alas, what wicked spirit told him thus?
Tomorrow, Uncle, if I can, I'll see
Some way to bring back all his trust in me   810
If ever a woman did—at least I'll try."
Her speech was interrupted with a sigh.

"O God," she said, "how worldly happiness,
Which learnéd men call false felicity,
Is shot throughout with shafts of bitterness.
And then full hurtful is, God knows—and me—
The very state of vain prosperity.
For either joys come halting, scant and slow,
Or else no one can keep them. Off they go!

"O brittle state of man's unstable joy!   820
Whoever you are with or how you play,

---

28. A person Chaucer invented. Not in Boccaccio.

Either he knows you for a passing toy,
Or he does not. There is no other way.
Now if he sees this not, how can he say
That he enjoys true happiness in aught,
When such a lack of knowledge clouds his thought?

"But if he knows full well how joy will flit,
As every joy in worldly things must flee,
Why then, each time that he remembers it,
His dread of losing joy must make him see   830
No earthly lasting happiness can be.
And if he counts world's bliss as but a mite,
That shows us that its value is but light.

"Therefore I would draw things up this way:
That right enough, for all I can espy,
No true joy springs from earthly things, or may.
But you, distrust that sparks a jealous eye,
Envenomed folly envious and sly,
Why make my Troilus think that I'm untrue?
I never gave him any reason to."   840

Pandarus said, "Yet, Niece, that is the case."
"Why, my uncle? Why? Who told him this?
How can my love think anything so base?"
"Now you know," he answered, "how it is.
I hope all will be righted that's amiss,
For you can quench the fire, if you but will.
I trust you shall. I know you have the skill."

"I will tomorrow, certainly," said she.
"I pray to God above that will suffice."
"Tomorrow! Not a chance of that," said he.   850
"No, no! This can't be done in such a guise,
Niece, hark the word of scholars who are wise:
'Put off the cure and you more peril glean'—
Bah! Help delayed is never worth a bean!

"Niece, all things have a time, as I avow,
For when a chamber's blazing, or a hall,
Do what you need to! Douse the fire now!

Don't wait to ask the people, one and all,
Who slipped and let the burning candle fall.
God bless our souls! For while you're in no rush,   860
The bird flies off, escaping in the brush.

"And so, my niece—don't take this in bad part—
If you leave him all night in such a fear,
God help us both, he never had your heart.
I say that while there's only you to hear,
But I know well you won't do that, my dear.
You're too wise to imperil such a knight.
To wait and risk his life would not be right."

"I never loved him! By holy God, that's mean!
You never had a love like mine," said she.   870
"Now by my life," he said, "that shall be seen!
For since you would compare yourself with me,
I'd not leave him all night to wait and see
For all the treasure piled up here in Troy.
I swear it, or may God deny me joy!

"Look to it now. If you who are his love
Would risk his life all night in such a case,
Just for a silly rumor, God above,
You'd not just be a fool and lacking grace,
But evil too! I say so to your face.   880
What! If you leave him in distress,
You fail at love! You lack all gentleness!"

Criseyde said, "I bid you do one thing,
And you'll relieve him of all this disease.
Have here, and bear to him, my good blue ring.   *blue indicates faithful love*
No other sign would leave him better pleased—
Except myself—or see him well appeased.
And say that there's no cause for his great sorrow.
I'll tell him so myself, good sir, tomorrow."

"A ring?" he said. "Ye quaking hazel stick!   890
To serve in this, that ring must have a stone
Whose virtue is to make a dead man quick,
And such a ring I know you do not own.

The sense I thought you had has clearly flown.
I feel that now," he said, "but on my oath,
We're losing time. A curse on all this sloth!

"Don't you know a high and noble heart
Neither grieves nor stops its grief for naught?
Now if a fool were jealous for his part
I wouldn't give his hurt a single thought,   900
But fob him off with words to soothe his lot.
Such fools are met with every day, you'll find.
This case is of a very different kind.

"Troilus has such a fine and tender heart
That surely he will die for sorrow's sake.
But, trust me, niece, however he may smart,
He'll speak no jealous words despite that ache,
And therefore act before his heart can break.
Speak to him, dear, tonight to show you care,
For with one word of love you'll set him fair.   910

"Now I have told what peril he is in
And how he came, escaping all men's sight,
By God, to see the man cannot be sin.
I will myself be with you, as is right.
Niece, you know the prince is your own knight.
Trust him, then, at least to this extent.
I'll fetch him if I may with your consent."

Her lover's plight so piteous to hear,
Then too, so truthful seeming on its face,
And Troilus' standing as her knight so dear,   920
His secret coming, the fastness of the place,
Made her think, though it seemed a special grace,
That, weighing all things rightly as they stood,
She could see him, meaning only good.

And thus she answered, "May my soul find rest
By God's good grace, I pity his great woe,
And, Uncle, I would gladly do what's best
If only I could see which course is so.
But whether you stay or bring him, stop or go,

I am, till good God wills my thoughts to mend,   930
In a dire dilemma, near wit's end."

"A dilemma!" said Pandarus. "Will you hear me?
Dilemmas are caused by wretches, start to end.
They're hard for those who cannot clearly see
For slothful, slapdash faults they won't amend,
And those they trap are never worth a hen.
But you are wise, and what we have on hand
Is clear enough for you to understand."

"Then," she said, "do what you think you must.
But when he comes I must not be in bed.   940
And, for the love of God, since all my trust
Is in you two, do right, upon my head,
But work it all discreetly, sir," she pled,
"And I will risk my honor for his joy.
I'm here for you to lead right or destroy."

"Well said," he answered. "Well indeed, my dear.
May God reward your wise and gentle heart.
But keep your bed. You can receive him there,
For that will show you trust him for your part;
Then each can ease the other's grievous smart,   950
For love of God. Dame Venus, I praise thee.
We'll be right merry, Niece, as you will see."

Troilus soon was there and on his knees,
Earnest enough, right by Criseyde's bed.
And as he could, he set himself to please,
But seeing him, she suddenly grew red.
She couldn't speak. No, not to save her head!
Not a single word could she bring out.
His sudden coming filled her heart with doubt.

Pandarus, whose perception was so fine   960
In every way, began to joke anon.
He said, "Lo, Niece, how kneeling is his line!
Now by your truth, look to this gentle one!"
He fetched the prince a cushion at a run,
And said, "My lord, now kneel there while you will,
And may God deign to cure your bitter ill."

I can't say why she did not bid him rise.
Sorrow, perhaps, had put it from her mind,
Or else his kneeling seemed in her fair eyes,
A form of duty of some courtly kind.   970
But well I know she didn't lag behind,
But kissed him sweetly, though she sadly sighed,
Then moved so he could sit down at her side.

Pandarus said, "Well, now you may begin.
Yea, make him sit, dear niece, if you desire.
No, not outside the curtains, but within.
Whisper there, don't bellow like a crier."
And with that word he drew back near the fire,
Took up a light and opened up his book
As if that was the only place he'd look.   980

Criseyde, now, was Troilus' own by right,
And stood assured of her full faithfulness.
Although she thought her servant and her knight
Should never doubt her love and truthfulness,
Yet, nonetheless, she pitied his distress,
And thinking how his love had made him weak,
To ease his jealous mind, began to speak.

"Lo, my heart," she said, "swayed by the force
Of love, against whose power no man may—
Or ought by any shift—rule his own course,   990
And too, because I know and prize the way
You've shown me love and service every day,
And since you're wholly mine, as you've made plain,
I'm driven now to pity your great pain.

"Your goodness I've found constant ever yet,
For which, my dearest heart and faithful knight,
I thank you just as far as I have wit,
Yet all my thanks fall short of what is right.
You know that I, in every way I might,
Have been, and ever shall be, though I smart,   1000
Your truest friend with all my faith and heart.

"My love is strong enough for any test,
And so, sweetheart, all that I have to say

Shall now be told, though it may wring your breast
To hear me speak against you in a way.
I mean to drive off all the pain I may
That holds your heart and mine in heaviness,
To cast it out and every hurt redress.

"I cannot think, my love—I don't know how—
This jealousy, alas, this wicked snake,   1010
Has (altogether causeless, dear, I vow)
Invaded your dear heart and made it break.
Alas that such an evil shaft or flake
Should find its refuge in so fine a place.
May Jove remove the hellish dart apace!

"But thou, great Jove, the font of all we see,
Is this in keeping with thy deity,
That guiltless folks should suffer injury,
While he who's done his worst goes off scot-free?
If it were lawful to complain on thee,   1020
That innocence should suffer jealousy—
Of that, I promise, thou should hear from me!

"My woe, indeed, is that folks sometimes use
To tell us this: 'Ah, jealousy is love!'
They would a vial of venom thus excuse,
Because one grain of love is part thereof.
I call upon the gods who sit above,
If jealousy is love, . . . or hate and shame.
Choose one of those and give it its true name.

"But certainly some forms of jealousy   1030
Are easier to forgive than others are,
As when there's cause or very like to be,
But love will keep it hidden, like a scar,
So it cannot be seen from near or far,
But bravely drinks up all its bitterness.
I say such acts as this are gentleness.

"But sometimes it's so full of foul despite
That it surmounts all reason and restraint.
Yet you, dear heart, were never in that plight.

Thank God for that! So this, your present plaint,   1040
Is less real jealousy than trust grown faint.
Your strong affection, dear, and busy care,
Have made your tender, fearful heart to err.

"For that, I am right sorry but not wroth.
Yet for my sake and for your dear heart's rest,
As you may please, by some ordeal or oath
Or prophesy—whatever you think best—
For love of God, let's put it to the test.
If I am guilty, love, then let me die.
What better way to give your fears the lie?"   1050

In her bright eyes the shining teardrops grew
To wet her cheeks. She then implored God so:
"Dear Lord, you know I never was untrue
In thought or deed to that clear faith I owe."
She then lay back and dropped her head full low,
Drew up the sheet to hide her face and sighed,
And spoke no more to Troilus at her side.

And now may God help quench their cares and sorrow.
I hope He will, for if not He, who may?
Yea, I have seen full many a misty morrow   1060
Produce a bright and merry summer's day,
As after winter follows joyous May.
Men may see or read in any place
How after rain the sun can show his face.

This Troilus, when he heard her speaking so,
As you might guess, had little taste for sleep.
He thought it better than a rod's sharp blow
To hear and see his well-loved lady weep.
But then about his heart began to creep,
The cramp of death. She seemed in such distress.   1070
Seeing her tears, he felt it grip his breast.

His mind misgave, and he began to curse
His coming there, or that he had been born.
For now it seemed his doubtful start turned worse.
All the loving trials he had borne

Had gone to waste, and he was left forlorn.
"Pandarus," he thought, "your scheming and this plot
Are useless now, for all is turned to naught."

And with that thought he dropped his sorry head
And fell upon his knees and heaved a sigh.   1080
What could he say? He felt already dead.
She seemed too hurt to make his sorrows fly.
He steeled himself, and when he felt he might,
He said to her, "God knows that in this game,
When all is known, I'm not the one to blame."

And then his woeful heart began to clot,
So from his eyes no tear could even fall.
His vital spirits clenched into a knot[29]—
Frozen, stunned, and helpless, one and all.
His sorrow's mighty power to appall   1090
With every sign of life he ever bore
Fled and left him crumpled on the floor.

His sad collapse filled both their hearts with doubt,
But all was quiet still, and Pandarus said,
"Be silent, Niece, or else we'll be found out!"
Then though the prince was limp and halfway dead,
He got him up and cast him on the bed,
Saying, "O thief, why swoon though you're unhurt?"
And as he spoke he stripped him to his shirt,

And said, "My niece, if you don't help us now,   1100
He'll die and you can live alone and mourn!"
"I would," she said, "if only I knew how.
I swear I would. Alas that I was born!"
"You," Pandarus said, "must pull the thorn
That's sticking in his heart. Act as his friend!
Say, 'I forgive you all,' and he will mend."

"I'd rather that," she said, "good uncle dear,
Than to own the earth and planets both."

---

29. The vital spirits were essences formed in the heart and distributed through
the blood to govern the heart itself (responsible for breathing and the pulse), the
liver (digestion), and the brain (perception and thought).

And with that thought she whispered in his ear,
"Dear heart, I'm not displeased with you or loath,   1110
I swear I'm not"—with many another oath.
"Now speak to me. Speak for Criseyde's sake!"
But all for naught. He couldn't come awake.

With that his palms and hands and wrists
They chafed full fast and wet his temples too.
To free him from extinction's bitter mists,
She kissed him often, in hopes he'd rouse anew.
In short, she did as much as she could do
Until at last he blinked and drew a breath,
Woke from his swoon, and thereby cheated death.   1120

His mind began to stir and reason wake,
But he was muddled, fresh from the abyss,
And with a sigh and stretch and sudden quake,
He said, "Have mercy, God. What is all this?
Why crowd me so? Say, what has gone amiss?"
"You'd be a man and yet play such a game?"
Criseyde said. "O Troilus, sir, for shame!"

And yet she wound her arm around his head,
Forgiving all, and often enough they kissed.
He thanked her for her change of heart and said   1130
Whatever fell to purpose, bathed in bliss;
Nor were her sweet replies a bit remiss.
No, with her goodly words she pleased her knight
And softened all his sorrows as she might.

Pandarus said, "For all I can espy,
This light and I serve no good purpose here.
Such light's not good for sickly patients' eyes.
But as all doubtful matters have grown clear,
And you're agreed, now let no heavy cheer
Be hanging in your hearts, but joy and grace"—   1140
And bore the candlestick back to its place.[30]

---

30. Chaucer says Pandarus bore the candle to the "chymeneye," or fireplace. He's clearly still in the room with Troilus and Criseyde. See line 1188 ff.

Soon after this, although there was no need,
She made Troilus swear as she devised.
He owned that she was true, and then indeed,
She found no further cause to bid him rise.
Yea, lesser things than swearing may suffice
To reconcile such lovers, as they should,
Whose love is true and who mean naught but good.

But in effect she bid him say anon
What man it was and also where and why   1150
He thought she loved—repeating there was none—
Then too for proofs supporting such a lie.
She asked him to explain these things or try,
Or else she'd think he meant it, at the best,
To weigh her love and honor as a test.

To shorten this and bring it to an end,
He must obey his ladylove's behest.
To ease the harm, that is, he must pretend.
At some late feast, he said at her request,
She looked his way but once or twice at best.   1160
No reasons that he gave were worth two haws.   *hawthorn berries*
They seldom are when fishing for a cause!

She answered, "Sweet, suppose that this were so,
What harm in that? What evil can it mean?
For, by the God who guards us here below,
My love was always constant, as you've seen.
You know such fancied sleights aren't worth a bean.
If you'd the jealous lover counterfeit,
You merit all you've suffered, and may yet,"

Then Troilus, now found out, began to sigh.   1170
Her chiding cast a chill upon his mind.
He said, "Perhaps my sickness bleared my eye.
Have mercy, though, Criseyde. Dear, be kind!
For if your faithful love has been maligned
In any way, I promise you I'll mend.
Do what you like with me. I'm yours, dear friend."

Criseyde said, "My mercy for your sin.
That is to say that I forgive all this.

But don't forget tonight and what has been,
And, dear, take care to no more go amiss."   1180
"I never will," he said, "upon my bliss."
"And now," she said, "since I have made you smart,
Forgive me too with all your will, sweetheart."

Troilus then, enchanted and absolved,
Put his trust in God, for He ordained
Nothing but good; and—suddenly resolved—
He took her in his arms, now unrestrained.
Pandarus, as his ends were now obtained,
Lay down to sleep,[31] and said, "If you are wise,
Don't swoon again, lest more folk should arise!"   1190

What does or can the simple skylark say
Whenas a hawk has clutched it in her foot?
I'd write no more of these two where they lay
For those who think it sweet or foul as soot,
But though it takes a year and I'm hard put,
My author does, so I must tell their joys
As fully as I've numbered their annoys.

In Troilus' arms, she thought her heart must break,
As clerics in their old books write and tell.
Like an aspen she began to quake,   1200
Folded in his loving arms full well.
But Troilus, cured of anguish by her spell,
Poured thanks upon the seven gods above   *the seven planets*
As all his pains dissolved themselves in love.

He held her in his arms, as I have shown,
And said, "O sweet one, now may I rejoice,
For you are caught, and we are all alone!
Now yield yourself. You have no other choice."
She answered in a low and tender voice:
"Had I not already, sweetheart dear,   1210
Been yielded up, I never would be here."

_____

31. It's not clear where Pandarus spends the rest of the night, but he's clearly
still in the room with the lovers at this point, although line 1555 below makes it
appear that he returns from somewhere else in the morning to speak to Criseyde.
In Boccaccio, he was never present at the meeting in the first place.

It's truly said, that if they would be healed
As of a fever or another ill,
Men must drink, for so their fate is sealed,
A bitter drink; aye, bitterness distilled.
To taste true gladness, one must drink his fill
Of dreary sorrow. So Troilus shows us here.
By suffering he won much better cheer.

For sweet itself may sometimes seem more sweet
Upon the heels of bitterness and scorn.   1220
Lo, through their woe their bliss was made complete.
They never felt such joy since they were born.
That's better far than both should stay forlorn.
For love of God, all women now take heed:
Give in to love, if love is what you need.

Criseyde, now, was freed from dread and woe,
And had fresh cause to know the prince her friend.
Lord, it was joy to see her please him so,
His truth affirmed and nothing to amend.
As about a tree, with subtle twists and bends,   1230
There cling and circle shoots of sweet woodbine,[32]
So they embraced each other, arms entwined.

And like the newly startled nightingale,
Who stops her sound when she begins to sing,
If she should hear a shepherd in the dale,
Or among the hedges any noisy thing,
But once secure, then lets her sweet voice ring,
Right so Criseyde, free of dread and care,
Opened her heart and showed him what was there.

And just as one who sees the awful shape   1240
Of death approach to take him in distress,
And suddenly by rescue does escape—
From certain death returned to life, no less—
For all the world, in such great happiness,
Was Troilus with his lady and his sweet.
With luck like his God send we all may meet!

---

32. A European variety of honeysuckle.

Her slender arms, her back, so straight and soft,
Her tender flanks, so long and smooth and white,
He began to stroke, and blessed and praised full oft,
Her snowy throat, her firm breasts, round and tight.[33]   1250
So in this heaven he roamed with great delight.
A thousand times he kissed her, as was due.
Joy swelled his heart. What next? He scarcely knew.

Then he spoke thus: "O love! O charity!
Your mother too, Dame Cytherea[34] sweet,
After yourself the next to praise is she—
Kind Venus and the planet that's her seat—
And next to her dear Hymen, thou I greet,   *god of weddings*
No man has had as much to thank you for,
As I, whom you have brought to such a shore.   1260

Most kindly Love, thou holy bond of things,
One seeking grace but loath to honor you,
Finds his desire won't fly without your wings.
If you don't succor him, however true,
Although he gives his loved one what she's due,
He loses all. His service is in vain,
Unless thy kindly grace outweighs our pain.

"I know my humble merits don't rank high
Among those lovers entered in your grace.
You helped me, though, when I was like to die   1270
And left me standing in so high a place
No other love or bliss can match my case.
I can't say more, but praise and reverence
Be to thy bounty and thy excellence."

With that he kissed Criseyde once again—
No kiss from him would likely hurt her ease—
And said, "Would God I knew just how or when,
To serve you best, to honor you and please!

---

33. All these characteristics—slim arms, long flanks, white throat, and small,
firm breasts—are marks of conventional late medieval beauty. See any painting
of Eve by Lucas Cranach the Elder or Albrecht Durer.

34. *SITH-er-EE-a.* Another name for Venus.

What man," he said, "has felt such joys as these
But I, on whom the fairest and the best   1280
Has deigned to place her love and her heart's rest?

"Here men may see that mercy passes right.
No one, dear, has felt that more than I,
Who know how little I deserve your sight.
But still, dear heart, through your good grace so high
Think though I am unworthy (I'll not lie)
Your virtue will improve me in each way
While I strive on to serve you as I may.

"And for God's love, my lady and my pride,
Since God has fashioned me to wait on you—   1290
By this I mean he wills you be my guide
To bid me live or die as I am true—
Teach me, love, what you would have me do
To win your gracious thanks and rightly ease you,
So I won't slip by chance and so displease you.

"For certain, lovely creature unsurpassed,
I dare to say my truth and anxious care
Will not diminish while my life may last.
I'll honor your commandments everywhere,
And if I don't obey you, free and fair,   1300
For love of God, why then let me be slain,
Should you, my highest light of love, so deign."

"You know," she said, "I love you as I must,
My source of ease and all my dearest heart.
I thank you, and I've given you my trust.
But, dear, lay all this anxious talk apart.
We've said enough. Let's make a fresh new start:
In one word then—no halting or regret—
Welcome my knight; I'm yours without a let!"

Of their delight and joys not in the least   1310
Can my wit stretch so far to truly say,
But you may judge who've tasted such a feast
Of loving gladness, how they liked their play.
I can't say more. That night they found a way,

Caught up between security and dread,
To feel the precious joys that love can spread.

O blissful night! Thou night they sought so long!
How blithely you relieved them of their care.
I'd give my soul for one such, right or wrong,
Yea, for the smallest pleasure that was there!   1320
All haughtiness and fear have flown elsewhere.
Now let them in their loving raptures dwell;
Those reached more high by far than I can tell.

But it is true, though I can't tell it all[35]
As can my author in his excellence,
I've written down, God willing, and I shall,
In everything his substance and his sense,
And if I, holding Love in reverence,
Have added in a word as I thought best,
Take it as you will at my behest.   1330

For my words here and in each other part
Are offered up as under your correction,
Assuming that you understand love's art,
And all I wrote I trust to your discretion.
Excise a word or add some new perfection
To what I've said, good reader, I beseech.
But back now to the purpose of my speech.

These two whose loving arms held so much bliss
Were so afraid to part again, I deem,
That both half thought that things would go amiss,   1340
Or else—and this among their fears rose up supreme—
That all they did there happened in a dream.
Each one asked the other, speaking low,
"It's you I hold? Or am I dreaming so?"

And Lord! He looked so eagerly on her
That he saw naught before him but her face,
And said, "My dearest heart, can I be sure
That this is true and you are in this place?"

---

35. This and the following stanza do not appear in Boccaccio.

"Yea, my heart, I thank God for that grace,"
Said Criseyde. With that she kissed him so   1350
That where his soul had flown he didn't know.

Troilus often kissed his lady's eyes
Full tenderly and said, "So bright and clear,
You are the orbs that took me by surprise,
You modest nets that serve my lady dear.
Though mercy may be written in your cheer,
God knows that text, in truth, is hard to find.
How was I bound where there's no cord to bind?"

Again he took Criseyde in his arms,
And sighed a thousand times with all his heart—   1360
Not sighs of sorrow that betoken harms
Or sighs of sickness heaved when men may smart,
But easy sighs without a touch of art
That showed his love and fullness and his peace.
Such sighs as these he breathed and could not cease.

Soon after this they spoke of sundry things[36]
That fell to purpose touching this affair,
And, playing, gaily interchanged their rings.
I can't recount the inscriptions written there,
But know a brooch of gold and lapis fair,   1370
Set with a ruby fashioned like a heart,
She pinned on him, a rich gift on her part.

Lord, do you think an avaricious wretch
Who blames all love and holds it in despite,
Looking on the pennies he can catch . . .
Could such a one encounter such delight
As lies in love, though prosper as he might?
No, I have no doubt for good or worse,
Such joy would not befit a mean clenchpurse.

Misers won't agree, but, Lord, they lie,   1380
Those busy skinflints full of woe and dread.

---

36. This stanza does not appear in Boccaccio. Chaucer may intend this to be
the same brooch Troilus later sees on Diomedes' captured armor. See Book 5,
line 1651.

They call all lovers mad to hear them sigh,
But they'll learn to reproach themselves instead.
They must forgo all ladies, white and red,
And live in woe. May God give them mischance,
And every honest lover's cause advance!

I would to God each wretch who will not heed[37]
Love's service had two hairy ears as long
As Midas,[38] who was famous for his greed,
And also had a drink as hot and long   1390
As Crassus[39] drank for his rapacious wrongs,
To teach them it's themselves who should fear fate
And not the happy lovers they berate.

These lovers, now, the two of whom I tell,
With hearts assured and empty of all care,
Began in play, but earnestness as well,
To remind each other how and when and where
They met at first, and each hurt, hard to bear,
Though which they passed. But now such heaviness—
May God be thanked—was turned to joyousness.   1400

And evermore, when they described the ache
Of any woe from times that now were gone,
With tender kissing that sad tale would break
And fall into another joy anon.
They both did all they might, since they were one,
To bring back bliss and all their love to show,
With counterweights of joy to cancel woe.

Reason forbids that I should speak of sleep,
For nothing's further from my purpose here.
God knows the two of them held slumber cheap,   1410
And lest this night that they both held so dear

---

37. This stanza does not appear in Boccaccio.

38. Midas, the king with the golden touch, had to wear an ass' ears for preferring Pan's music to Apollo's.

39. Marcus Licinius Crassus (ca. 115–53 BC), a general and the richest man in Rome. When his army was destroyed by the Parthians, legend has it they cut off his head and poured molten gold in its mouth to symbolize his greed.

Should pass without its fill of bliss (no fear!),
They used it all in joy and busy play
And courtesy and love till nearly day.

But when the cock, our first astrologer,
Woke to beat his breast and loudly crow,
And Lucifer, the day's bright messenger,   *Venus, the morning star*
Upreared himself to shoot his beams below,
And eastward rose—for those who such things know—
Fortuna Major, then Criseyde anon,   *a constellation*
Grown sad at heart, saw night was almost done.

"My heart, my trust," she said, "and all my pleasure,
Alas that I was born! I feel such woe,
For day has come to rob me of my treasure.
Dear, now it's time for you to rise and go,
Or else I'm lost and always will be so.
O night, alas, why won't you stop and hover
As when Alcmene[40] lay beside her lover?

"Black, welcome night, as every reader knows,[41]
You were shaped by God the world to hide   1430
At given times, wrapped in your sable clothes,
So in your sway men could in rest abide.
Beasts might well complain and people chide
That you fleet so and carry off our rest,
Whenas by day with labor we're oppressed.

"Alas, your work is ended in a trice,
You restless night! May God, who made us all,
Bind you for your haste and unkind vice,
And drape our hemisphere in one great pall,
So that beneath the earth you'd never fall!   1440
For now you hie yourself away from Troy
And steal away too quickly all my joy."

---

40. *Alk-MEE-nee.* Jove lengthened the night he spent with her and conceived Hercules.

41. This and most of what is in the following seven stanzas (through line 1484) do not appear in Boccaccio. Chaucer turns a fairly objective description of the parting into a lively but conventional lover's complaint against the coming day.

This Troilus sighed and felt within his heart—
It seemed to him for piteous distress—
The bloody tears of sharpest anguish start.
Never had he felt such heaviness
Crowd the heels of blissful joyousness.
He turned to strain Criseyde on the bed
In both his arms and sighed full sore and said:

"O cruel day, O traitor to the joy   1450
That night and love have hidden fast away,
How I curse your coming into Troy!
Now every chink lets in another ray.
Envious day, why make our love your prey?
What have you lost? What are you seeking here?
God, quench this light. I pray that You may hear!

"Alas, what did we lovers do to you,
Despiteful day? Go taste the pains of hell!
You've slain full many loves and lovers too.
Your pouring in leaves them no place to dwell.   1460
What? Have you brought this light to us to sell?
Go sell your light to jewelers carving seals.
We don't need anything daylight reveals."

Just so, the sun, that titan, he dared chide
And said, "O fool, whom men may well despise,
Who holds the dawn all night fast by thy side,[42]
Yet suffers her so soon from thee to rise,
Affronting eager lovers in this wise.
Nay! Keep thy bed and there enjoy the morrow!
Or if you won't, God give you endless sorrow."   1470

Therewith he sighed full sore and added this,
"My ladylove and of my weal or woe
The font and root, Criseyde, O my bliss,
Shall I arise, alas, and must I go?
Now I feel my heart is splitting so
My life cannot endure another hour
For only you can give it lasting power.

---

42. Chaucer is confusing the sun (sometimes classed as a titan) with Tithonus, the aging mortal loved by Aurora, goddess of the dawn.

"What shall I do? For, love, I don't know how,
Nor when, alas, my dearest, we'll be free,
Placed as we are, to meet as we have now.   1480
And on my life, God knows, how can that be
Since fresh desire already swells in me?
I know I'll die unless you ease my heart.
I'll never thrive while we remain apart.

"Yet nonetheless, my lady sweet and bright,
Could I but have some certain sign,
That I were fixed, your servant and your knight,
As firmly in your heart as you in mine,
To me your peerless love would be as fine
As all this world if there were two of them.   1490
I'd bear my troubles better so, my gem."

To that Criseyde answered right anon,
And with a sigh she said, "Ah, Troilus dear,
The game we play between us now has gone
So far that Phoebus must desert his sphere,   *the sun*
And doves consort with eagles without fear—
The very rocks indeed must burst apart—
Before you shall be driven from my heart.

"You're now so deeply in my heart engraved
That if I tried to tear you from my thought,   1500
As truly as I wish my soul were saved,
The pain would kill me—yet I still could not.
But for the love of God, who all us bought,
Sweep all other fancies from your mind.
I'd die if you considered me unkind.

"And that you hold me firmly in your heart
As I do you, love, I must now beseech,
For if I knew you faithful in each part,
My joys could grow no bigger, all or each,
But now, my heart, we must cut short our speech.   1510
Be true to me or be forever shamed,
For I am yours, by God and my good name!

"And so be glad and live in surety.
I never said as much or shall again

To any man. If of your charity
You'd come to visit soon, love, tell me when.
I'll be as glad as you to greet you then,
As God may bring my heart into his bliss!"
She took him in her arms once more to kiss.

Against his loving will, since it must be,   1520
Troilus left the bed and quickly dressed;
And folded in his arms his lady free
A hundred times at least, though haste was best.
And sighing with the pain that filled his breast,
He said, "Farewell, my heart, my lovely sweet,
God grant we both be well, and soon will meet."

She said no word; for sorrow her heart churned.
His leaving left it sorely bruised and strained,
And Troilus to his palace soon returned
As woebegone as she was in his brain,   1530
For now he burned with fresh desire and pain.
Ah, how his sweet remembrance of her swells.
By God! The prince could think of nothing else!

Back in his royal palace once again,
He passed straight to his bed to lie and think.
He thought he'd sleep away his worries then,
But all for naught—he may well lie and blink,
But sleep would not come in by any chink.
He lay and thought how she for whom he burned
Was worth far more than he at first discerned.   1540

And in his thought he started to unwind
Every word she'd said, each countenance,
And firmly pressed upon his working mind
All that she spoke of love, her slightest glance,
Reliving all the night as in a trance.
And as he did, desire rose like a tide,
But he could only put his lust aside.

Criseyde also, in the selfsame way,
Began to recast Troilus in her heart,
His potency and worth, his loving play,   1550

His gentleness, how Love had plied his art
And served her inmost wishes for his part,
Desiring once again to have him near,
Lord, if he were, she'd make him ready cheer!

Pandarus came the morning of that night,[43]
And hailed his niece, all humor and caprice,
And said, "Last night it rained hard as it might.
My greatest fear of all was you, my niece—
That you could hardly sleep and dream in peace.
I know all night the rain kept me awake.   1560
Some heads among us now must surely ache!"

Then he drew near and said, "How stands it now
This merry morrow? Niece, how do you fare?"
She said, "No better, sir, for you, I vow—
Fox that you are! God give you every care!
Upon my life, you staged this whole affair!
I believe that's so, despite your upright speech.
Your practice puts the lie to all you preach."

With that she dodged beneath the sheet to hide.
For shame—put on or not—she blushed full red.   1570
Pandarus, peering, pulled the sheet aside.
"My niece," he said, "I think you wish me dead.
Just take a sword and smite away my head!"
With that he bent, his arm around her neck,
And kissed her soundly, more than just a peck.[44]

I pass all that which I've no need to say.
God forgave his death, and she did too,[45]
And with her uncle she began to play.
There was no further cause for them to stew.
But now to bring my story back in view—   1580
When it was time, Criseyde homeward went.
Pandarus had accomplished his intent.

---

43. This and the following three stanzas do not appear in Boccaccio.

44. It's not clear what's happening here, but Chaucer certainly implies that Pandarus goes well beyond what we would consider mere avuncular affection.

45. That is, Christ forgave his executioners, and she forgave Pandarus—a notably irreverent comparison.

To Troilus once again now let us turn,
Still awake and restless where he lay.
He sent for his good friend, for whom he yearned
To come to him and make what haste he may.
Pandarus came at once—he'd not say nay—
And entered Troilus' room with sober tread
And finding him alone sat by his bed.

This Troilus then with all the earnest care   1590
Of friendship's love his full heart could devise,
Fell down upon his knees in grateful prayer.
Before he would consent to cease and rise,
He offered honest thanks in his best wise
A hundred times, and then began to bless
Pandarus' birth, who'd saved him from distress.

He said, "O friend, of all my friends the best
That ever was, if I the truth may tell,
You've now in heaven brought my soul to rest,
From Phlegethon,[46] that fiery flood of hell.   1600
Yea, if I had a thousand lives to sell,
Why, serving you, although at such a price,
Would no more than a mote, my lord, suffice.

"The sun, that all the world below may see,
Saw never in my life—I do not lie—
Such a goodly paragon as she
Who holds my heart and will until I die.
And that I'm hers as well by every tie,
I thank great Love for his benign attention,
And you, my lord, for your kind intervention.   1610

"This thing you've given me is hardly slight.
On its account I owe you all I may—
Indeed, my life. You've helped me live aright,
Or I would now be dead these many days,"
And with that word down in his bed he lay.
Pandarus nodded gravely as he heard
And made the prince his answer in these words:

---

46. *FLEG-a-thon.* A burning river in hell.

"My dearest friend, if I've advanced your plea
In any way, God knows I'm overjoyed,
As glad, indeed, as any man may be,   1620
God help me so; but—sir, don't be annoyed
At what I say—I'd not see this destroyed.
My lord, as you enjoy the highest bliss,
You must ensure that nothing goes amiss.

"Of all of Fortune's sharp asperities,[47]
The foulest sort of evil luck is this:
For a man to triumph in prosperity,
And fall, and then remember his lost bliss.
You're wise enough, my lord. Just use your wits.
Do nothing rash, although you sit full warm,   1630
For if you do, you'll surely come to harm.

"You are at ease. Now hold you well therein.
For sure as red flames lick in every fire,
It takes as much of craft to keep as win.
Curb your speech and bridle your desire,
For worldly joy hangs by a slender wire.
Every day we see that wire break.
Go softly, sir, or sure your heart will ache."

Troilus said, "I mean at any cost,
Dear friend, to fully carry out my part   1640
So not through me will anything be lost.
I won't be rash and wring my lady's heart.
I have no hasty urge for you to thwart.
If you could know my inmost thoughts, my friend,
You'd hardly find a thing there to amend."

And then he told Pandarus of his night
And how at first his heart was filled with dread.
"My honest friend, as I'm a faithful knight,
And by my faith in God, and on my head,
I never had it hot as now," he said.   1650
"Yet all the more desire may sting and bite me
To love her best, the more it will delight me.

---

47. This and the following stanza do not appear in Boccaccio.

"I myself can't say just what it is[48]
But now I feel a fresh, new quality,
Yea, not like anything I felt ere this."
Pandarus said, "It's plain enough that he
Who's had a taste of heaven's bliss will be
A man of finer feelings—that's but fit—
Than dullards who have only heard of it."

Troilus, now, to put it in one word,   1660
Never tired of speaking on this head.
He talked in tones his friend had never heard.
He praised her peerless bounty, have no dread,
And praised his good friend too in all he said.
The tale seemed ever fresh with each retelling
Till Pandarus left to go to his own dwelling.

Soon after this, as soon as Fortune would,
The day was come—a bright and blissful day—
That Troilus was apprised of how he should
Meet Criseyde in the former way.   1670
By God, he felt his heart would fly away!
He praised the gods and blessed their noble aerie.
Just ask the folks he met if he was merry!

Their preparations went just as before—
For Criseyde's coming, his as well—
All as at first; I needn't tell you more.
But to the point! This, then, is what befell.
In joy and surety Pandarus worked his spell.
Briefly, he put the two of them to bed,
Where they were glad to be, upon my head![49]   1680

You needn't ask me, now that they were met,
If they were happy. That will soon appear.
If first was well, why, this was better yet,
A thousandfold—as no one needs to hear.
Gone was every sorrow, every fear,

---

48. This stanza does not appear in Boccaccio.
49. In Boccaccio, as earlier, this second meeting takes place at Criseyde's house.
Pandarus isn't there at all.

And they both had, and so they felt and thought,
As much of joy as hearts can take in aught.

This is no little thing I hope to say.[50]
It's more, indeed, than wit can well devise—
The way they both the other's wish obeyed—   1690
"Felicity," a word old scholars prize,
Will not suffice. In this their books aren't wise.
This joy cannot be written down in ink.
It passes all our hearts can hold or think.

But cruel day—alas, the passing time—
Approached headlong as all the signs foretold,
And this they thought a hard and deadly crime;
The woe they felt turned each one pale and cold,
And so again they both began to scold,
Calling day a traitor, thief, and worse,   1700
And bitterly the sun's bright light they curse.

Troilus said, "Alas, now I'm aware[51]
That Pyroïs[52] and those other three swift steeds,
That make the sun's bright flaming chariot fare,
Have gone some hidden way to spite our needs.
Day's come too soon with all the hurt it breeds.
Because the day's so eager to arise,
I'll give him no more praise or sacrifice."

Yet it was day indeed, and they must part.
They drew the process out with speeches sweet,   1710
Then went their ways again with heavy hearts
But set a time—right soon—when they could meet.
And many a night they used the same deceit.
Thus Fortune for a time led them in joy,
Criseyde and this royal prince of Troy.

Contented now as Bacchus' lusty priests,[53]
Troilus made his life a celebration.

---

50. This stanza does not appear in Boccaccio.
51. This stanza does not appear in Boccaccio.
52. *PYR-oise*. One of the four horses that draw the sun's chariot.
53. This and the following stanza do not appear in Boccaccio.

He spends, he jousts, he laughs, he drinks, he feasts,
Gives alms and decks his clothes and habitation,
Gathers a great crowd in keeping with his station,   1720
A world of folk, all suited to his mind,
The fairest and the best that he could find.

Then such a noise went up throughout all Troy
Of how he fared—his honor and largess—
That heaven itself resounded with his joy,
And as his love swelled almost to excess
It seemed that in his inmost heart, I guess,
No lover in the world had felt such ease.
In love like his each smallest thing must please.

The goodliness or beauty he might find   1730
In any other woman that he met
Had not the slightest power to unbind
The welcome bonds Criseyde's love had set.
He was so tightly tangled in that net,
For it to be unloosed in any way
Could hardly be imagined, come what may.

He would take Pandarus by the hand
And lead him to some garden unespied,
And there spread such a feast, full rich and grand,
Of Criseyde's great virtues and his pride   1740
And of her beauty, not to be denied,
That heaven's grace appeared in every word.
Then too, he'd often sing, as I have heard:

Canticus Troili[54]

"*Love, who rules the earth and all the sea,*
Love, who can command the heavens high,
Love, who causes people to agree
In wholesome unions, those he would ally,

---

54. The Song of Troilus. Chaucer and Boccaccio both base Troilus' song on a poem in *The Consolation of Philosophy* by Boethius, Chaucer's favorite philosopher. Chaucer's version is shorter, partly because he had already used much of Boethius' poem in his prologue to Book 3 (lines 1–231).

Love, who knits the laws that friends stand by,
And makes well-coupled lovers keep their word,
Bind now and sanctify my own accord.   1750

"The world consents with rules no force can mar
To change its seasons at the proper time;
The very elements, so like to jar,
Preserve their bonds in every place and clime;
Phoebus brings forth his rosy day each prime;
The sailing moon commands the dark of night;
All by Love's power. Yea, praise his holy might!

"The sea, apt as it is to rage and flow,
Constrains itself and keeps within its shore.
Its fiercest floods cannot spread wide and grow   1760
To drown the earth at once forevermore.
But let Love drop his reins on any score,
And all united things would spring apart,
Disjoining all he binds by his great art.

"I would that God, the author of all nature,
Would use His loving power as He might
To bind the hearts of every living creature
So from that bond no rebel could take flight.
And colder hearts . . . I wish He'd set them right,
To make them love as they all should and rue   1770
The hearts of those they hurt who would be true."

To serve the needs of Troy's warlike affairs,
Troilus took the lead in every fight.
And certainly, unless my author errs,
Save Hector, he was held their greatest knight.
And this increase of hardiness and might
He gained through love, to win his lady's grace,
Who fired his eager soul with each embrace.

When truces came, he took his horse to hawk
Or else hunt bristling lions, boars, or bears,   1780
But smaller beasts he quite disdained to stalk.
And when he rode back gay and free of cares,
He often saw Criseyde by her stairs,

Fresh as a falcon coming from her pen.
He was keen enough in bowing then!

Virtue and love were always in his speech
And he held in scathing scorn all wretchedness.
For certain there was no need to beseech
A man like him to honor worthiness
And ease all whom he could in their distress,   1790
And he was glad if anyone fared well,
Lovers at least, of whom he heard men tell.

For truth to say, he held all others lost[55]
Unless they set themselves to serve Love's ends—
I mean those folk who should have loved the most.
Amid all this, so fervently he penned
And spoke of love that no one could amend
His rare discourse, and so all lovers thought
He was their guide. No better could be sought.

And though he came of highest royal blood,   1800
No man, however low, would he mistreat.
He scattered good will everywhere he could.
For that, he garnered praise in every street.
This was Love's work—Salute his graces sweet!—
That Pride and Anger, Envy, Avarice
Should be put down, all vices such as this.

Thou lady bright, thou daughter of Dione,[56]
With Cupid brisk, thy blind and wingéd son,
You sisters nine that fast by Helicon   *stream sacred to the nine Muses*
Upon Parnassus dwell—you holy ones—   *mountain in central Greece*
You've guided me so well my book is done.
I'll say no more, but since you wish to go,
While men shall live may your sweet praises grow.

Through you I have told fully in my song
Of Troilus' joy and how it came to pass.

---

55. This stanza does not appear in Boccaccio.
56. *Di-O-ne*. Jove's first consort and the mother of Venus. This stanza and the
next do not appear in Boccaccio.

By course it brought a few sharp pangs along.
My author told them. So must I, alas.
Like all things, though, my book must end at last,
With Troilus now content and gratified,
And Criseyde, his fair darling, at his side.   1820

Explicit liber tercius[57]

57. Here the third book ends.

BOOK 4

Incipit prohemium quarti libri[1]

But all too little, wellaway the while,
Does such joy last; and Fortune is to blame,
Who seems most stable when she would beguile,
Though fools trust her false singing all the same,
And so she blinds them cruelly, to her shame.
And when deluded hearts fall from her wheel,
She laughs in scorn despite the hurt they feel.

For she soon pleased to turn her smiling face[2]
Away from Troilus, paying him no mind.
She cast him down, clean out of his lady's grace,   10
And raised up Diomedes[3] while he pined.
My own heart bleeds to see her so unkind
So now the very pen with which I write
Quakes with dread at what I must indite.

For how Criseyde Troilus forsook—
Or how at least her liking went astray—
Must henceforth be the matter of my book,
To go by what all other writers say.
Alas each one maligns her in his lay
And speaks her harm, . . . but if they say untrue,   20
Then they deserve their share of censure too!

O ye Furies,[4] daughters of the night,
That ceaselessly complain in endless pain,

---

1. Here begins the prologue to the fourth book.
2. This and the following three stanzas do not appear in Boccaccio.
3. *Di-o-MEE-deez*. One of the chief heroes on the Greek side of the war.
4. The Erinyes, or Furies, named below, avenged crimes and broken oaths. Chaucer named Tisiphone as his muse for Book 1.

Megaera, Alecto,[5] Tisiphone, aright,
And Mars, great father of the Roman strain,[6]
Help me with this fourth book; rouse my brain
To show how in a world embroiled in strife,
Troilus lost his love and then his life.

> *Explicit prohemium quarti libri*[7]
>
> *Incipit liber quartus*[8]

Encamped in siege, as I have said ere this,
The Greeks sat strong about the Trojan town.   30
It happened then, unless my author miss,
When Phoebus fair in Leo's house was found,[9]
That Hector, with his knights of high renown,
Decided he would ride outside the walls to fight.
He often did, to grieve what Greeks he might.

I do not know how long it might have been
From his decision to the fight he planned,
But on a day, they donned bright arms and then
Hector sallied forth amid his band
With sturdy bows and sharpened spears in hand.   40
And fighting face to face and nose to nose,
The Trojans did their best to rout their foes.

All day long, with keen new-whetted spears,
And arrows, darts, and swords and heavy maces,
They heaved and struck at men and mounted peers.
Axes tasted brains; sharp, fine-ground blades split faces;
Yet still the Greeks stood steady in their places.
But then, alas, the Trojans broke and ran.
They'd fared the worse. Now save himself who can!

---

5. *Ma-JEER-a, A-LEC-toe.*

6. Mars was the father of Romulus, the founder of Rome.

7. Here ends the prologue to the fourth book.

8. Here the fourth book begins.

9. That is, the sun was in the zodiacal sign of the lion, Leo, as it is in July and early August.

And on that day the Greeks took Antenor[10]   50
In spite of Polydamas or Mnestheus
Antiphus, Sarpedon, or Polymestor,
Polites, or the just lord Ripheus,
And other lesser folk like Phebeus.[11]
And so the day brought harm to those of Troy,
Who felt they'd lost a great part of their joy.

King Priam gave the Greeks a truce they claimed,
And emissaries were sent out to treat
And trade the noble prisoners by name
And for the others set such sums as meet.   60
Soon all the terms were known in every street.
The Greeks all heard, and Trojans far and near.
Among the first, it came to Calchas' ear.

Seeing this exchange should be discussed
Among the Grecian council, whom he knew,
Calchas pressed his case with lords who must
Attend to him as they were wont to do,
And with an altered face he bid them to,
For love of God, show him such reverence
As hold their noise and give him audience.   70

"My lords," he said, "I once belonged to Troy.
That's known to every man of you indeed.
I'm Calchas, sirs, and now in your employ,
Who first looked to your comfort in your need
And told you well just how your arms could speed.
Through you without a doubt as I have found
Troy will be burnt and beaten to the ground.

---

10. *AN-ten-or.* An important Trojan elder. According to some traditions, his
house was later spared in the sack of Troy either because he advocated giving Helen
back to the Greeks or because he somehow betrayed the city at the end of the war.

11. Most of these are known figures. Polydamus and Menestheus were Trojan
warriors; Antiphus and Polites were two more of Priam's sons; Sarpedon was the
son of Zeus and Laodamia and king of Lycia (in modern Turkey); Polymestor
was the treacherous king of Thrace; and Ripheus was a Trojan known for justice.
Phebeus was a warrior Chaucer invented and gave a fake-Italian name, Phebuseo.
I gave him a fake-Greek name instead.

"And in what form, my lords, with no disguise
You best will bring it down and have your way,
You've surely heard me fashion and devise.   80
All this is widely known, my lords, I say,
And since the Greeks are dear to me as day,
Alone and quite unarmed I came to you
To teach you if I could what you must do.

"I set aside my treasure and my rents,
Overlooked them, sirs, to serve your needs.
All my goods I left yet was content
If I could aid your efforts with my deeds;
But that was no great burden I concede,
For I was more than willing, by my joy,   90
To lose for you all that I had in Troy—

"Except my daughter, whom I left, alas,
Asleep at home, my leaving was so swift.
O cruel father! Hard and cold as brass!
How could I leave my dear one thus adrift?
I should have brought her, even in her shift!
I swear, my lords, I'll die before tomorrow
Unless you now take pity on my sorrow.

"Because I never saw a chance till now
To rescue her, I haven't said a word.   100
But now or never is the time, I vow,
For me to see my well-loved girl transferred.
O grant me help and grace for what you've heard!
Pity this old varlet in distress.
It's for your sake I have this heaviness.

"Your prison holds the Trojans you have won,
Enough and more; now if you should agree,
Let my child return to me for one.
For love of God, I pray you, hear my plea:
One of those many Trojans grant to me.   110
What need have you to disallow this boon
When Troy and all her folk must fall so soon?

"On peril of my life, I shall not lie.[12]
Apollo, mighty god, has said in truth
What's also written in the stars on high,
In number lore, and other ways in sooth:
The time is near to all the Trojans' ruth
When fire and flame and war's tumult and clashes
Shall turn their town to smoking brands and ashes.

"For Phoebus and Neptune, joined with him just now,   120
Who once built up the walls that guard the town,
Are angry with the folk of Troy, I vow,
And they will surely smash those same walls down.
Incensed against the king who wore Troy's crown
Because he once refused to pay their hire,[13]
They'll now consume his precious town with fire."

He told his tale right well, this gray old man,
Seeming in his speech aggrieved, yet meek,
While salty tears from both his old eyes ran,
To streak his face and moisten either cheek.   130
So long he stood to argue and beseech
That, to heal his hurts and ward off more,
The Greeks in counsel gave him Antenor.[14]

And who was glad indeed but Calchas then?
Full soon enough he laid his present need
Before the embassy of Greeks, all chosen men,
Imploring them, when Antenor was freed,
To bring back Thoas[15] and Criseyde as agreed.

---

12. This and the following stanza do not appear in Boccaccio.

13. Laomedon, Priam's father, promised lavish wages to Poseidon (Neptune) and Apollo (Phoebus) for building Troy's city walls, but when the work was done he refused to pay. As a result, the two gods favored the Greek invaders.

14. After originally arguing that the Trojans should send Helen back to Greece, in some versions of the story Antenor later turned traitor and opened the gates to let the Greeks sack the city.

15. *THO-as*. A Greek hero and one of Helen's former suitors. Virgil identifies him as one of the Greeks inside the Trojan Horse. He is part of the exchange as described by Benoît, but not mentioned in Boccaccio, where the trade involves only Criseyde and Antenor.

And when King Priam sent his guarantee
The ambassadors went at once, as we shall see.   140

Learning of their coming and its cause,
King Priam issued forth a general call,
To summon his assembly by their laws.
Now I'll relate what happened in their hall.
The ambassadors were answered, one and all:
The Trojans welcomed this exchange indeed.
They liked it well. Let bargaining proceed!

Now, Troilus was present in the meeting place
When Criseyde was pledged to ransom Antenor.
This brought a sudden change into his face   150
As those words gripped his heart and wrung it sore,
But he stayed silent as he'd been before
Lest men should get some hint of his affair,
And with a manly heart he hid his care.

But full of anguish, pierced by grisly dread,
He sat to hear what other lords would say.
If they would grant—and, Lord, how his heart bled—
That sad exchange (he thought in his dismay).
How could he save her honor in some way
And yet oppose her leaving? He sought some clue,   160
Thinking in a panic what to do.

Love made him swear that she should stay;
He'd rather die at once than see her go.
But Reason pulled his mind the other way:
He couldn't speak without her saying so,
Or, speaking, he might make his love his foe.
He'd show their love to evil-minded spies,
And she would cringe before all Trojan eyes.

So as the prince considered what was best,
He thought that if the trade would win assent,   170
He'd hold his peace, agreeing with the rest,
But be the first to tell her what it meant
And hear her wish and honor her intent.
And then he'd work her will, and work with joy,
Though what he did might outrage all of Troy.

Hector, who had heard the Greeks right well,[16]
How they would have Criseyde for Antenor,
Stood out against the plan as it befell.
"She is no prisoner," he said; "therefore,
Whoever made this plan must think once more.   180
For my part, sirs, this answer must suffice:
We sell no women here for any price."

A stir of loud objections rose at once
As fierce as straw that crackles on the fire.
As ill luck chose to guide them for the nonce,
They laid their own destruction on the pyre.
"Hector," they said, "now how can you desire
To shield this woman with Antenor at stake?
Explain yourself; you must, for heaven's sake.

"Antenor is proven, wise and bold,   190
And we have need of him, as all can see.
He's been a strong support to us of old.
O Hector, let these foolish fancies be!
King Priam, be persuaded. Grant our plea:
We're all agreed Criseyde has to go
And Antenor return. Sire, make it so!"

O Juvenal,[17] my lord, your word is true,
That people little know what they should will
So good instead of evil should ensue,
For clouds of error shroud their eyes and spill   200
Their judgment. Now Troy displayed that ill:
These lords demanded Antenor's return—
The very man who then caused Troy to burn!

For he was later traitor to the town.
Alas, those people brought him back too soon.
O silly world, your judgment is unsound!
Criseyde, who was honest as the noon,

---

16. This and the following five stanzas do not appear in Boccaccio, who occupies
the same space telling of a fainting spell that came over Troilus on hearing Criseyde
would be exchanged.

17. *JUV-a-nul.* Roman satirist.

Will suffer now with all her hopes marooned.
Antenor must come home, a shining sun,
While she's cast out—and so says everyone.   210

For that was what the parliament decided:
They'd trade Prince Troilus' love for Antenor.
This was proclaimed by him who then presided.
Though Hector balked and voted "nay" once more,
No vote from him or voices from the floor
Could sway the group. It must be so and should,
For far the larger faction ruled it would.

Soon everyone had left the parliament,
And yet the prince did not oppose the plan
But to his private room he quickly went,   220
Alone, save for a loyal serving man
Whom he desired to vanish out of hand,
For he would sleep at once, or so he said,
And hastily he threw himself in bed.

And as in winter green leaves are bereft,[18]
One after another, until the tree stands bare,
So that there are but bark and branches left,
Just so lay Troilus stripped of comfort there,
Cloaked in the blackest bark of his despair,
Reeling in his wits and halfway mad—   230
This trade would cost him all the joy he had!

He rose at last and closing every door,
The windows too, this heartsick, grieving man
Sat down upon his waiting bed once more
Much like a statue, silent, pale, and wan,
Till, bursting from his breast, his woe began
To break his heart and work in such a wise
As I will shortly lay before your eyes.

Just as the wild bull charges every way,
Now here, now there, when wounded to the heart,   240
And, dying, lifts his head to roar and bray,

---

18. This stanza does not appear in Boccaccio.

Just so the prince about his chamber starts;
Smiting his breast with fists so that it smarts,
Beating head to wall and frame to ground,
He bruised himself, his body to confound.

Both his eyes for pity of his heart
Welled up with tears, swift running every way.
The rough, harsh sobs of his great sorrow's smart
Stopped his speech so he could scarcely say,
"O death, alas, please come for me today.   250
Accursed be the moment of my birth,
When I became a creature of this earth!"

But later, when the fury and the rage
That wrung his heart and left it sorely pressed
Began in time to soften and assuage,
He laid him down in bed once more to rest.
And yet again the tears swelled from his breast,
So hot his body hardly could sustain
Even half this woe and grief-filled strain.

And then he said, "Fortune, alas the while!   260
What have I done? Say, what is my guilt?
How could you so deceive me with your guile?
Is there no grace? Shall all my hopes be spilt?
Must my Criseyde go because thou wilt?
Alas, how can you find it in your heart
To use me with such cruel and unkind art?

"Have I not honored thee through all my life
Above all other gods, both large and small?
Why turn my soul from happiness to strife?
O Troilus, what must thou henceforth be called   270
But wretch of wretches, dishonored by this fall
From joy to weeping? Now I must bewail
Criseyde, lost to me, until I fail!

"Alas, Dame Fortune, if my life in joy[19]
Displeased you, with your unforgiving eye,

---

19. This stanza does not appear in Boccaccio.

Why not remove my father, king of Troy—
Cut off his life—or make my brothers die,
Or else kill me, who thus complains and cries?
I clog the world. I'm good for nothing now,
Dying, yet not dead enough, I vow.   280

"If only Criseyde's self were left to me,
I wouldn't care a whit how thou wouldst steer.
But she's been banished hence today by thee,
For that's thy way—alas, I see it clear—
To rob us of the things we hold most dear,
And prove to all thy veering, willful power.
So I am lost forever from this hour.

"O very lord, O Love! O god, alas!
You understand my heart and all my thought.
How shall my lingering, idle life now pass   290
If I must lose what I've so dearly bought?
Since you my love and me have fully brought
Into your grace, uniting either heart,
How can you now allow her to depart?

"What shall I do? I shall, while I may last,
Live on in torment and in cruel pain.
I'll never put this trial in the past,
But alone, as I was born, I will complain.
I will not see the sunshine or the rain;
Like Oedipus,[20] I'll wander dark and blind   300
And end bereft of spirit and of mind.

"O weary soul, that ranges to and fro,
Why won't you flee this body I possess,
The saddest corpse that still can stand and go?
O soul immersed in woe, now leave your nest!
Fly forth and leave my hopeless, aching breast,
And follow your Criseyde, lady dear.
Your place is where she is. Don't linger here!

---

20. *EE-di-pus.* He blinded himself on learning he had slept with his mother,
Jocasta.

"O woeful eyes, because your greatest sport
Was once to see Criseyde's sparkling glance,   310
What shall you do but cut your looking short
And serve for naught but weep as in a trance
Since she's expelled by this sad happenstance.
Henceforth in vain shall I have eyes at all.
Criseyde will be gone beyond recall!

"O Criseyde, sovereign lady, all my gain,
Ruler of this soul that hurts and cries,
Who shall give me comfort in my pain?
Alas, no one! But when my sad heart dies,
That soul will hasten to you in some guise.   320
Receive it then! It always will stay true.
What matter that my body's life is through?

"O you lovers, who are high upon the wheel
That Fortune turns, I hope it may be so
That God grant you a loved one true as steel,
And may you live long lives full free of woe.
But when I'm dead and laid to rest below,
Remember I was one who loved like you,
Unworthily, perhaps, but always true.

"O old, unwholesome, wicked, evil man—   330
Calchas, I mean—what could have tempted you
To turn to Greece from Troy, where you began?
O Calchas, who has set my world askew,
I curse your birth and all your doings too.
I would that Jove would grant me for his joy,
To have you where I would—back here in Troy!"

A thousand sighs, each hotter than a coal,
Rose from his breast, one fast upon the next,
Mixed with plaints arising from his soul.
His streaming tears showed forth these sad effects;   340
In short, his many pains left him so vexed
And so tired out, no joy or happy chance
Could wake him from his heartsick, hopeless trance.

Pandarus, too, who in the parliament
Had heard what every lord and burgess said,

And how they ruled, almost with one assent,
To give Criseyde up, take Antenor instead,
Thought all his wits must leave his downcast head.
He couldn't guess, for woe, how things could mend,
But in a rush he went to see his friend.   350

A certain knight, who kept the chamber door,[21]
Let him in, for Pandarus was known.
Stepping soft, he paced across the floor.
The room was dark and still as any stone.
Toward the bed, he groped his way alone,
So confused he knew not what to say.
Sick with woe, his ready wit gave way.

With sorry cheer and looking all forlorn,
Sad at heart, arms folded on his breast,
He stood before this Troilus crushed and worn,   360
And looked down on his face, so sore distressed,
And felt his own heart chill within his chest
To see his friend in woe, whose heavy pain
He feared would stop his life and prove his bane.

This woeful man, this Troilus, when he felt
Pandarus, his foremost friend, there at his side,
Began like snow beneath the sun to melt;
And Pandarus himself, now sorely tried,
Wept along with him, so both men cried,
And speechless in the grief they felt that day   370
Neither spoke. There were no words to say.

But then at last this Troilus in his woe,
Near dead for pain, began to heave and roar
And with a choking noise he spoke just so—
Among his sobs, while he was sighing sore:
"Lo, Pandarus, I am dead. I am no more.
Have you not heard in parliament today,
While Antenor returns, Criseyde goes away?"

This Pandarus, now full wan and pale of hue,
Answered, "Such a pity, by my bliss.   380

---

21. This and the following stanza do not appear in Boccaccio.

If only it were false as it is true, . . .
But I was there, and know how sure it is.
O mercy, God, who would have guessed all this?
Who could have thought by such a sudden ploy
Fortune would deprive us of our joy?

"In this world there's no one, as I think,[22]
Who ever saw so strange an overthrow.
This is the worst, and struck ere we could blink.
But who escapes misfortune, high or low?
Such is the world! Henceforth I will know   390
No man can keep Dame Fortune for his own:
Her fancy's light; her gifts are but on loan.

"But tell me this: why are you so mad
With sorrow now? Why grieve you in this a way,
Since everything you wished to have you've had?
That should content you now. You've had your play.
But I, who never felt in all my days
A friendly look or glance of shining eyes—
Let *me* weep thus and wail until I die.

"Remember, lord, as you know well yourself,   400
This town abounds in ladies all about,
And, by my fate, there must be ten or twelve
As fair as she. Well, I will seek them out.
Yea, one or two at least, without a doubt.
And so be glad my own, my dearest brother.
If she be lost, we'll quickly find another!

"God forbid that all our pleasures here[23]
Should rest in one thing or one lady's sight.
One dances well; one's singing soothes the ear.
If one is modest, another's glad and light.   410
If one is fair, her sister acts aright.
Each has her virtue. To each a special grace.
A hawk for herons. Greyhounds for the chase.

---

22. This stanza does not appear in Boccaccio.
23. This stanza does not appear in Boccaccio.

"Then too, as Zanzis wrote—a man full wise—   *unidentified*
'The new love always chases out the old.'
A new event requires some new advice.
Nor are lives ours to end, as we are told.
The hottest fire will die and soon grow cold.
Love is pleasant, but it turns on chance.
It may become a prey to happenstance.   420

"For just as sure as day comes after night,[24]
A newer love or labor, or some woe,
Or just to have the loved one out of sight,
Soon dims an old affection, as you know.
You'll pick up one of these to serve you so:
The new concern will ease this bitter smart,
And absence itself will drive her from your heart."

He said this lacking any better plan
To help his friend, for sorrow halfway dead.
Hoping he could pacify the man,   430
He hardly cared what foolishness he said.
But Troilus, weak and wilting on his bed,
Took little heed of anything he meant.
It struck his ear, then out again it went.

Yet finally he answered, saying, "Friend,
To take the medicine you've offered me
Would suit a devil eager to offend.
Betray a lady true as she can be!
To such advice I never will agree.
I'd rather die at once, right here and now,   440
Than do as you would have me do, I vow.

"She whom I serve, whatever you may say,
To whom my heart belongs by every right,
Shall have me wholly till my dying day.
My lord, since I am pledged her faithful knight,
I'll not be false—supposing that I might—
But as her man I'll live until I die.
I'll love no other, sir, beneath the sky.

_____

24. This and the following stanza do not appear in Boccaccio.

"You say you'll find another fair as she.
Let be, my lord! Make no comparison! 450
No earthly thing that fine could ever be.
Now one word more, Pandarus, and I'm done:
I won't take such advice from anyone—
Not touching this—no, that's absurd.
So hold your peace or kill me with your words!

"You bid me, sir, that I should love another
All freshly new, and let Criseyde go!
That's not within my power, honored brother,
But even if I might, I'd not do so.
What! Bat my love with rackets, to and fro? 460
Nettle in dock out;²⁵ now here, now there?
Let any girl who loves you, lord, beware!

"You act toward me, Pandarus, I declare,
Like one who when his friend is woebegone
Comes to him and says, to show his care,
'Ignore your hurts, and then you will feel none.'
You'd have to change me first into a stone,
And still my passions—somehow make them go—
Before you could so lightly cure my woe.

"Death may come to me and stop my heart, 470
Destroy my life, so undermined with care,
But nothing will remove Criseyde's dart.
Like Proserpine,²⁶ I'll go to Pluto's lair
When I am dead, and sorely suffer there,
Eternally complaining of this ill:
How we've been set apart by Fortune's will.

"Now you have argued this way as I find:
That it should be a lesser pain to me
To lose Criseyde, because she once was mine,
And served my ease in full felicity. 480
That's nonsense, sir. I've heard you say, you see,
'A man's worse off to lose the joy he's owned
Than someone else who no such joy has known.'

---

25. Popular saying based on treating stinging nettles with dock leaves.
26. *PRA-ser-pine*. Pluto, god of the underworld, carried her off to hell.

"But tell me now, since you think it so light
To change your mind in loving, to and fro,
Why haven't you determined, as you might,
To change from her who now works all your woe?
Why not uproot her from your heart just so?
Why not love another lady best,
One who'll set your wounded heart at rest?   490

"If you've had nothing but mischance in love
Yet cannot drive that feeling from your heart,
I, who lived in pleasure with my dove,
As much as any creature can impart,
How can I now make such a love depart?
Where have you been? How have you hid your light?
Who else could mount an argument so tight?

"No, no, by God, your words are nothing worth,
And so, no matter what may next befall,
Without more speech I'll die and rest in earth.   500
O Death, the happy end of sorrows all,
Come to me now, since I so often call!
Blessed be Death, and so may he remain,
That, often called, responds and ends our pain.

"I know well, Death, that while I felt complete
I'd offer any price to make you stay.
But now your coming seems so good and sweet
That dying is my fondest wish today.
O Death, since sorrow burns in me this way,
Call up my tears indeed until I drown,   510
Or with your cold stroke dash me to the ground,

"Since you slay so many in sundry ways
Against their will, unprayed for, day and night,
Slay me too, I ask, and earn my praise.
Rid the world of me—that's only right.
Take me now, for I'm the saddest blight
That ever was. It's time that I should die
Since no one's less of use on earth than I."

With this his bitter tears began to spill
Like liquor from an alembic, just as fast,   *a device for distilling liquids*

And Pandarus held his busy tongue quite still,
Eyes looking down upon the ground, aghast,
But nonetheless, he thought this way at last:
"What now? Before he casts his life away,
I'll try again to save him if I may."

"Friend," he said, "since you're in such distress,
And since you find my arguments so lame,
Why don't you help yourself and take redress?
Use your manhood! Don't just bleat and blame.
Go ravish her! No? Can you not? For shame!   530
Either lead her off, I know not where,
Or keep her hid, but stop this sorry fare!

"Are you in Troy and have no hardihood
To take a woman sick for love of thee?
She herself, my lord, would think it good.
Now isn't this a pretty sight to see?
Rise up at once, and let this weeping be!
Show you are a man! Today, by Mars,
I will be dead, or Criseyde will be ours!"

To this his grieving friend replied full soft: 540
"By God's good grace, beloved brother dear,
I've thought all this myself, you know, and oft,
And more things, too, than you have told me here,
But why this cannot be I'll now make clear.
And when you've heard all that I have to say,
Why, then advise me further if you may.

"First, you know this town is now at war
All for a woman ravished by men's might,   *i.e., Helen of Troy*
I'd never be allowed to steal one more.
As things now stand, that hardly could be right.   550
I'd justly win the blame of every knight.
Nor can I false my father's word, nor should,
Since she's been traded for Troy's common good.

"I've also thought, supposing she'd agree,
To ask her of my father, of his grace,
But that would show the love she's given me.

I'd not subject her to such loss of face.
Then too, my father in so high a place
As parliament approved this—you saw how.
He hardly could repeal his ruling now.   560

"My biggest fear is that she'd be perturbed
By any violence that I might inflame,
For if the town were publicly disturbed,
That too would bring dishonor on her name.
I'd rather die than see her thus defamed.
God forbid I bring about such strife.
I much prefer her honor to my life.

"And so, I'm lost for aught that I can see,
For certainly I am Criseyde's knight.
I must regard her honor more than me,   570
In every case, as lovers should of right.
Desire and reason join to bind me tight:
Desire would have me steal her, as I said,
But reason bids me keep the peace instead."

Thus his bitter weeping could not cease.
He said, "How shall a wretch like I am fare?
Always I feel my love for her increase
As hope grows less—flown I don't know where.
And always there's new reason for despair.
So wellaway, why won't my hard heart break?   580
Love doesn't ease the heart but makes it ache."

Pandarus answered, "Friend, you may, for me,
Do as you like, but if I loved so hot
And was a prince, by God, I'd set her free
Though all the town cried out that I should not!
I'd pay them no attention, not a jot!
When all their noise is done, men settle down.
No wonder lasts for nine nights in this town.

"Don't poke and probe your reason quite so deep.
Don't be so soft, but help yourself anon.   590
Let others weep, if anyone must weep,
And shortly, since the two of you are one,

Assert yourself, my lord, she's not their pawn!
Rather be a bit to blame, I say,
Than shrivel like a gnat and waste away.

"It's no shame to you, my lord, or vice
To keep her here, her whom you love most,
Perhaps she'd think you had a heart of ice
To let her go thus to the Grecian host.
Think how Fortune, as all heroes boast,   600
Helps the hardy man to work his will
But leaves a coward's fondest hopes to spill.

"And though your lady might be grieved a bit,
Well, that will pass. Fresh peace is yours to make.
But as for me, I can't believe as yet
She'd think you wrong in acting for her sake.
Why should you fear? Why should your weak heart quake?
Think how Paris, sir, your noble brother,   *Helen's abductor*
Won his great love. Shall you not win another?

"And one more thing I swear to you is sure:[27]   610
If Criseyde, your greatest good, beyond compare,
Loves you, my lord, as well as you love her,
She won't, so help me God, so greatly care
If you can save your love in this affair.
But if she is content to go away,
Then she is false; so love her less, I say.

"And so take heart and bear you as a knight.
Lovers often trample every law.
Show the world your courage and your might.
Have mercy on yourself. Shake off your awe.   620
Don't let woe have your heart to grind and gnaw,
But stake your all on rolling six or seven—   *winning numbers at dice*
And if you die a martyr, go to heaven!

"I myself will help you in this deed,[28]
Though I and all my kin may die for it—

---

27. This stanza does not appear in Boccaccio.
28. This stanza does not appear in Boccaccio.

Lie about the streets like dogs and bleed
From gaping mortal wounds, our bodies split.
I'll be your friend, my lord, and never quit.
But if you'd rather starve here like a goat,
I wouldn't pay to save you, not a groat!"   *small coin or hulled grain*

This Troilus felt his blood begin to rise.
"My thanks, my friend," he said, "and I assent,
But you should not berate me in this wise.
No pain I feel, however it is sent,
No circumstance, can alter my intent:
I will not ravish her, upon my word
Unless the two of us are in accord."

"That's just what I've been saying, lord, all day!"[29]
Pandarus said, "but do you know her mind?
You sorrow so!" But Troilus answered, "Nay."   640
"Then why," his mentor asked, "be so resigned?
For all you know, my lord, she'll think you kind
To ravish her. What! Are you a seer?
Did Jove say 'Leave the lady' in your ear?

"And so, rise up. There's naught amiss so far,
And wash your face and go to see the king,
Or he may fall to wondering where you are
(Take care that he does not suspect a thing),
And he might call you there to kiss his ring
Before you're set. In fine, my brother dear,   650
Be glad, and let me work as I will here.

"For I'll shape all things so that certainly
You shall this very night, some time, somewhere,
Meet Criseyde alone, as you will see,
And by her words and also by her cheer
You'll quickly sound her thought, my lord, and hear
All she may say, what course she thinks is best;
Now fare thee well, for on this point I'll rest."

Fleet-flying Fame that many trumped up things
Spreads through the world with those that are most true,   660

---

29. This stanza does not appear in Boccaccio.

Had flown through Troy on swiftly beating wings
From man to man, each telling each anew
How Calchas' lovely daughter, bright of hue,
At parliament, upon the common floor,
Was offered up in trade for Antenor.

Soon as Criseyde heard what all men said,
She, who gave her father little thought
Nor cared if he was living still or dead,
Full busily high Jupiter besought
To punish those who made her so distraught.   670
But then, alas, for fear the tale was true.
She daren't ask. Say, what was she to do?

For she had all her heart and all her mind[30]
Set on her Troilus, and set so wondrous fast,
That all the world might not her love unbind,
Nor Troilus from her loyal spirit cast,
She would be his as long as life might last.
Burning now with love and now with fear,
There seemed no proper course for her to steer.

But as we see in towns and all about,   680
Women like to gossip and convene.
To Criseyde now they gathered in a rout
To comfort her and let their love be seen.
And with their tales—in truth none worth a bean—
These women who all thought they knew her well
Sat them down and spoke as I shall tell.

The first one said, "My dear, I'm truly glad.
Because of this you'll see your father now."
Another said, "Well, I am rather sad,
She's been too little with us here, I vow."   690
And then a third: "I hope this will allow
A time of peace to fall on either side,
And may almighty God now be her guide."

These idle words and flighty women's things
She heard although her mind was hardly there.

_____

30. This stanza does not appear in Boccaccio.

God knows, her heart had flown with heavy wings,
Leaving her body almost unaware.
It sat with them; her spirit was elsewhere.
For Troilus now full fast her bruised soul sought.
She'd naught to say. On him was all her thought.   700

Those women, though they surely meant to please,
Chattered of their wishes there in vain,
Their gossip had no power to bring her ease,
For all the while she burned with inward pain.
Her passion was of quite another strain
Than they could guess. And so she thought she'd die,
Beset by fears while they remained nearby.

But then at last she could no more restrain
Her burning tears, so hotly they would well.
These evinced the gnawing, bitter pain   710
In which her spirit was, and now must dwell,
And signaled from what heaven to what hell
She was hurled, since she had lost his sight—
Her Troilus—so she sighed sore as she might.

But all those foolish women round about
Thought only that she wept and sighed so sore
Because she'd soon be leaving them. No doubt,
She'd miss the town and miss their gossip more;
Thus those who knew her best and had of yore
Saw her weep for them, as they must guess,   720
And wept along with her in her distress.

And busily they offered consolation
For things, God knows, on which she little thought;
And with their talk and friendly exhortations
They prayed her to be glad, as well she ought.
But all the comfort that their chatter brought
Was just as if to cure an aching head
You'd claw a man upon his heel instead!

When after all their foolish, wasted work,
They took their leave and went home, one and all,   730
Criseyde, in her grief near gone berserk,

Went to her chamber fast beside the hall
And on her bed she mourned her painful fall.
She never hoped from thence to rise again.
I'll tell you how she fared in her great pain.

She tore her hair, that glinted like the sun,
And wrung her fingers hard, so slim and fine.
And prayed to God for pity, when she'd done,
To bring her death to ease her lovesick mind.
Her color, waxing pale, lost all its shine   740
In witness of her woe and sore constraint,
And thus she spoke—with sobs—her sad complaint:

"Alas," she said, "out of this well-loved town,
I, woeful wretch and sad ill-fortuned one,
Born under baleful stars and heaven's frown,
Must go and leave the precious love I've won.
I curse the very day by whose bright sun
I saw him first, riding with such noblesse,
Who causes me, and I him, such distress!"

Therewith the hot tears rained down from her eyes   750
Like showers in April, falling hard and fast.
She beat her breast and heaving doleful sighs,
She prayed that God would send her death at last
Since he who had so soothed her in the past
She must forgo; and anguished at this cost,
She held herself a creature maimed and lost.

She said, "What shall he do, since I must go?
How shall I live without him if we part?
O blessed, tender heart that I love so,
Who will cure this hurt by any art?   760
O Calchas, father, you heaped up this smart!
O mother Argive,[31] my sorrows are so rife,
Curséd be that day you gave me life!

"To what end should I live and sorrow thus?[32]
Without its water, can a fish endure?

---

31. *AR-jive*. Chaucer seems to have made this name up.
32. This stanza does not appear in Boccaccio.

What am I worth, deprived of Troilus?
No plant or creature on the earth, it's sure,
Without its nurture can flourish or mature.
Now here's a saying no one can deny:
'For want of roots the leaves must surely die.'   770

"I will do thus—since neither sword nor dart
I dare to handle for their cruelty—
From that same day, my lord, that I depart,
If such a sorrow fails to set me free,
No meat or drink shall be consumed by me,
Until I loose the soul from my sad breast
And bring my body to its final rest!

"And, Troilus, all the clothing I will wear
Shall be as black as death to show, sweetheart,
That I have been released from other care,   780
Who once could soothe your mind and ease your smart,
My order, till I meet death's welcome dart,
Will be forever, once I have gone hence,
Sorrow and complaint and abstinence.

"My sore heart and the woeful soul it bears
I offer to your spirit for my part,
To wail with yours their hard, unceasing care;
For though on earth, perforce, we live apart,
Yet in the field of pity, by God's art,
We'll join in great Elysium above   *the heaven of the Greeks*
Like Orpheus and Eurydice,[33] his love.

"So, sweetheart, for Antenor, alas,
I'll be exchanged and therefore go in pain.
But what of you when this shall come to pass?
What prospects will your tender heart sustain?
Live on, my love; don't let this be your bane.
Forget me now, for dear one, this is true:
I'd gladly die so things go well with you."

---

33. *OR-fee-us, Eu-RID-i-cee.* After Orpheus' wife, Eurydice, died, he went to
Hades and persuaded Pluto to let her return to the living world with him on
condition that he walk first and not look back. He couldn't keep from looking,
and so lost her forever.

How could it now be either read or sung—
The plaint she made in this, her great distress?   800
I cannot say, for if my feeble tongue
Attempted to describe her heaviness
I fear I'd make her sorrow seem far less
Than indeed it was, and thus deface
Her high complaint, so I'll pass on apace.

Pandarus, whom Troilus sent on his way,
Sought Criseyde—as you heard before—
For they had both agreed he should that day
And he was glad to undertake the chore.
Now coming to her by a secret door   810
Where she lay in anguish, without fail,
He set himself to briefly tell his tale.

He found his loving niece was sore beset—
A piteous sight—for with her bitter tears
Her lovely face and breast were streaming wet.
Her radiant tresses, once so bright and clear,
Unbraided, hung in clumps about her ears.
She seemed an image of her martyred passion
And death, for which she longed in any fashion.

Seeing him, she began for grief anon[34]   820
Her tear-streaked face between her arms to hide.
Pandarus started back, so woebegone
That he could scarcely in the house abide.
He felt warm pity rising in his side,
For if his niece had once complained full sore,
By now her grief had risen even more.

And in her bitter first complaint she said:
"Pandarus, you once brought me joy, I know,
First mover of that wondrous love, now fled.
It's been transmuted now to cruel woe.   830
Tell me, shall I welcome you or no?
You brought new love into my life that day—
Alas that it should end in such a way!

_____

34. This and the following three stanzas do not appear in Boccaccio.

"Ends love in woe? It does, unless men lie,
Like every worldly bliss, it seems to me.
Each joy produces sorrow by and by,
And any who maintain that cannot be,
Let them come here. Lord, what a wretch they'll see!
I hate myself; my very birth I curse.
From feeling always bad, I go to worse.   840

"Who sees me, sees my grief in full array:
Pain and torment, woe and black distress!
Every form of harm has come my way:
Anguish, languor, cruel bitterness,
Annoyance, smart, dread, fury, and the rest.
In short, I think that heaven's tears must rain,
For pity of my suffering and pain."

"But now, my niece, so battered and so scarred,"
Pandarus said, "what do you think to do?
Why don't you treat yourself with more regard?   850
Why can you, my dear, look after you?
Leave this sad work, and hear some good news too.
I've brought you, dear—hear me with good intent—
A message that your lord, your Troilus, sent."

Criseyde turned herself a bit his way.
Her woeful face was pitiful to see.
"Alas," she said, "what has my lord to say?
What message will my dear heart send to me,
Whom I must dread I nevermore will see?
Does he want tears or sorrows from his friend?   860
God knows I have enough and more to send!"

She was, to look upon her pallid face,
Like one new dead and bound up on his bier.
Her looks, that rivaled heaven in their grace,
Were wholly changed by suffering and fear.
Her playful laughter, all her wholesome cheer,
Her every joy and comfort now were flown,
As she lay there defenseless and alone.

Her pretty eyes were marred by purple rings,
True tokens of her grief and mortal pain.   870

To see her was itself a deadly thing,
And Pandarus found that he could not restrain
Tears of his own that fell like heavy rain.
But nonetheless he struggled to convey
All that he had heard Prince Troilus say.

"Lo Niece," he said, "you've heard what they will do:
The king and other peers have thought it best
To make exchange of Antenor for you.
This caused you painful trouble and unrest.
But how it has invaded Troilus' breast,   880
No tongue of earthly man could ever say.
For very woe, his wits have flown away.

"And thus we have so sorrowed, he and I,
It almost killed us to a certainty.
I gave him my best counsel, Niece, whereby
He's somewhat cured of weeping presently.
And now he wishes this most eagerly:
To be with you all night and hatch a plan
To do away your grief, if any can.

"This, in short, is all I have to say—   890
At least as much as I can comprehend.
Because you suffer such great smart today,
I fear a longer version would offend.
But it's enough. What answer will you send?
And for the love of God on high, my dear,
Leave off your grief before the prince is here!"

"My woe is great," she said, and sighed full sore,
Like one who feels a deadly, sharp distress.
"But yet to me his sorrow is much more.
I love him better than myself, not less.   900
Alas, for me has he such heaviness?
Can he for me so piteously complain?
My lord, his sorrow doubles all my pain.

"It hurts enough," she said, "that we should part,
But as God knows it's harder still to me
To know what sorrow must afflict his heart,

For that will be my bane, as you will see.
I'll die. I will for certain," murmured she.
"But bid him come ere death, that's lurking there,
Drives out my soul and stops my heart with care."   910

When this was said, she on her two arms
Fell face down while weeping piteously.
Pandarus said, "Away with these alarms
Since as you know the time is now fast by
When he shall come. Now wipe each tearful eye.
Quick! Don't you weep yourself quite blind
Unless you'd have him clear out of his mind!

"For if he knew you fared in such a way,
He'd kill himself. I tell you if I'd known
You'd take on so, he'd never come today   920
For all the goods King Priam ever owned.
Arouse yourself! His death must be postponed.
I know that well. Be more yourself, or try.
If not, I tell you flatly, he will die.

"Now shape yourself to help him as you pledge.[35]
Don't increase his sorrow so, my sweet.
Touch him with your flat sword, not the edge.
Work wisely so his woe will lose its heat.
What help to weep enough to flood a street?
Or would you pour out tears until he drown?   930
It's time to cure him, Niece. Now don't break down!

"Here's what I mean: as soon as he is here,
Since you both are clever and assent,
Hit on some plan to stay in Troy, my dear,
Or come back quickly after the event.
Women are wise, at least to that extent.
Use your wit to prosper and prevail,
And know if I can help, I will not fail."

"Go," said Criseyde. "Go, and on my faith
I'll use my utmost courage to refrain   940

---

35. This and the following stanza do not appear in Boccaccio.

From weeping and complaining like a wraith.
I'll make him glad, my lord, despite my pain,
And in my heart I'll seek through every vein
To soothe his woeful soul and fitly salve it.
If such an ointment's there, then he shall have it!"

Pandarus went forth, and Troilus sought
Till in a temple he found him all alone,
As one who gave his life but little thought,
But to the tender gods above, each one,
He prayed in fervent heat and made his moan—   950
To leave the wretched earth behind apace.
For he could see no other hope of grace.

And shortly, all the truth at once to say,[36]
He was so deeply plunged in black despair,
He thought he'd surely die that very day.
All his former thinking led him there.
He held that he'd been born to suffer care:
"For all that happens, happens as it must,
And so if I am lost, that's only just.

"For certainly, I know this well," he said,   960
"The foresight of divine predestination
Knew from the first this ruin loomed ahead,
Since God sees all throughout His whole creation.
All that occurs has heaven's dispensation.
Things happen as they should, as we may see.
It's all controlled by God's high destiny.

"But nonetheless, alas, whom to believe?
For there are mighty teachers—many a one—
Who peer at things and destiny perceive;
But others look abroad and say there's none: 970
Free choice determines everything that's done.
So cleverly they argue—clerks of old—
I can't tell whose opinion I should hold.

---

36. This and the following nineteen stanzas (through line 1092) do not appear
in Boccaccio. Troilus' arguments on free will and predestination are loosely based
on *The Consolation of Philosophy,* but unlike Boethius, Troilus, through a rather
muddled series of deductions, seems to come down on the side of predestination.

"For some men say if God sees all to come
(Nor can He be deceived, we must agree),
Things happen as they have to, all and some.
Predestination rules how they must be.
And so I say if from all time that He
Has known our every thought and all our deeds,
There's no free choice in spite of all our creeds.   980

"No other thought nor other deed, just so,
Could ever be but by predestination,
Which never is deceived, as all men know.
It's pre-perceived without equivocation.
For if there might be some slight deviation
That wriggles out of what God wills and knows,
Not everything conforms to what He chose.

"Then all would be but guesses and opinion,
Uncertain, surely—chancy and unfast.
And that would shrink great God to Fortune's minion.   990
His knowledge might prove faulty at the last—
As weak as ours, so wavering in the past.
To say God may be wrong and so must guess,
Would truly be a blatant wickedness.

"Yet still, another theory's held by some
Whose tonsures are shaved close and held up high.   *monkish shaved heads*
They tell us thus, that no event can come
Just because of God's foreseeing eye.
It happens of itself, and yet that's why
He knows it's coming; all of nature draws it.   1000
But just to know a thing is not to cause it.

"Yet reasoning in this way, Necessity
Rises up before us once again.
Although free will implies it cannot be
That God dictates each choice we make—that's plain—
Yet His foreknowing mind can't be constrained.
It's needful that each thing that may befall
Be known to God of old, yea, one and all.

"I mean, although I labor hard in this,
To learn what causes all the things we see: 1010

As whether that sure prescience of His
Accounts itself for the necessity
Of things to come, whatever they may be,
Or if the needs that govern things aright
Are cause themselves of heaven's vast foresight.

"Now I don't think it's possible to show
Which cause comes first, but yet I know and say,
That everything that happens here below,
If it's foreknown, falls out beneath God's sway.
But that itself can't prove in any way   1020
His knowing it predetermines that it could—
Each new event we witness, bad or good.

"Now, if a man is sitting on a seat,
Necessity would then so order it
That you would be quite right in your conceit
To judge or to conjecture that he sits.
That seems to be the case indeed, and yet
Another man might judge the other way,
And so—now harken, for I won't delay—

"I say that if the thing you think is true   1030
(That he is sitting), then the case is this:
He sits indeed just as it seems to you.
Necessity works here, I must insist,
He needs is sitting there, unless I miss,
And you must see him so, forsooth,
This all must be as you perceive, in truth.

"But you may say, 'He's hardly sitting there
Because I think he is, though I think true.
The very fact he's sitting in that chair
Is what has made it seem so to my view.'   1040
He sits because he sits, that's so, and too
You see him for you must, and so you see
That everything is just what it must be.

"Now, in the selfsame way and out of doubt,
I may construct my thought, it seems to me,
Unless my closest reasoning is out,

About God's knowledge of all things that be.
I now have said enough indeed to see
That everything on earth that may befall
Comes as it must. Necessity rules all.   1050

"For everything that comes about, of right,
Must be foreseen by God, that's true.
Not that it's controlled by his foresight,
But nothing happens that God never knew.
He foreknows all his creatures say or do,
And what His wisdom says will happen must.
So all is predetermined, set, and just.

"And this suffices, yes, in every way,
To undercut free choice for good or ill.
It would be simple blasphemy to say   1060
Things happen so, and thus dictate God's will,
Or reach beyond His foresight and His skill.
No! No one but an infidel would hold
The present shapes what God has known of old.

"What must I conclude if I think this—
That God knows all the things that are to come
Because they are to come, no more, no less?
I must believe that happenings, all and some,
Although themselves insentient and dumb,
Enable our foreknowing God to see,   1070
Almost despite Himself what is to be!

"And I must add one more thing that I know
That just as when I see things on my own,
They must exist—once seen, they must be so—
Just so, when some firm consequence is known,
It must occur. So striking to the bone,
Foreknown events—deny this rule who can—
Aren't caused by their foreknower, God or man."

Then he said thus: "Great Jove upon your throne,
Who knows the start of all things and their end,   1080
Kill me, lord, I'll die without a groan,
Or bring my love, Criseyde, to her friend."

And while he shook with woe he couldn't mend,
Debating with himself in doubt and fear,
Pandarus came in, and spoke as you shall hear:

"Great Jove, indeed," he said, "upon your throne!
Who ever heard a wise man grovel so?
What do you hope to bring off with such moans?
Are you so set on being your own foe?
Criseyde isn't lost as yet, you know!   1090
Why give yourself to mourning and to dread?
The very eyes seem lifeless in your head!

"Have you not lived full many years ere now
Without her quite as well as you could please?
Is she your all, that you grieve so? I vow,
You weren't put on earth to serve her ease.
Let be, and think this way in your disease:
That just as dicing brings you loss and gain,
Love like yours brings not just joy, but pain.

"The thing that makes me wonder most of all   1100
Is why you sorrow when you don't know yet,
Touching her going, how all things will fall,
Nor if she can herself refrain from it.
You haven't sounded her intent a bit.
Though a man can offer up his neck indeed,
None but a fool would do so for no need.

"So listen now to what I have to say,
I've spoken with the lady for a space,
As we agreed I should, my lord, today,
And can't help thinking, judging by her face,   1110
That she has hidden in her heart someplace
A plan wherewith, if I have read aright,
She can avert this trial and your fright.

"For which my counsel is, when it is night,
You go to her and bring this to some end.
And blissful Juno through her power and might
Shall, as I hope, her gracious care extend.
My own heart says you shall not lose your friend,

And therefore put your mind a while at rest,
And hold your purpose, hoping for the best."   1120

This Troilus answered, with a sigh full sore,
"Your words are good, and I will do just so,"
And added to his speech a few words more.
And when he saw the time had come to go,
Full secretly he went, so none would know,
By hidden ways that he knew now so well,
And what they did that night I'll shortly tell.

True it is that when the two were met,
Pain made their hearts beat high and sorely twist.
The only greeting they could share as yet,   1130
Was, in each other's arms, a tender kiss.
The one who felt least bad, unless I miss,
Was wholly lost in sadness, grief, and fears.
They couldn't speak a word for all their tears.

The tears themselves that each one then let fall,
Were doubly bitter—more than tears should be.
They savored more of aloes or of gall.
No hotter tears than theirs went running free
From Myrrah, who was turned into a tree.[37]
In all the world there's not so hard a heart   1140
That wouldn't pity their most doleful smart.

But when their woeful, weary souls again
Returned to them, where they were wont to dwell,
They felt a little weakening of their pain.
Through long complaints and ebbing of the well
Of painful tears, their throbbing pulses fell.
Criseyde, hoarse with sobs and speaking low,
Addressed her loving lord, her Troilus, so:

"O Jove, I die, and mercy I beseech!
O help me Troilus"—thereupon her face   1150
She laid upon his breast and lost her speech.

---

37. *MEER-a*. She slept with her father and was transformed into a myrrh tree.
The dripping medicinal gum for which myrrhs are known was said to be her tears.

Her woeful spirit, from his proper place,
With every word was poised to fly apace.
And thus she lay, her color pale and green,
Who once had been the fairest lady seen.

This Troilus had not released her from his hold.
He called her where she lay, but she seemed dead.
She gave no answer, and her limbs were cold.
Her eyes rolled up and backward in her head.
Her woeful lover looked on her in dread,   1160
And kissed her chilling lips, but kissed in vain.
God alone knows how he bore his pain!

He raised himself and laid her long and straight.[38]
No signs of life! No hint that he could see
That his Criseyde had not met her fate.
All he thought to say was "Woe is me."
Speechless she lay, as still as she could be.
With sorrowing voice and empty heart he said,
"Alas, alas! My dearest love is dead!"

His heart was filled with woe as he complained,   1170
Wringing his hands, his speech in disarray.
He wet her breast with tears that fell like rain,
Then wiped them off, unknowing, in dismay.
And piteously began to plead and pray.
"O Lord," he said, "now death would be a boon.
Lord, pity me, for I shall follow soon."

She lay there pale and cold, deprived of sense.
For all he knew, his love had ceased to breathe.
He surely thought her life had flitted hence
And she had gone and left him there to grieve.   1180
Then, losing any hope of a reprieve,
He dressed her limbs, alas, with many tears,
As bodies are, when laid out on their biers.

And after this with stern and cruel heart,
He drew his fatal sword out of its sheath.

---

38. This and the following stanza do not appear in Boccaccio.

He'd slay himself, however it might smart.
His soul to dead Criseyde he'd bequeath,
To go where Minos[39] said it should, beneath,
Since Love and cruel Fortune now had willed
His race should end and his sad life be spilled.   1190

Then said he thus, now filled with high disdain:
"O cruel Jove and Fortune so adverse,
This is my cry: Criseyde lies here slain
Through your ill will; and since you can't do worse,
Fie on your might and evil works diverse!
You'll never win me with your cowards' art.
No death can keep my love and me apart!

"For I, since you have slain my lady thus,
Will leave this world and follow, low or high,
It never must be said that Troilus   1200
Dare not for his dearest lady die!
I will bear her company, or try.
But since we can't live on in Troy a pair,
Please grant that we can be together there.

"And you, you city that I leave in woe,
My father Priam, brothers gathered here,
And you, my mother, farewell, for I go;
And Atropos,[40] prepare my mortal bier.
And thou, Criseyde, love of mine most dear,
Receive my grieving spirit"—so he said,   1210
Sword at his breast and yearning to be dead.

But as God willed, Criseyde's life returned.
She breathed a sigh, and "Troilus, dear," she cried.
He answered, "Dear!" and how his rasped heart burned!
"Are you alive?" The sword fell by his side.
"I am, my heart, thank God," Criseyde sighed.
And therewithal she sobbed and wept in fright
While he worked to soothe her as he might.

---

39. *MY-nus.* Judge of souls in the underworld, especially concerned with suicides.
40. *AT-ro-pus.* The Fate who cuts the thread of life.

He took her in his arms and kissed her often
And then to glad her heart did all he could.   1220
Her flitting soul came down to earth again,
Returned to her cold body as it should.
But, lo, her eye, which darted as it would,
Fell on his sword, that glinted, lying near.
The blade shone bare. At that she cried for fear.

She asked him then to say why it was drawn,
And Troilus told her all there was to tell:
He'd meant to kill himself and not live on.
Criseyde's heart and eyes began to swell.
She took him in her arms and pressed him well.   1230
"O mercy, God!" she said. "Lo, by my head
How close we two just came to being dead!

"Then if I had not spoken, just by chance,
You would have killed yourself anon?" said she.
"I would," he said. She looked at him askance,
And said, "By God above, who fashioned me,
I'd not have lingered long, ungraciously,
When you were dead—no, not to be crowned queen
Of all the lands the sun on high has seen!

"Rather with that sword that's lying there   1240
I would have killed myself, upon my head.
But stop! We've had a surfeit of this care.
Let's rise up now and get ourselves to bed,
To speak of woe, if speak we must, instead,
For by the lamp I see is burning low,
Day's near at hand, my dear, when you must go."

But yet in bed and in a close embrace,
It wasn't like the nights they'd spent before.
Full piteously each scanned the other's face.
They knew they'd lost their bliss and likely more,   1250
Complaining of their birth and sighing sore,
Until Criseyde put aside her grief
To raise their hopes of finding some relief.

"Lo, my heart," she said, "full well you know[41]
That if one merely clamors and complains
And seeks no help at hand for all his woe,
He'll only cause himself to feel more pain.
Since we are here and some time yet remains,
Let's think about a cure for our distress.
Let's use this chance—we can't just acquiesce.   1260

"I am just a woman, as you're not,
But sometimes inspiration visits me.
I tell you now, my love, while it is hot,
I think that it cannot be right that we
Must suffer half the woe that we foresee.
Surely we'll be able to redress
What yet is wrong, and slay this heaviness.

"In truth the pain and sorrow we are in,
For all I know, amounts to only this:
That we must part. This causes our chagrin,   1270
But truly, dear, there is no more amiss.
Well, what's the nearest way back to our bliss
But to fix things so we don't remain apart?
Then we can live in joy again, my heart.

"Now, that I've wit to bring this all about—
To come again soon after I must go—
I haven't got the slightest fear or doubt.
Ah no, my dear, within a week or so,
I shall be back. And just so you may know
How many ways there are to end this pain   1280
As quickly as I can, let me explain.

"Love, I don't mean to make a lengthy speech.
Once time has passed, it's lost, as you'll agree.
But here are some conclusions that I've reached.
The first is best for all that I can see.
Now for the love of God, dear, pardon me,
If what I say shall give your heart unrest,
For truly I mean all things for the best.

41. This and the following five stanzas do not appear in Boccaccio.

"One word more. My dear, I must attest
That every plan I put to you today   1290
Comes from the great desire in my breast
To serve our loving hearts the nearest way.
Please take it in no other wise, I pray.
I'll gladly work however you may plan.
I never will resent your least command.

"Please listen to me. You have understood
That I must go by act of parliament
So clearly ruled it may not be withstood
For all the world, despite our discontent.
Now since no counteraction we invent   1300
Can hinder this, accept that fact as read,
And let us find a better way instead.

"The truth is this: that we must part today[42]
Will kill our ease and fill us with annoy;
But all Love's servants suffer some dismay,
Before they share his boons and all his joy.
Since I shall go no farther out of Troy
Than half a morning's ride, no greater piece,
That itself should make our woe decrease.

"Now, as the Greeks must mean I shall go loose,   1310
Then almost every day, my well loved dear,
Especially since now we have a truce,
You'll hear of my condition, never fear;
Then, ere the truce is done, I shall be here!
Both Antenor and I will be in Troy.
Be glad! This whole affair will bring us joy.

"Think this way: 'Criseyde may be gone,
But what of that? She'll soon be back again.'
'But when?' you ask. By God, dear, right anon!
Not ten more days, as I may say. That's when!   1320
And then you'll be the happiest of men.
We'll dwell together always, my dear lord,
Not all the world can tell our sweet reward.

---

42. This and the following three stanzas do not appear in Boccaccio.

"You know, my dear, as things are now, we two
Must veil our love—dissemble it and hide.
You can't speak with me nor I to you
A fortnight at a time or be espied.
May you not for ten short days abide—
To save my name, endure in such a state?
If not, your faith in me cannot be great.   1330

"You know that all my kinfolk are in Troy—
Except my father, who has run away—
And every other thing that gives me joy.
And you're the foremost there, as I must say.
From you I'd never choose to be away
For all the world, its riches, or its space,
Or may I never see Jove's sacred face!

"Why do you think my father in this way
Wants so much to see me, but for dread
Lest every Trojan hate me—as some may—   1340
Because of him, who traitorously has fled?
What does he know of what I want instead?
For if he guessed how well I fare in Troy,
He'd hardly make me leave and lose my joy.

"You see each day that passes, more and more,[43]
Men treat of peace, and now, my dear, it's thought
That we are set Queen Helen to restore
If Greeks repair the damages they wrought.
If there were no more comfort to be caught,
The fact that men on both sides favor peace   1350
Should ease your heart and offer some release.

"If war should cease, why, nothing could be better.
The nature of the peace itself must drive
Both sides to mingle and confer together.
And to and fro they'd ride to make things thrive
As thick as bees that swarm around a hive.
And everyone who wished could come and go
As he liked best, with none to tell him no.

---

43. This and the following stanza do not appear in Boccaccio. The idea of an
impending peace is Chaucer's addition to the story.

"If peace holds off, why, that's the status quo.
Hither, though the war drags on a year,   1360
I still must come, for where else could I go?
How could I live apart from you, my dear,
Among those men in arms in constant fear?
And so, as God may guide me, by my head,
I cannot see what causes you such dread.

"And here's another way that we could go,
If what I've said so far may not suffice:
My father as I think, my dear, you know,
Is old, and old men always have a price.
I just now have imagined a device   1370
To catch him up indeed without a net.
If you agree, we'll trick that wise one yet.

"Lo, Troilus, as men say, 'It's truly hard[44]
To feed the wolf and save the sheep as well.'
For lest a man's chief purpose should be marred,
He often yields up something, truth to tell:
Gold may loose the grip and judgment quell
Of greedy men who covet greater wealth.
And that's another way to work by stealth.

"All the goods I have in Troy today   1380
I'll take unto my father and pretend
That they were sent for safety in this way
From one or two of his familiar friends.
These wish, I'll say, that he should further send
For more, and soon, to keep for them, you see,
While our dear Troy remains in jeopardy.

"These takings will be huge if he'll agree
(Or so I'll say), but lest this be espied,
They can't be sent by anyone but me,
And I'll assure him too, if peace betide,   1390
That I have friends in Troy on every side,
In court and town, to soften and erase
King Priam's wrath and win back all his grace.

---

44. This and the following six stanzas (through line 1421) do not appear in
Boccaccio.

"So, one way or another as I deem,
I'll have him so enchanted, fooled so clean,
He'll think himself in heaven, or so dream.
And what Apollo's prophesies may mean . . .
Why, he'll conclude they aren't worth a bean.
Desire of gold will work upon his greed.
No matter how I trick him, I'll succeed.   1400

"And should he use his augury to prove
That I am lying, dear, I'll find a way—
Whatever fine distraction may behoove—
To cross him up and lead him quite astray.
I'll tell him he's misjudged what his gods say.
Gods often speak to blind our mortal eyes.
For every truth they may tell twenty lies.

"'It's fear that formed the gods,' I'll carp at him,
And say his coward heart from first to last
Made him mistake Apollo through some whim   1410
Back when he fled the Pythia[45] so fast.
And if I can't convert him by some cast
To do my bidding in a day or two,
You may have my life, I promise you."

And truly, it's been written, as I find,
That what she said was said with good intent,
And all along her heart was true and kind.
She loved the prince and spoke just as she meant
And nearly died for woe the day she went.
She resolved for certain she'd be true,   1420
For so they said, those ancient men who knew.

This Troilus—heart abroach and ears outspread—
Heard all these things considered to and fro,
They penetrated so inside his head
That he agreed. . . . But yet, to risk her so!

---

45. *PI-thi-a*. In Chaucer's version of the story, the Trojans sent Calchas to Delphi
to consult Apollo's oracle, a priestess called the Pythia, about the course of the
war. When he was told that Troy would lose, he came back to Troy at once and
later defected to the Greeks.

His heart cried out he couldn't let her go.
Yet finally he determined in his breast
To trust in her and take it for the best.

His fury was abated, and perchance
He felt new hope. And then, intent to please,   1430
They both began love's reassuring dance,
And as the birds in sunshine and at ease
Pour out their love amid the verdant trees,
Just so the words they spoke with better cheer
Relieved their hearts in truth and made them clear.

But nonetheless Criseyde's leaving soon,
For all she said, still preyed on Troilus' mind.
His thoughts misgave him. He prayed her as a boon
That she'd be true to him and not unkind.
"It's certain," so he said, "that if I find   1440
You fail to keep your day to be in Troy,
Then farewell all my honor and my joy.

"As surely as the sun will rise tomorrow—
May God as surely bring a wretch like me
To easeful rest out of this cruel sorrow—
I'll slay myself if you prove false, you see.
Of course, my life is hardly worth a pea.
But yet before you cause me such a smart
Stay here with me in Troy, my own sweetheart.

"For true it is, my lady and my dear,⁴⁶   1450
No matter how discretely you may fare,
Your plans are like to fail, we both must fear.
The leader may think one thing for his share;
'But that won't make it happen,' says the bear.
Your father's wise, and, dear, all men admit it:
'The wise can be outrun, but not outwitted.'

"It's hard to feign a limp and not be spied
Before a cripple, for he knows the craft.
Your father is full sly and Argus-eyed.⁴⁷

---

46. This and the following stanza do not appear in Boccaccio.
47. *AR-gus*. A giant with a hundred eyes.

Although he's lost his goods and lives bereft,   1460
He has his sleights and catchy dealings left.
You won't deceive him with these plans you've laid.
He'll see your machinations, I'm afraid.

"I'm not sure yet if peace will soon betide,
But peace or no, in earnest or in game,
I know, now he has joined the Grecian side—
Gone over there and earned so foul a name—
He dare not come to Troy for his great shame.
And so, my dear, as far as I can see,
To trust in that is but a fantasy.   1470

"As you shall see, he'll argue and persuade you,
To be a wife. He's apt enough to preach.
He'll choose some Greek to praise until he sways you,
And you'll succumb, I fear, to his fine speech,
Or make you do by force as he will teach.
And Troilus, dear, of whom you take no care
Shall causeless die, with such a blow to bear.

"And over all, your father shall despise[48]
Us Trojan folk, and say we are but lost
And that the siege shall bring on our demise   1480
Because the Greeks have sworn at any cost
To spoil our lives and all our homes accost.
He'll blear your eyes and frighten you that way,
You'll quake in such great fear you'll choose to stay.

"And then as well, you'll see such lusty knights
Among the Greeks—so full of worthiness—
And each one filled with heart and wit and might
To please your sight, each eager to impress,
That you'll devalue Trojans, as I guess,
For we're but rude, unless you pity us,   1490
Or else your pledge of love may make you generous.

"To me all this is such a grievous thought
That it will wrench the soul out of my breast.

_____

48. This and the following stanza do not appear in Boccaccio.

I can't convince myself, so sore distraught,
That you'll return once you have left your nest.
Your father's sleights will outweigh your unrest.
If you go now, as I have said before,
I am but dead, my dear, and nothing more.

"For which, with humble, true, and piteous heart,
A thousand times your mercy let me pray.   1500
Commiserate my sharp and bitter smart.
Agree with me and do as I shall say:
Confirm our love! My dear, let's steal away.
It's foolishness, when you are free to choose,
To reach for hopes and present comfort lose.

"Here's what I mean, dear: since we might ere day
Be out of Troy and still together so,
Why not elope? Why hazard all on *may*?
Why let your father rule and make you go,
Why make me doubt if you'll return or no?   1510
What a mistaken folly it would be
To take that chance and live in jeopardy.

"Next, my dear, to think of vulgar wealth,[49]
We're rich enough in goods to take a store—
Enough to live in honor and in health
Until the time when we shall be no more.
Thus we'll escape this risk that I abhor.
Truly, there's no other way I see
To which my fretful heart can now agree.

"Don't think we'll live in poverty or dirt,   1520
For I have friends and kinfolk everywhere,
So, though we come with little but a shirt,
We should lack for nothing, I declare,
But live in honor while remaining there.
So let us go, for that is my intent.
I think it best—if you will but consent."

Criseyde, sighing, answered in this wise:
"Certainly, dear heart, I know it's true.

---

49. This and the following stanza do not appear in Boccaccio.

We could steal away as you devise
And try your plan or think of something new,   1530
But afterward our hearts would ache with rue.
Besides, God help me, dear, as I have said,
There's not the slightest need for all this dread!

"The day indeed that I on any head—⁵⁰
For love, or fear of father or some plight,
Or for estate, or pleasure, or to wed—
Am false to you, my Troilus and my knight,
May Saturn's daughter, Juno,⁵¹ through her might,
As mad as frenzied Athamas⁵² bid me dwell
Eternally in Styx,⁵³ the deepest pit of hell!   1540

"And this on every other god as well,
I swear to you—and every goddess too.
On every nymph and deity in hell,
On satyrs, dryads, fauns, and all the crew
That haunt the forest—laurel, oak, and yew.
May Atropos cut short my mortal thread
If I am ever false, as I have said.

"And thou, Simois,⁵⁴ like an arrow clear
That runs through Troy and downward to the sea,
Bear witness to the pledge that I've made here: 1550
For every day that I untrue shall be
To Troilus, he who holds my heart in fee,
Run backward in your channel to your well,
And send me, soul and body, down to hell!

---

50. This and the following two stanzas do not appear in Boccaccio.

51. Jove's wife and testy queen of the Olympian gods.

52. *ATH-a-mas.* King of Thebes, hounded into hell by the Fury Tisiphone at Juno's request.

53. One of the rivers (along with the Phlegethon, Acheron, and Cocytus) that flow into a central marsh in hell, which is also called the Styx. The name means *hatred.*

54. *Si-MOY-is.* Both a god and one of two rivers (with the Scamander) crossing the Trojan plain.

"But when you say we two should run away
And leave your friends, may God forbid that deed.
No woman's worth a cost like that, I say—
Especially when Troy stands so in need.
And here's another point that you should heed:
If this were known, then bid my life good-bye,   1560
Your honor too—defend us, God on high!

"And then suppose that peace should come again.
It always does, as histories proclaim.
Lord, how you'd suffer then from woe and pain.
You wouldn't dare return to Troy for shame.
No, no, I beg, don't jeopardize your name;
Don't be so reckless in this hot affair.
A hasty man must always suffer care.

"What do you imagine people all about
Would think of it? Why, that's not hard to say: 1570
They'd think, indeed, and swear, I have no doubt,
It wasn't love that made you act that way,
But wicked lust and fear as plain as day.
You would have lost, my noble Troilus dear,
Those honors that you've won that now shine clear.

"This also bears on me and on my name.
It's clean as now, but how I'd foul it then!
My honor would be marred with clinging shame.
Our flight would bare our dealings to all men.
If I should live until the whole world's end,   1580
My credit lost and not to be regained,
I'd live on in regret, disgraced and pained.

"Call on your reason to restrain this heat.
'Patience prevails,' men say, and that is so,
And 'He who wins must stomach some defeat.'
Need can be a virtue, as you know.
Resign yourself. Who would be Fortune's beau,
Must never stoop to bow and scrape to her.
She scourges every wretch who does, that's sure.

"And trust in this—be certain as I am—[55]   1590
Ere Phoebus' sister, Lucina,[56] calm and pale,
Has sailed into the Lion from the Ram,[57]
I'll be back. I swear that I won't fail.
As sure as Juno, heaven's mistress, can prevail,
By the tenth day, dearest Troilus, I'll contrive
To see you back in Troy if I'm alive."

"Well then, if this be so," Prince Troilus said,
"I'll set myself to wait until that day.
Since you would have it thus, I will be led.
But once more for God's love, my dear, I say   1600
Let us steal full secretly away!
For once and all, if we're to live in rest,
My heart says to elope would serve us best."

"O mercy, God, what's all of this?" said she.
"Alas, you'll slay me yet with your great fear!
I see it well: you have no faith in me,
For all your words proclaim it's so, my dear.
Now for the love of Cynthia's[58] silver sphere,
Don't mistrust me. Truly there's no need.
I've sworn I will be true to you indeed.   1610

"Remember, dear, sometimes the better course
Is 'spend a time some later time to gain.'
As I have said, this isn't a divorce
Though I must leave a while and you remain.
Drive off those carping fears you feel in vain,
And trust in me, and leave off all this sorrow,
Or on my word, I'll die before tomorrow!

"For if you knew how sore you make me smart,
You wouldn't go on so. God only knows

---

55. This stanza does not appear in Boccaccio.

56. *Lu-SI-na.* The moon, especially when associated with menstrual cycles and childbirth.

57. That is, before the moon has gone from rising in Aries to rising in Leo— about ten days.

58. Yet another name for the moon. The moon, of course, is also a symbol of changeability.

The inmost spirit weeps within my heart   1620
To see you hurt, the man whose love I chose,
And think that I must join our Grecian foes.
I swear that if I didn't know a cure—
My quick return—I scarcely could endure.

"But, dear, I'm not so helpless and so tame
That I can't invent or find a way
To come again—yes, on the day I named—
For who can hold a thing that will not stay?
My father can't, for all his cunning play!
And on my head, my leaving now from Troy,   1630
Shall soon or later turn our cares to joy!

"And so with all my heart, my lord, I pray
That if you will do aught to help me here,
For all the love I bear for you today,
Before I have to part from you, my dear,
Show some crumb of comfort and good cheer
To pacify my heart and give it rest,
Or it will surely break within my breast.

"And last, but over all, I ask," she said—
"My anguished heart's own true and noble lord—   1640
Since I belong to you until I'm dead,
When I am gone, dear, let no loving word
Or pleasure make another be preferred.
I fear that always. As men say, upon my head,
'Love is full of jealousy and dread.'

"For in this world there is no lady—none—
Who, if you were untrue—as God forefend!—
Would be so sore betrayed or woebegone,
As I, who've placed all trust in you, my friend.
For if your taste some other way should bend,   1650
I'll surely die. Before you act that way,
Think of the love you owe me, as you say."

Troilus quickly answered her and said,
"Now God, who knows our every act and thought,
Desert me if I ever turned instead

To someone else since that first day I sought
Criseyde's love to cherish as I ought.
Yet, dear, you're free to doubt me if you must,
And I must let my actions prove my trust."

"Thank you, my great treasure," answered she,[59]   1660
"And blissful Venus now my life preserve
Until I can arrange in some degree
To pay you well who all I have deserve.
While God will foster life and wit conserve,
I'll do my best, since you have been so true,
To live in honor, emulating you.

"You must believe that not your royal estate
Nor vain delight nor yet your worthiness
In all this war or tourneys small or great,
Not pomp, array, nor riches, I profess,   1670
Have made me, dearest, pity your distress,
But moral virtue, grounded on great trust—
That's what made me love you as I must.

"Your gentle heart and manhood of great price
And how you felt the worthiest despite
For every action savoring of vice,
As rudeness, dear, and boorish appetite,
And how your reason bridled your delight:
These made me choose, of all the men alive,
To be your own as long as I survive.   1680

"And none of this may length of years undo
Nor any trick that Fortune plays deface.
Yet Jupiter—who, love, can make it true
That sorrow turns to joy—will grant us grace
Ere ten nights pass to meet back in this place.
So feed your heart, my dear, on that surmise
And now farewell—it's time for you to rise."

And after their lamenting and behests
And many kisses—embracing as of old—

---

59. This and the following three stanzas do not appear in Boccaccio, who gives
a similar speech to Troilus instead.

Day began to rise and Troilus dress.   1690
Now he was as pained, Criseyde to behold,
As one whom Death has struck and now grows cold.
He said his last good-byes then nonetheless.
Whether these were sad, I'll let you guess.

No other head can feel or know aright,[60]
No mindfulness consider or tongue tell,
The cruel pains that racked this grieving knight.
They passed the sharpest agonies of hell,
But when indeed he took his last farewell,
Which pierced his soul and left him brokenhearted,   1700
He turned away and silently departed.

Explicit liber quartus[61]

---

60. This stanza does not appear in Boccaccio.
61. Here ends the fourth book.

BOOK 5

Incipit liber quintus[1]

Now looming near was fatal destiny[2]
Which mighty Jove holds in his dispensation
And commits to you, dire Parcae,[3] sisters three,
To oversee its due dissemination.
Criseyde must resign her home and station
While Troilus suffers hurts and dwells in dread
Till Lachesis[4] no longer spins his thread.

Gold-tressed Phoebus, now full high aloft,
Had thrice renewed his genial rays and seen
Cold winter melt, and Zephyrus[5] as oft   10
Had summoned back to earth the tender green,
Since the son of Hecuba, the queen,[6]
Began to love her first, for whom he grieved.
Now she must go and leave the prince bereaved.

Diomedes[7] waited near the town at dawn
To lead Criseyde to the Grecian host.
Sick at heart with how she had been won,
She hardly knew what course would help her most.
And truly, if old authors do not boast,
No woman born has ever felt such care   20
Or felt so loath to leave from anywhere.

---

1. Here begins the fifth book.
2. This and the following stanza do not appear in Boccaccio.
3. *PAR-see*. The Fates.
4. *LA-cha-sis*. The Fate who spins the thread of life.
5. The west wind, associated with spring.
6. I.e., Troilus. Hecuba (*HEK-cue-ba*) was Priam's queen.
7. *Di-o-MEE-deez*. One of the greatest heroes of the Greeks.

With no one to advise him and no plan
This Troilus was like one whose hopes are mute.
He waits with all the patience he commands,
For she was all his pleasure, flower and root.
He loved her more than life beyond dispute.
Now, Troilus, bid farewell to all your joy:
You'll never see your love again in Troy!

It's true that while he suffered in this way,
He hid his sorrow as a man should do.   30
His face showed little sign of woe's grim sway,
But at the gate the Greeks would lead her through
He waited for her passing with some few,
So desolate, although he'd not complain,
He scarce could sit his horse for all his pain.

Anger made him quake and gnawed his heart,
As Diomedes mounted on his horse.
He looked away and said, a bit apart:
"Alas, alas! This foul and wretched course!
Why suffer it? Why not strike back with force?   40
Far better that I die at once, I'm sure,
Than hold my peace and silently endure.

"Why don't I stir them up, both rich and poor—
Give all enough to do before she goes?
Why not set the whole town in a roar?
Slay Diomedes? Why not? Heaven knows!
I could with one or two as I suppose,
Steal her away. Why stand here and look on?
Why not intervene before she's gone?"

But when he came to do so fell a deed,   50
I'll tell you plainly why he didn't dare:
He had at heart a fear if he'd proceed,
Criseyde, when the Greeks saw how he'd fare,
Would be slain at once. That was his care.
If not for that, as I have said above,
He would have held her back and fought for love.

Criseyde, when she was mounted up to ride,
Sighed sorrowfully, proclaiming, "Wellaway!"

But she must go, for aught that might betide.
There was no hope at all that she could stay,   60
But she rode forth full woefully that day.
Who'd be surprised to see her sorely smart,
When she must leave the one who held her heart?

This Troilus, for the sake of courtesy,
With hawk on hand, and riding in a rout
Of other knights to give her company,
Passed on to where the valley widened out.
He would have ridden farther still, no doubt;
It hurt him so to see her leaving Troy,
But he must turn away. Farewell his joy!   70

At just that moment out came Antenor.
He left the Grecian host, and every knight
Rejoiced to have him back with them once more.
And Troilus, though his heart was far from light,
Pained himself with all the skill he might
To keep from weeping—outwardly at least.
He kissed Lord Antenor and acted pleased.

But then at last, he had to take his leave.
He watched his love full piteously indeed—
Rode at her side, but there was no reprieve.   80
He took her hand as if he meant to plead,
And, Lord above, her heart began to bleed.
His voice was low, but she still heard him say:
"Don't let me die, my love, but keep your day."

He shifted then and reined his horse about.
He turned from Diomedes pale as lead,
Without a word to him or all his rout.
At this, the son of Tydeus[8] shook his head.
He knew full well all Cupid's credo[9] said.
He took Criseyde's horse up by the reins,   90
And Troilus went home to grieve across the plains.

---

8. *TIE-di-us.* One of the Seven Against Thebes and Diomedes' father.
9. *CREY-doe.* Statement of central beliefs as in the Latin Mass.

Holding Criseyde's palfrey by the bridle,[10]
Diomedes watched the Trojans ride away.
He thought, "My work today shall not be idle
If I can help it. Somewhat I shall say—
For at the worst, such talk will pass the day.
I've heard a dozen wise men cite this rule:
'Forget to serve yourself, and you're a fool.'"

But he had judged Criseyde well enough:
"I'm sure," he mused, "that I'll accomplish naught　　　　　100
To speak of love albeit sweet or rough.
For if she holds a lover in her thought—
The one I guess—he won't be lightly brought
So soon away. But I'll work to that end,
So she will hardly guess what I intend."

This Diomedes, as one who knew his good,
When it was time, engaged in trifling speech
Of this and that, and asked her why she stood
In such distress, and then began to reach
For any means he could supply or teach　　　　　110
To make her easy. If, he said, he could,
In any way she wished, he surely would.

For truly, as he promised as a knight,
Nothing he could do to make her pleased
Would be withheld. He'd work with all his might.
He'd do his best to see her sore heart eased.
He prayed that she should shortly be appeased,
For as he said, "We Greeks will find great joy
In honoring you as well as folks in Troy."

He added then, "I know you think it's strange—　　　　　120
No wonder that, for this is new to you—
To leave your friends in Troy and have to change
For Greeks instead, for folks you never knew.
But God forbid that Greeks can't be as true,
While living in our camp you'll surely find,
As any Trojan is, and just as kind.

---

10. This and the following thirteen stanzas (through line 189) do not appear in Boccaccio.

"And as I swore to you, and rightly so,
To be your friend and helper if I might,
And as I've seen much more of you, you know,
Than any other Greek or foreign knight,   130
Dear, from today, I pray you, day or night,
Ask anything you'd like for me to do,
And I'll perform it, just to comfort you.

"And so you'll learn to treat me as a brother,
And never hold my friendship in despite,
Although you grieve for one thing or another
(I don't know why)—I pray hear this aright:
I'll ease you all I can with great delight.
But if that proves beyond me, I profess,
At least you'll know I rue your heaviness.   140

"Although you Trojans view us Greeks with hate,
And have for quite some time, yet as you see,
The selfsame god of love rules either state.
Now for the love of Venus, lady free,
Hate whom you will as long as it's not me.
Truly, lady, no man in your path
Would be as loath as I to feel your wrath.

"And if we weren't now drawing to the tent
Of Calchas—who perhaps has seen us both—
I wouldn't spare to tell my whole intent,   150
But that must keep a while yet, by my troth.
Give me your hand. I am, upon my oath,
So help me God, as long as I endure,
Your own above all others, true and sure.

"I've never said as much upon that score
To any woman born. My dear that's so.
I never loved another so before—
No one at all—nor will again, I know.
Now for the love of God, don't be my foe!
If I can't speak as well as I can yearn,   160
Forgive me, lady. I have much to learn.

"It's not a wonder, my own lady bright,
That I'm compelled to speak of love apace,
For love, indeed, has stricken many a knight
The moment he first saw his lady's face.
I have no power to stand against the grace
In Cupid's gift. O no! I must obey
And always will. Forgive that too, I pray.

"Such worthy knights abound about this place
And you're so fair, that soon enough they all   170
Will do their best to stand well in your grace.
But if, as I must pray, it should befall
That I become the servant whom you call,
Not one will be as true, upon my head,
As I swear I will be till I am dead."

Criseyde rode along and answered little,
For sorrow left her woeful and oppressed.
She hardly understood a jot or tittle,
Though here and there a word sank in her breast.
She thought the heart would burst within her chest,   180
And when she saw her father coming near
She shrank upon her horse in sudden fear.

Still, she thanked Diomedes, that is sure,
For all the pains he took and for his cheer
And for the friendship that he offered her.
She'd be his friend, she said, true and sincere.
She promised she would always hold him dear
And trust him as she knew full well she might.
He stilled her horse and helped her to alight.

Her father held her tight in his embrace,   190
And kissed her twenty times. His joy was sweet.
"Welcome!" he said and looked into her face.
She murmured she was glad that they should meet
And stood before him silent and discreet.
I'll leave her there for Calchas to enjoy,
And tell you next how Troilus fared in Troy.

Back to the town came Troilus, grim and sad,
In sorrow far above the common force.
With sullen looks and gestures far from glad
He threw himself, all careless, from his horse   200
And through his palace steered a hasty course.
Up to his room he went with little heed.
None dared to speak a word to him indeed.

And there the sorrows that he held inside
Issued at last, and "Death!" he roared at first.
Then in frenetic throes and fiery-eyed
Cupid, Apollo—Jove himself—he cursed,
Blaspheming Lady Venus even worse.
He damned himself, his fate, his very birth
And—save Criseyde—everything on earth.   210

He lay down on his bed to twist and turn
With fury as King Ixion[11] must in hell.
And in this state till morning he sojourned
But then his heart began to soften and unswell
Because of all the tears that left that well.
He called out to Criseyde by and by
And, speaking to himself, he made his cry:

"O now where is my lady, sweet and dear?
Where is her white breast? Her loving air?
Where are her arms and sparkling eyes so clear   220
That this time yesternight were in my care?
Now may I weep alone for my lost fair
And reach about all ways, though in this place
I've nothing but a pillow to embrace.

"What shall I do? When shall she come again?
I don't know how I ever let her go!
I wish God had seen fit to slay me then.
O my heart, Criseyde—sweetest foe!
My dearest love, my soul is scored by woe.
I dedicate my burning heart to you,   230
But though I die, there's nothing you can do.

---

11. *IX-ee-on.* He lusted after Juno and was bound forever to a fiery wheel in hell.

"Who sees you now, my darling, bright lodestar?[12]
Who sits or stands beside you, dear, today?
Who comforts you and soothes away each scar?
Now I am gone, who talks to you in play?
And who can speak for me while you're away?
No one, alas, and that is all my care.
I ache, but just as evilly you fare.

"How shall I thus a full ten days endure,
When this first night gives me such grief and pain?   240
And how shall she, who pines as well I'm sure?
How shall her tender, loving heart sustain
Such woe for me? O pitiful and plain
Shall be your lovely face, dear one, I fear
For anguish, till you make your way back here."

When from time to time he fell asleep,
He soon began to toss about and groan
And dream of dreadful things that made him weep:
He dreamed he was imprisoned and alone
In direful straits to ever make his moan,   250
Or that he had been wounded in some brawl
And now must face his foemen, one and all.

And therewithal he felt his body start,
And with that start come suddenly awake,
And such a tremor felt about his heart,
For very fear his stricken body quaked.
And then in torment he would moan and shake,
As if from high above he'd fallen deep.
That fear would take his breath and make him weep.

He pitied his own state so ruefully   260
I don't know how he overcame his fears
But now and then he shook his fancy free,
Consoled himself and wiped away his tears
And thought it folly to be set so by the ears.
But then his bitter sorrows would come back
So anyone would pity him, alack!

12. This and the following six stanzas (through line 280) do not appear in Boccaccio.

For who could tell aright or well describe
His woe, his plaints, his languishing, his pain?
No man, I think, who's ever been alive.
You, reader, can well imagine, if you deign,   270
How I fall short. Mere words must be in vain.
It cannot help for me to spend more ink.
His woe went far beyond all I can think.

In heaven now the fading stars were seen,
And faint and growing paler shone the moon.
The sky began to rouse itself and preen
Across the east, with early light festooned.
And Phoebus in his rosy carriage soon
Would show himself awake and start to fare,
When Troilus called for Pandarus in his care.   280

Pandarus, all throughout the previous day
Could not come to Troilus, as he said.
For though he'd sworn he would with no delay,
He had been summoned to the Court instead.
So as it chanced, he claimed upon his head,
He couldn't come as promptly as he meant,
But here he was, the minute Troilus sent.

For in his heart he knew that he would find
That Troilus lay in pain all night awake,
And that his friend's sore heart was not resigned.   290
He saw this and lamented for his sake.
He took the shortest path that he could take
To Troilus' room, and somberly he greeted
His lovelorn friend, and shortly he was seated.

"Pandarus," Troilus said, "the dreadful sorrow
That plagues my heart is too much to endure.
I doubt that I will live until tomorrow,
No, I must die at once unless I err,
So now I will design my sepulcher.
As for my belongings and the rest   300
Dispose of those however you think best.

"But for the pyre and quick-consuming flames
In which my body burns, and all such deeds,

And for the feast and prayers and funeral games
At my vigil, lord, yourself take heed
That all be well; and offer Mars my steed.
And last, my brother, give my helm and sword
And my bright shield to Pallas for reward.   *Pallas Athena*

"The powdered ashes of my poor burnt heart,
I pray you take those up to be conserved   310
And put them in an urn of gold apart
And give them to the lady whom I served.
And say I died for love, as she deserved.
And, friend, when you perform this task for me,
Pray she'll keep me in her memory.

"For by these ills in which you see me lie,
And by my dreams, both now and long ago,
I know for sure, my lord, that I must die.
Ascalaphus,[13] the omen-owl, you know,
Has shrieked for me two nights, portending woe.   320
Now Mercury,[14] guide my soul, so weak and wretched
The proper way when you are pleased to fetch it."

Pandarus answered, "Troilus, my dear friend,
As I have told you often heretofore,
It's foolishness to sorrow to no end
Or for no cause. Now, what can I say more?
But whoso will not heed advice or lore,
For him I see no present remedy
But let him live caught up in fantasy.

"Yet sir, I must pray you'll tell me now,   330
Whether you believe that any knight
Has loved his paramour as well as thou?
God knows some have, yet went without her sight,
Because they fared away, a whole fortnight!

---

13. *As-CAL-a-fus*. Owls were generally considered birds of ill omen. Ascalaphus
was transformed into an owl because he let it be known that Proserpine had eaten
a pomegranate seed in the underworld and so was condemned to stay there.
14. One of Mercury's duties was to lead souls into the afterlife.

And still those lovers made not half the stir
That you have raised for being gone from her.

"Now, every day you cannot fail to see[15]
That from his love, or even from his wife,
A man must travel of necessity
Yet even though he loves her as his life,   340
He doesn't give himself such woe and strife.
For you know well, or should, beloved brother
That friends can't always be with one another.

"How fare those folk who see their lovers wedded
By others' choice, as it betides full oft,
And see them with those other spouses bedded?
God knows, they bear it wisely, as they ought,
Because good hope holds their bruised hearts aloft.
Although a time of grief is theirs for sure,
As time can hurt, so time supplies a cure.   350

"Just so should you endure and let this slide—
Your time apart—and flourish, gay and light.
Ten days is not a long time to abide,
And since she promised to escape her plight,
She'll never break her word to her own knight.
Don't be afraid that she won't find a way.
She'll soon be back. My life on that, I say!

"As for your dreams and all such fantasy,
Why, drive them out and leave them to their fate.
They're naught but melancholy fumes, you see,   360
Arising from the hurts you've felt of late.
A straw for all such trifles of no weight!
I swear, by God, they aren't worth a bean,
For no man knows at all what such things mean.

"Priests who haunt the temples tell us thus:[16]
That in our dreams we hear the voice of gods.
But then they say as well, with equal fuss,

---

15. This and the following stanza do not appear in Boccaccio.
16. This and the following two stanzas do not appear in Boccaccio.

That they're infernal sendings by all odds.
'Ill humors!'[17] doctors claim with learned nods—
Or too much fasting . . . or else gluttony!   370
Who knows what their significance may be?

"Still others trace them to some thing you've seen,
For say a strong impression fills your mind—
That may send visions rising from your spleen.
But others turn to ancient books they've mined
And say it's by the time of year, they find,
That dreams are formed—according to the moon—
Lord, put no faith in dreaming, late or soon!

"Leave all foolish dreams to mad old wives,
And leave them, too, all augury by fowls,[18]   380
For fear of which men think they'll lose their lives
For croaking ravens or for stritching owls.
No true soul trusts in such foreboding howls.
Alas, that man, a creature good and sure,
Should count on lying dreams and such manure.

"For which with all my heart I pray to you,
Forget these dreams and omens that you fear,
And rise up now without much more ado
And let us think and act with better cheer,
And use our time in hope and joy sincere,   390
Until Criseyde's back, which won't be long.
To doubt her truth would do the lady wrong.

"Let's speak, my friend, of lusty days in Troy
That we had once and make these moments pass,
And view the time that's still to come with joy.
For it will bring her glad return full fast.
These twice five days will wear away at last,
And when they're gone, my lord, this must be plain,
No thought of them will give us further pain.

---

17. According to classical and medieval theory, illnesses and obsessions came
about from an imbalance of the four "humors," or active fluids, in the body: blood
(the sanguine humor), yellow bile (the choleric humor), black bile (the melancholy
humor), and phlegm (the phlegmatic humor).
18. Foretelling the future by the flight of birds or by examining their organs.

"The town is full of nobles all about,   400
And while this truce that we enjoy may stay,
Let's amuse ourselves among the rout
At Sarpedon's[19] house. It's not a mile away.
And so we'll pass the time and ease its sway,
And make it fly until that blissful morrow
When you'll see her who's caused you so much sorrow.

"So now get up, Prince Troilus, brother dear,
For certainly no honor comes to you
To weep in bed and cower so in here,
For trust me in one thing—I swear its true: 410
Hide yourself for just a day or two,
And folk will say you've lost your nerve, no doubt,
And hunker here for fear of going out!"

"Pandarus," Troilus answered, "noble friend,
It can't be news to those who've suffered pain
That though he weep for grief he can't amend—
One who feels great harm in every vein—
It's no great wonder that he must complain
Or always weep. I don't deserve your blame
Because my aching heart is all aflame.   420

"But since I can't resist but must arise,
I'll get up betimes and not delay.
Now God, to whom my heart I sacrifice,
Grant us she's back, and on the proper day.
No bird was ever half so glad of May
As I shall be when she returns to Troy—
Criseyde, my dear torment and my joy.

"But wither do you think we two should go?
Where shall we find the greatest sport we may?"
Pandarus answered, "I just said, you know.   430
King Sarpedon's house is always gay."
They spoke of this till it was fully day

_____

19. *Sar-PEE-don.* A king of Lycia (southeastern Turkey). A son of Zeus and one of Troy's principal allies. Chaucer neglects to say so, but Sarpedon's feast was intended to last several days.

And Troilus at the last gave his consent,
And forth to King Sarpedon's house they went.

Sarpedon was as rich as he was able,
And all his life held love of friends full high.
He held back nothing from his open table.
There was no dainty he would not supply,
And those he fed there praised him to the sky.
Such nobleness, they said from first to least,   440
Had not been shown before at any feast.

Nor in this world was there an instrument,
Delectable through wind or sounding cord,
That you could find no matter where you went,
None known to tongue of peasant, serf, or lord,
That failed to sound before his high-piled board.
Nor ever such a comely company
Of ladies, dancing there for all to see.

And yet what help was this to grieving Troilus?
His sorrow made him hold the feast for naught.   450
For all the time his heart pined as it must.
His missing love Criseyde filled his thought.
He yearned for her alone, as well he ought,
Brooding on this and this and that and that—
No festive mood could reach him where he sat.

Seeing ladies there who graced the feast,
Since his own Criseyde was away,
Could only make his woeful pain increase;
Nor could the music much improve his stay.
For since the one who held him in her sway   460
Was absent, he contrived this fantasy:
That no one should be making melody.

Nor was there an hour, day or night,
When he escaped to where friends couldn't hear,
He failed to cry, "O lovesome lady bright,
How fare you now that you have disappeared?
Welcome when you will, my lady dear."
He almost thought he saw her, but was wrong,
Fortune was just leading him along.

The letters that she'd sent in former times,   470
Alone, he read as often as he could,
Each time of day or night, from noon to prime,
Imagining her shape and womanhood.
Within his heart he called up as he would,
Her every loving deed, and in that way
He passed four days of his intended stay.

But then, "My brother Pandarus," he said
"Do you intend to make this house our seat,
Or stay until the other guests have sped?
Are you still hungry? I'm not. I'm replete!   480
For God's love, sir, this evening after meat,
Let's take our leave for home and end this stay.
I won't remain, no matter what you say."

"Did we come here, my lord," Pandarus said,
"To beg a light and run back home again?
By God, I know no better place instead
Where we may go or, may I suffer pain,
Where any would so joy to see us twain
As does Sarpedon. If we leave him now,
He'll think we are ungrateful, lord, I vow.   490

"You know we told Sarpedon we'd remain
A week with him, and now, so suddenly,
To leave the fourth day and go home again—
He'll wonder what's gone wrong with you and me.
No, let us stay at least another three.
For since we made a promise we'd abide,
We should remain all seven ere we ride."

Thus Pandarus, in spite of Troilus' pain and woe,
Made him stay until the full week passed.
And then they took their leave, prepared to go,   500
And rode away toward their homes at last.
"Now God," said Troilus, "send me what I've asked:
That I may find before I've been home long
Criseyde has returned!" and so burst into song.

"What twaddle!" Pandarus said beneath his breath,
And muttered to himself full softly then,

"God knows that his desire may burn to death
Ere Calchas sends Criseyde back again!"
But yet he joked and chattered like a wren,
And swore his heart persuaded him aright   510
That she would come as quickly as she might.

Riding to the prince's palace door,
They both reined in their horses to alight.
And later, in his chamber as before,
From early evening far into the night,
They spoke of Troilus' love, Criseyde bright.
And after this, when both of them thought best,
They took a hasty supper—then to rest.

That morning, as the day began to clear,
This Troilus woke from dreaming with a start,   520
And then to Pandarus, his own brother dear,
"By God," he said full piteously for his part,
"Let's go to see the house of my dear heart,
For now that we have given up the feast,
We'll both enjoy a glimpse of that at least."

And therewithal to fool his household men
He found some cause to say he had to go,
And rode to Criseyde's palace with his friend,
But, Lord, that only caused the prince more woe.
It gave his anguished soul another blow,   530
For when he saw her doors fast locked and barred,
He never felt his heart more sorely charred.

And when he roused up somewhat to behold
The shutters on each window of the place,
He felt his weary heart was turning cold,
And so, with aching heart and deathly face,
Without a word, he spurred his horse apace
And rode right by, head down and posting fast,
So no one there would know him as he passed.

"O palace," said he then, "so desolate,   540
O house of houses, once you shone so bright;
O palace, empty now—disconsolate—

Discarded lantern, robbed of all its light;
O you, once clear as day, now dark as night!
Now you ought to fall and I to die
Since she who ruled us is no longer nigh.

"O palace, once the crown of houses all,
Illumined with the sun of my great bliss;
O ring, from which I let the ruby fall;
O cause of woe now all has gone amiss!   550
Since I can't do more, your doors I'd kiss
If all these watchful folk were not about.
Farewell my sacred shrine; your saint is out!"

Therewith he cast on Pandarus his eye.
His face was changed and piteous to behold.
And when he could his time aright espy,
As he rode on, to Pandarus he told
His freshest sorrows and all his joys of old,
So piteously and with so dead a hue,
That anyone might on his sorrow rue.   560

And then he rode at random up and down,
But everywhere he met some memory,
For as he passed the places of the town,
Old joys came flooding back he couldn't flee.
"Here," he said, "my lady danced for me;
And in that temple—there—her glancing eyes
First caught my heart. Lord, that was my demise!

"And in that house I heard her laugh for joy.
And there she acted playfully one day.
She teased me as she would, now bold, now coy.   570
And yonder, by my faith, I heard her say,
'Sweetheart, you must love me well, I pray.'
And there she looked such tender love at me,
She'll hold my heart forever in her fee.

"Around that corner, down two doors or three,
I heard my most beloved lady dear,
So woman-like and so melodiously
Sing so sweetly—with goodly voice and clear—

That in my soul I think I still can hear
That blissful sound. And in that yonder place   580
My lady took me first into her grace."

Then he thought thus: "O Cupid, blissful lord,
When I rehearse our dealings I bewail
How thou so pierced my heart with dart and sword,
That men might make a book of it—a tale.
Why be proud to vanquish one so frail,
Since I am thine and wholly at thy will?
What joy is it thy servants so to kill?

"Well hast thou, my lord, shown me thine ire,
Thou mighty god, so dreadful to aggrieve!   590
Grant mercy, lord! Thou knowst that I desire
Thy grace above all other things I crave,
And I will live and die, my lord, thy slave.
For which I ask thee but a single boon:
That my Criseyde should be home full soon.

"Lord, move her heart as strongly to return
As thou doest mine to long to see her here.
Inspire her, lord, to shorten her sojourn.
And, blissful lord, I pray don't be austere
Unto the blood of Troy, which you've held dear,   600
As Juno was unto the Theban lords[20]
Pursuing them with monsters, war, and swords."

And after this he went out to the gate
By which Criseyde left, and at that place
Now up and down he walked, bewailing fate,
And to himself he said, "Great God, how base!
From here my solace rode from my embrace!
If only blissful God now, for His joy
Would let her come again to me and Troy!

"Yet to that yonder hill I was her guide,   610
Alas, and there I took my leave of her.

_____

20. Juno disliked Thebes. She hounded the Theban hero Hercules in one way
after another, at one point driving him mad. She also sent the Sphinx to Thebes
to kill and eat anyone who failed to answer her riddle.

She rode to join her traitor father's side,
A sorrow I cannot for long endure.
But I came home that night without demur,
And here I dwell apart from all my joy
Until I see her safely back in Troy."

He felt himself grow weaker day by day,
Defeated, pale with grief, and somehow less.
And then, he often fancied, men must say,
"What can this be? Pray tell me who can guess   620
Why Troilus toils in such great heaviness?"
But that was nothing but his melancholy,[21]
Rising to his brain and spawning folly.

Another time his fevered mind would hold
That every knight that went along the way
Pitied him and said, if they were bold,
"The prince will surely die; mark what I say."
And yet he must endure another day
As you have heard; and thus, so nearly dead,
He lived with shrinking hope and swelling dread.   630

Sometimes he cast his sadness into song,
Describing all his grief as best he might.
The words and tune, both somber but not long,
Made his anguished heart a bit more light.
And far away from any watcher's sight,
Full softly he would sing about his dear,
Absent as she was, as you may hear:

    Canticus Troili   *The song of Troilus*

"O star, of which I have lost all the light,
With sorest heart I properly bewail
That in this dark and torment, night by night,   640
Toward my death with wind astern I sail.
And if on that tenth night, my star, you fail

---

21. One of the four humors, melancholy—or black bile—was thought to give off
vapors that could permeate the body and cause sadness and depression.

So that I miss thy guidance but an hour,
My ship and me Charybdis²² will devour.

He sang this song and then he fell full soon,
Back into piteous sighing as of old,
And every night he stood beneath the moon,
Whose light befit his mood, so pale and cold,
And, looking up, his grief and sorrow told.
"O moon," he said, "when next your horns are new,²³   650
I shall be glad—if all the world be true.

"I saw your horns grown old on that same morrow
When she rode hence, my loveliest lady dear,
The cause of all my torment and great sorrow.
But now, O bright Latona,²⁴ pale and clear,
For love of God run fast about your sphere!
For when your horns are newly sprung again
She shall be here. Lord, I'll be happy then!"

His days were long and longer still his nights.
Far longer than they used to be, he deemed.   660
The course the sun took daily wasn't right.
It took a longer path each day it seemed.
"I'm sure," he said, "all this must be a dream,
Or else the sun's son Phaeton²⁵ now once more
Drives his car as badly as before."

At times he'd go to walk the city wall
And look far out upon the Grecian host,
And sadly muse like one who was in thrall.
"Lo there," he'd say, "is she whom I love most,
Or yonder, where those tents lie near the coast;   670
Ah, thence must come this air that is so sweet
It soothes my soul, foretelling how we'll meet.

---

22. *Ka-RIB-dis.* A famous whirlpool in the strait between Italy and Sicily.

23. Troilus is looking ahead to a new crescent moon that he hopes will mark Criseyde's return.

24. *La-TON-a.* Diana's mother and one of the moon's several names.

25. *FI-ton.* He drove the sun's chariot so erratically that the world was in danger of burning up until Jove killed him with a thunderbolt.

"And certainly this breeze that more and more
With every hour increases on my face
Comes of my lady's sighs, so deep and sore.
It must be thus for in no other place
In all the town, save in this little space
Is there a wind that sounds a like refrain.
'Alas,' it says, 'when shall we meet again?'"

And thus he wore away the time, and thus,   680
Until he passed the ninth and final night,
Ever at his side went Pandarus,
Who busily used all his wit and might
To comfort him and make his heart more light,
Keeping hope alive for that tenth morrow
When she would come again and end his sorrow.

Criseyde languished on the other side,
With few attendants, though the Greeks were strong.
"Alas the day," full many times she cried,
"Why was I born to suffer such a wrong?   690
I yearn for death for now I've lived too long.
But this, alas, is nothing I can mend.
My plight is worse than I can comprehend.

"My father won't unbend in any way[26]
Or let me go no matter what I do.
But if I am held back and miss my day,
My Troilus' heart shall tell him I'm untrue.
He'll think that's so, and with good reason too.
And thus I shall be scorned on every side.
O that I'd not been born at all!" she cried.   700

"And if I put myself in jeopardy
To steal away by night and it befall
That I am caught, I shall be held a spy,
Or else—and this would be the worst all—
Some wretched man will seize me for his thrall.
I am but lost although my heart is true.
O mighty God! Please tell me what to do!"

_____

26. This and the following two stanzas do not appear in Boccaccio.

Now grown pale as ash was her bright face.
Her limbs grew lean as she stood every day—
As often as she dared—to view the place   710
Where she was born and lived a life full gay;
And all the night in tears, alas, she lay,
And thus despairing, hoping for no cure,
She found her life a hardship to endure.

Full often she would sigh in great distress,
And all the while fast fixed within her mind
Was Troilus and his spotless worthiness.
There all his goodly words had been enshrined
Since that first day their lives were intertwined.
And thus she set her woeful heart afire   720
Recalling all she could of her desire.

In all the world there's not so cruel a heart
That hearing her complain in all her sorrow
Would not take pity on her grievous smart,
So tenderly she wept by night and morrow—
So rich in tears she never had to borrow.
And yet this was the worst of all her pain:
She had no one to whom she dare complain.

Full ruefully she looked across at Troy,
Beheld its noble towers and mighty halls.   730
"Alas," she said, "the pleasure and the joy
That I have often had within those walls
Is bitter now. That life has turned to gall.
What are you doing Troilus, dear?" she sighed.
"Do you think of Criseyde as you ride?

"Ach, I should have listened to your voice
And gone with you, dear, as you asked me to.
Then I wouldn't so regret my choice.
How could I think worse fortune would ensue
If I had flown with such a one as you?   740
But it's past the time to seek the cure we crave
When we're already lying in the grave.

"It's too late now to think of this, I fear.
Prudence,[27] alas, one of your three eyes
I always lacked before they brought me here.
My past is plain enough. It never dies.
My present I can see and well apprise.
But future times are blind and but a snare.
That eye is blurred, and thence comes all my care.

"But nonetheless, whatever shall betide,   750
I shall tomorrow night, by east or west,
Steal from these tents if I am not descried,
And go with Troilus wherever he thinks best.
This purpose is now fast within my breast.
Away with all men's wicked tongues can say.
They envy love and treat it as their prey.

"For whoso will of every word take heed,[28]
Or rule himself by other people's wit,
He shall never prosper or succeed;
For some folks will find any course unfit   760
In spite of how all others value it.
No, I won't care what others may profess.
My surest guide is my own happiness.

"And so, without more words, here's what I'll do,
I'll go to Troy, and that's my final say"—
But, God knows, in another month or two
She looked at things in quite a different way!
For Troy and Troilus both, as I must say
Shall knotless slide and drop down from her heart.
She'll choose the Grecian side on her own part.   770

Diomedes, of whom you've heard me speak before,
Went about debating without let,
With all the skill he had (and few had more)
How he with no undue delay could get
Criseyde's tender heart into his net.

---

27. Prudence was often thought of as a goddess with three eyes to take in the past, present, and future.
28. This stanza does not appear in Boccaccio.

Toward this purpose, always, rain or shine,
He chose his bait and laid out hook and line.

Yet all the while, deep inside he thought
That she was not without a love in Troy.
For never, since he fetched her so distraught,   780
Had he seen her laugh or show a sign of joy,
Nor could he soothe her by his shrewdest ploy.
"Still," he said, "it's worth my time indeed,
For not to try is never to succeed."

And yet he told himself one starry night,
"Now am I not a fool? I know full well
Her pain in love is for another knight.
What hope so soon that old love to expel?
It's not within my power to break his spell.
Wise authors in their books all say it's so: 790
'It's vain to woo a lady deep in woe.'

"But anyone who won so fair a flower
From him for whom she mourns both night and day,
Ach, he would be a lover of some power!"
And then anon—for he was bold that way—
He thought at heart: "Lo, happen now what may,
If I should die, I will her love beseech.
There's naught to lose in this except my speech!"

This Diomedes, as all books declare,[29]
Was bold enough at need and stout of heart.   800
His voice was stern; his limbs were strong and fair—
Hardy, headstrong, daring for his part,
Like Tydeus, his father, in war's arts.
He was proud and often hasty to respond,
And heir to Argos and wide Calydon.[30]

---

29. This and the following seven stanzas (through line 854) do not appear in Boccaccio. The descriptions of Diomedes, Criseyde, and Troilus are drawn from The *Ylias (Iliad) of Dares the Phrygian* by way of a twelfth-century Latin retelling by Joseph of Exeter of Dares' lost Greek account, but in greatly expanded form.
30. Two ancient Greek city-states.

Criseyde was but middling in her height.[31]
As to her shape and face and noble cheer,
There never was a more alluring wight.
Her heart was soft and tender, not austere.
She went about in braids behind each ear   810
And down her back, delightful to behold,
All bound up with a slender thread of gold.

Save somewhat heavy brows that joined together,[32]
She lacked no point of beauty, so I've read.
And for her eyes, as gray as autumn heather,
Yea, truly those who write of her have said
That Paradise was in them, softly spread.
Her beauty struck men speechless to the core,
But love would leave them yearning all the more.

She was sober, simple, kind, and wise,   820
As well bred and well nurtured as might be,
And honest in her speech—without disguise—
Generous yet stately, gay and free,
And always open to a worthy plea;
Quick to help, though risk could make her pause,[33]
But truly I can't say how old she was.

And Troilus was well grown, straight, and tall,
Correct and well proportioned in design.
Nature had not erred with him at all,
But made him strong and hardy as a lion,   830
True as steel, inflexible of spine.
A fitly furnished noble, unsurpassed
While men strive for esteem or world shall last.

And certainly in stories it is found
That Troilus never stooped to yield in any fight.
Nor was he second best on any ground
In doing all that most becomes a knight.

---

31. In Book 1, line 281, Chaucer, like Boccaccio, implied she was tall.

32. An odd detail adopted from Dares. Medieval treatises associate joined brows
with fickleness and instability.

33. Chaucer says she was "slydynge of corage," a detail he derived from Benoît.

A giant might possess the greater might,
But not a greater heart. His was the best,
And helped him to prevail in any test.   840

But I was telling Diomedes' tale.
It fell that on the tenth and fatal day,
As Criseyde endured her sharp travail,
This Diomedes, fresh as blooms in May,
Came to the tent where she and Calchas lay,
Pretending to discuss some kind of boon,
But what he really meant, I'll tell you soon.

Criseyde, to put it shortly as I may,
Welcomed him to sit down at her side.
Lo, sitting so he was most glad to stay.   850
And after this as often may betide
Spices, sweetmeats, wine were spread out wide,
And they began to speak as friends well met,
And some of what they said, I'll tell you yet.

He first began to talk about the war
And how his side oppressed the folk of Troy.
He asked her what her people thought of yore
Of Greece and Greeks and prayed she'd not be coy.
With that much done, he said he would enjoy
Hearing how she liked the Grecian style—   860
How Greeks behaved—now she'd been there a while.

Then he asked why Calchas had delayed so long
To wed her to some worthy Trojan knight.
Criseyde—still in pain she felt full strong
For Troilus, whom she'd loved since their first night—
Made as good an answer as she might.
But truly, as for his concealed intent,
It seemed she had no notion what he meant.

But this same Diomedes, nonetheless,
Grew surer of himself, and then he said: 870
"I've formed a strong impression, I confess—
Criseyde mine, I think, upon my head,
That since you had to follow where I led,

When you came riding out of Troy that morrow,
I've never seen you, lady, but in sorrow.

"Now, I can't say just what the cause could be,
Unless you love some noble Trojan peer.
But that, my dear, would sore dishearten me—
That you for any knight that's dwelling there
Should spill the merest quarter of a tear,   880
Or so mistakenly yourself beguile.
Believe me, dear. It isn't worth your while.

"The folk of Troy, no matter how they strive,
Are prisoners, as you yourself can see.
No one in that town will long survive
For all the gold between the sun and sea.
Please listen well, my dear, and trust in me:
No mercy will be shown—none left alive,
If he were lord of all this world times five!

"Such vengeance shall we take upon this plain   890
For loss of Helen, for whom we now contend,
The Manes,[34] gods in charge of causing pain,
Shall stand aghast at how our swords can rend,
And men will dread until the world shall end
From this time forth to ravish any queen,
So cruel shall our counterblow be seen.

"Unless your father's prophesies betray us—
That is to say, with double words and sly,
Words, as men may say, that bear two faces—
You'll know right well, and soon, I do not lie.   900
You'll see these things unfold before your eye.
You won't believe how quick it all will be,
Troy's end is coming shortly; trust in me.

"How could one who knows all things to come
Have given up Lord Antenor for you,
If he'd not known the Trojans, all and some,

---

34. *MAN-ez.* Gods of the underworld. Often described as inflicting pain on
dead souls.

Will be destroyed? Love, give him what he's due!
Calchas knows his prophesies are true.
No Trojan will escape. With that to fear,
He took you out of Troy and brought you here.   910

"What will you more, my lovesome lady dear?
Let Troy and Trojans go. Forget the place.
Drive out that bitter hope. Regain your cheer.
Restore the blissful beauty of your face.
All traces of these salty tears erase.
Troy stands now in such great jeopardy,
It's lost indeed beyond all remedy.

"Consider this: here with us Greeks you'll find
A far more perfect love, ere it be night,
Than any Trojan is—a love more kind   920
And fit to serve and of a greater might.
If you would but permit me, lady bright,
I'd undertake to serve you without cease
Before I'd rule a dozen times in Greece."

And with that word he grew a little red,
Began to fidget just a bit and quake,
And slightly frowned and turned away his head
And stopped a while, then gave himself a shake
And looked into her eyes, now wide awake,
And said, "I am, though it gives you no joy,   930
As highly born as any knight in Troy.

"For if my father, Tydeus, had not died,
My dearest lady, know that I would be
King of Argos and Calydon beside,
And hope I will be yet, as some foresee.
But he was slain by cross-grained gods' decree,
By Theban Melanippus' lucky arm
To Polynices' and his forces' harm.[35]

---

35. *Mel-an-IP-pus, Pol-ee-NEE-ses.* It isn't clear what Chaucer was thinking here.
In line 805 he said Diomedes was heir to Argos and Calydon, while classical stories
describe the hero as already being king of Argos (but not of Calydon) before he
left for Troy. The other details in the stanza come from the story of the *Seven*

"But, my heart, since I'm to be your man,
And you're the first from whom I've sought such grace—   940
To serve your needs as fully as I can
(I always will, my dear, in any case)—
Before I leave you, dear one, in this place—
Please grant this boon: say that I may tomorrow,
And at more leisure, tell you all my sorrow."

Why should I recount each thing he said?[36]
He said enough, indeed, for that one day,
And he spoke well, for his petition sped:
Criseyde said she'd hear him anyway.
He could come again and have his say.   950
She'd listen, so she said, if he'd steer clear
Of topics that she banned as you may hear.

She spoke as one whose heart was set on Troilus,
A deep commitment nothing could erase.
But she spoke coolly, too, and answered thus:
"O Diomedes, how I love that place
Where I was born. Jove grant, of his grace,
That it will find deliverance from its care.
God foster Troy and save it from despair!

"That Greeks would raze the town the cruelest way[37]   960
If that could be, my lord, I know it's so.
But maybe things won't fall out as you say.
May God forbid it! And I also know
My father's wise, as all his doings show,
And that he bought me dear I'll not forget.
He cares for me, and I am in his debt.

Against Thebes, which is complicated. Briefly, Tydeus and other heroes enlisted with Polynices—one of the sons of Oedipus—to regain Thebes, from which he'd been expelled by his brother Eteocles. Tydeus distinguished himself in the fighting until he was mortally wounded by Melanippus, whom he killed. A gory detail: Athena was poised to carry Tydeus off to Olympus until he gorged on Melanippus' brains and so lost his chance at immortality. Polynices eventually lost the war and was also killed.

36. This stanza does not appear in Boccaccio.

37. This stanza does not appear in Boccaccio.

"That there are many Greeks of high condition,
I know full well, but surely you will find
Worthy Trojans in the same position—
As well learned and as perfect and as kind   970
As any in all other states combined.
Still, I believe you could a lady serve,
And earn from her the thanks you would deserve.

"But as you speak of love to me," she sighed,
"I had, my lord, a husband—we were wed—
And gave him all my heart until he died,
And other love—may Pallas spare my head—
I never had since my good lord's been dead.
And that you are of high and noble birth,
I grant that's true enough, for all the earth.   980

"But knowing so has surely made me wonder
That you would disrespect a woman so.
God knows that love and I are far asunder.
It suits me best, as I shall live and go,
To mourn until I die and weep for woe.
What I'll do hereafter, I can't say.
Be courteous. Don't worry me this way!

"My heart is now in dire tribulation,
And you're in arms and busy every day.
When you've reduced my city to prostration,   990
Perhaps it might so happen in some way—
When I see things I never saw, I say—
That I'll do things I've never done, my lord.
That's all the comfort I can now afford.

"If you're here tomorrow, we'll speak then—[38]
As long as you forbear to speak of love.
And when you like, sir, you may come again.
And ere you go, I'll say this much thereof:
So help me Pallas and all the gods above,
If I should for any Greek take care,   1000
You would be the one I'd choose, I swear.

---

38. This and the following sixteen stanzas (through line 1113) do not appear in Boccaccio.

"I will not say that I will love you, sir,
Nor will I say I'll not. . . . I'll not be bound.
I mean right well—God help me if I err!"
With that she cast her eyes down to the ground,
And then she sighed and burst out: "O my town!
I pray to God I see you back at rest,
Or may my poor heart burst within my breast."

But in effect, to put it shortly as I may,
This Diomedes, feeling good as new,   1010
Pressed his suit so hotly, without stay,
That afterward—and this is surely true—
He took her glove,[39] which he rejoiced to do.
Then finally when day gave way to eve
And all was well, he rose and took his leave.

Bright Venus rose and sparkled as it taught   *the evening star*
The way that flaming Phoebus should alight,
And Cynthia urged her horses as she sought   *the moon*
To whirl out of the Lion as she might,   *the sign of Leo*
And Signifer[40] fired its constellations bright,   1020
When Criseyde, feeling weary, rose and went
To rest inside her father's glowing tent.

She turned things in her mind, now up, now down,
The sudden statements Diomedes made—
His great estate, the peril of the town—
And how she was alone, in need of aid
With little help. And truly she was swayed.
Such things as these, and others of that stamp,
Convinced her not to leave the Grecian camp.

The morrow came, and with it without fail,   1030
Came Diomedes to Criseyde once again.
And shortly, lest it interrupt my tale,
So well he spoke, inveigled, and complained,
That he broke down the doubts she still retained,
And finally, in truth I must assert,
He soothed away the most part of her hurt.

---

39. As a token of her regard.
40. *SIG-ni-fer.* Latin for *sign bearer,* a name sometimes applied to the zodiac.

And after, as the oldest authors tell us,
She gave him back the prancing, fair bay steed
That he once won in battle from Prince Troilus.
And Troilus' brooch as well—with little need—   1040
She pinned on Diomedes' shirt indeed,
And later, as she hoped his sorrow to relieve,
She made the knight a pennant of her sleeve.

I also find in those old tales, I fear,
When Troilus wounded Diomedes in a fight
That Criseyde sorely wept full many a tear—
His bloody gashes gave her such a fright—
And that she nursed him ably as she might;
And then to heal him of his sorrows smart
(I hope this isn't so), she gave her heart.   1050

But truly, as those ancient stories tell us
No woman ever suffered greater woe
Than she, when she betrayed her lover Troilus.
She said, "Alas, alas, for now I know
My name for truth is gone. Alack, that's so,
For I've betrayed as surely as I might
The world's most worthy man and gentlest knight!

"Alas, of me, until the world shall end,
There never shall be written now or sung
A kindly word. No author will defend   1060
One whose faults are rolled on every tongue.
Throughout the world my falseness will be rung.
All women shall despise me, every she.
Ach, that such a fate should fall on me!

"They'll say, since I'm so much to blame in this,
That I've dishonored all my sex, alas!
Although I'm not the first who did amiss,
That can't abate my shame or make it pass.
But since my guilt is settled, hard and fast—
A falseness far too grievous to undo—   1070
To Diomedes now I swear that I'll be true.

"But, Troilus, in that I no better may,
And since we must be parted, you and I,

I pray that God will guard you every day,
The gentlest knight that ever met my eye,
The faithfulest and quickest to comply,
The best to serve his lady and to keep
Her honor bright." . . . But here she stopped to weep.

"And certainly, my lord, I'll hate you never.
A friend's best love you'll always have from me,   1080
And my good words if I should live forever,
And truly I'll be sad enough to see
You suffer any great adversity.
You can't be blamed for anything I do,
And so, my prince, I take my leave of you."

How long it was between her firm decision—
Goodbye to Troilus; Diomedes, hail!—
No book or author tells us with precision.
Let every man look closely; without fail,
He won't find that set forth in any tale.   1090
Diomedes' suit was soon begun,
But he had much to do ere she was won.

Nor am I quick to judge her or to chide
More than the tale itself would cause me to.
Her name, alas, is scorned so far and wide,
She's punished well. There's little I could do.
If she could be excused on any view,
Because she mourned her lack of faithfulness,
I'd treat her with compassion, I confess.

This Troilus, as I told you here before,   1100
Endured his sorrow stoutly as he might.
His heart grew hot then icy evermore,
Especially on that ninth and crucial night.
The morrow after that, she said aright
She'd come again. God knows, but little rest
Had he that night. His heart burned in his breast.

Laurel-crowned Phoebus with his rays
Began to rise, and ever upward thrust,
To warm the eastern waters and their waves,

And Nysus'[41] daughter proclaimed the morning thus,   1110
When Troilus rose and sent for Pandarus
To walk the walls and look out toward the sea
And welcome Criseyde back, if that might be.

Till it was noon they stood aloft to see
Whoever came, and as each sort of wight
Approached from far, they both said it was she
Until they could advise themselves aright.
Troilus' heart fell with the spreading light.
And thus well fooled they shade their eyes and stare
At nothing, for that's all that met them there.   1120

To Pandarus Troilus turned and shortly said:
"For all I know, the hour's too early, sir.
Criseyde's been detained, upon my head.
She has enough to do, my lord, I'm sure,
To pacify her father ere she stir.
Perhaps the old magician makes her dine
Before she leaves—may God now let him pine!"

Pandarus answered, "That might surely be,
And therefore let *us* dine, my lord, I pray,
And later we'll come back if you agree."   1130
So home they went with little more to say—
Then back again, but they'll look long that way
Before they find what they are searching for.
Fortune meant to balk them evermore.

Troilus said, "Lo, now I see that she
Is hampered by her doddering father so
That ere she comes it well nigh eve will be.
Come down to the entrance gate, my lord. Let's go!
Those porters are but cloddish men, you know,
I'll see to it that she won't have to wait   1140
When she arrives at last, however late."

---

41. *NEE-sus.* King of Megara, on the Isthmus of Corinth. His daughter, Scylla, attempted to betray the city to King Minos of Crete and was turned into a lark for her perfidy. Larks sing at daybreak.

The day goes fast, and after that the eve,
And yet Criseyde still does not appear.
Troilus looks by hedges, trees, and leaves
And hangs his head outside the wall to hear.
But then he turned and showed a better cheer.
"By God, I know her meaning now," he said,
"And just in time—I almost felt real dread.

"Now doubtlessly she's thinking as she should.
I'm sure she means to ride here privately.   1150
And I commend her. This is for the good.
She won't have people crowding round to see—
Gaping fools who know she's come to me.
Night will fall before she nears the gate.
Patience, brother; there's not long to wait.

"We've nothing else to do now, by my bliss.
Ho! Pandarus! There! You must believe me.
By all my faith, I see her. There she is!
Look! Just use your eyes, man. Can't you see?"
"Nay," Pandarus answered. "By that tree?   1160
All wrong. These are the urgings of your heart.
Lord, all I see is but a market cart."

"Alas, you're right again, I fear," said Troilus.
"But surely, it can't simply be for naught
That I now find my heart rejoicing thus.
Some coming good must bring about these thoughts.
Since I was born, I've not been less distraught
Nor felt such comfort. Surely there's a cause.
She comes tonight! I lay my life she does!"

Pandarus answered, "It may be, well enough,"   1170
And held with him in everything he said,
But in his heart he thought this sorry stuff,
Imagining far otherwise instead:
"From the hazel woods where Robin[42] made his bed,

_____

42. Traditional name for country fellows in pastoral romances, which were
sometimes set in hazel woods. Or possibly Chaucer had Robin Hood in mind.
Either way, Pandarus thinks it just as likely that Criseyde will return to them from
some old story as from the Greek camp.

She'll sooner come, than from that camp to here.
She's gone for good, like snows of yesteryear."

The warden of the gates began to call
To folks still out upon the darkening plain.
He bid them bring their beasts in, one and all,
Or all that night outside they must remain.   1180
And later on by far, in dreadful pain,
This Troilus homeward took his anguished way.
He saw at last it wouldn't help to stay.

But nonetheless, he cheered himself in this:
He thought his count was wrong—he'd missed his day.[43]
"I have it now," he said. "I've gone amiss.
On our last night I heard Criseyde say,
'I'll be back here, dearest, if I may,
Before the moon—so sure of it I am—
Shall pass out from the Lion to the Ram.'   1190

"And so she may yet keep her last behest."
And on the morrow to the gate he went,
And up and down he looked, both east and west,
And back and forth he paced the wall's extent.
But all for naught. His time was vainly spent.
When darkness fell, his sorrows sprang anew,
He plodded home with nothing more to do.

Clean from his heart his fading hopes had fled.
Nothing he thought now could hold them back.
His sorrow grew until his sore heart bled,   1200
Lanced through and through by misery's sharp attack.
Somehow her resolution failed, alack.
He wondered why she waited—what occurred.
But it was clear as day she broke her word.

He watched out for her yet a full six days
After those first ten of which I told.

---

43. In *Il Filostrato* Troilus says Criseyde meant to spend ten days with her father, so it would be on the eleventh day that she would come, not the tenth. Chaucer recasts the matter in astrological terms.

Twixt hope and fear his heart was pulled both ways,
Recalling all she pledged to him of old.
But then his trust and dwindling hopes grew cold.
She was gone; that he could not deny.   1210
Now he must resign himself to die.

Therewith the wicked spirit, I confess,
Known to men as brainsick jealousy,
Crept into him amid his heaviness.
Thenceforth, since only death could set him free,
He neither ate or drank, so stung was he,
And equally all company he fled,
So sorry was the life the poor knight led.

He was so defeated and so drawn,
Men scarcely knew him, for he looked so sick.   1220
He became so feeble, pale and wan,
He had to walk supported by a stick.
Sharp jealousy had cut him to the quick.
If any asked him then what made him smart,
He said it was a pain about his heart.

King Priam often, and his mother dear,
His brothers and his sisters, asked in vain
Why he sorrowed so as it appeared
And what had caused him so much dreadful pain.
But all for naught. He never would explain,   1230
But said he felt a hurt—and fetch a sigh—
About his heart, alas, and now must die.

And then one day when he lay down to sleep,
It happened so, that in his dreams he thought
That in a wood he walked alone to weep
For love of her who all his pains had wrought,
And as he went about there sore distraught,
He saw a long-tusked, fearsome, brawny boar
Asleep upon the sunlit forest floor.[44]

---

44. In *Il Filostrato* the dream boar attacks Criseyde, rooting out her heart, but
she seems pleased by its action.

And by this boar and fast in its embrace—   1240
And kissing it—the lady of his heart.
With that in view his pulse began to race,
And misery made him wake up with a start.
He called aloud for Pandarus in his smart.
"O Pandarus," he cried, "I know it well
That I am dead. There is no more to tell.

"Criseyde has grown false, my lady bright,
To whom I gave my faith and all my love.
Her heart has fastened on some other knight.
The blissful gods have sent a sign thereof—   1250
A bitter, fearful vision from above.
For in my dreams Criseyde was consoled . . ."
And all the rest to Pandarus he told.

"O my Criseyde, alas, what tortured thought,
What trick of lust, what beauty, or what skill,
What honest cause for this have you in aught?
What guilt in me, or what outrageous ill
Made you desert me, turned aside your will?
O trust, O faith! The promises you made!
O who has won you now I am betrayed?   1260

"Alas, why did I ever let you go?
That nearly drove the wits out of my head!
I'll never trust in oaths again, I know.
By God, I thought without a trace of dread
That there was gospel truth in all you said!
But who can fool a man, if that's her pleasure,
As well as one he trusts beyond all measure?

"What shall I do, my Pandarus, alas?
I feel a new and even sharper pain,
And since there is no cure to make this pass,   1270
It's right that I should kill myself, that's plain,
Better to die than sit here and complain.
For through my death my woe would have an end.
Each day I live reproaches me, my friend."

"My lord," Pandarus answered, "alas the while
That I was born! Have I not said, by my bliss,

That dreams are formed to flatter and beguile?
And why? Our anxious readings often miss.
How dare you say your lady's false in this
For any dream? You're moved to by your fear.   1280
It's dread that speaks, not gods, for you're no seer.

"Perhaps, sir, when you dream of such a boar
It may well be it only signifies
Her father Calchas. He is old and hoar.
He doesn't feel the heat. His death is nigh.
And Criseyde for sorrow weeps and cries
And kisses him, there lying on the ground,
And that's where your dream's meaning may be found!"

"What can I do," said Troilus to his friend,
"To bring the proper sense of this to light?"   1290
"Now that's the way to talk," said Pandarus then:
"Hear my advice. Since you know how to write,
Send my niece a letter. Ask outright.
That's the surest way to tease this out
And know the truth where now you can but doubt.

"And here is why, as you will ascertain:
If indeed Criseyde is untrue,
I can't believe that she will write again.
And if she writes, she'll make things plain to you,
As whether there's still some course she can pursue   1300
To come to Troy. Or else she'll make it clear,
If she's held back, why she cannot be here.

"You have not written to her since she went,
Nor she to you, and this I dare to say:
She may name such a cause that you'll assent—
Agree yourself it's better in some way
For both of you, my lord, that she should stay.
So write to her, and shortly you will know
The truth of all—if she's still true or no."

They both agreed this was their proper course,   1310
And they'd see to it soon. They'd not be slow.
So hastily Troilus sits him down perforce,

And rolls within his sad heart to and fro
How he may best describe his present woe,
And to Criseyde, his lovesome lady dear,
He wrote his inmost thoughts, as you shall hear:

Litera Troili[45]

"*Fresh flower, whose I have been and shall be ever,*
You have my loving service, you alone,
With heart and mind and life, my whole endeavor.
I'm but a woeful knight, unworthy yet your own,   1320
As true as tongue has told or heart has known.
As sure as matter must exist in space,
I recommend myself unto your noble grace.

"*Please call this to mind, my own sweetheart:*[46]
As you well know, it's been some time since fate
Took you from here in grief and fearful smart.
You're gone, and I've no hope except to wait,
And ever in a worse and sadder state.
I mourn from day to day and must live so
As long as you shall please, my joy and woe.   1330

"*And so, my dear, with fearful heart but true,*
I write as one whom grief compels to write
To speak my woe, that each hour grows anew.
I must complain, though I have little right.
This letter's many smudges show my plight;
They're made by tears that rain down from my face.
Those tears would speak if they could ask your grace.

"*I first beseech you not to think your eyes*
Befouled by this sad letter that you hold.
Be gracious to me. Dear, do not despise   1340
To read these words, though some be overbold.
And for the sake of all my sorrows cold

---

45. Troilus' letter. In Boccaccio the letter is much longer and more confrontational. Boccaccio's Troilus makes it clear he thinks some Greek lover has taken his place with Criseyde.
46. This and the following stanza do not appear in Boccaccio.

That slay my wit, if I say aught amiss,
Forgive me, sweetheart and my dearest bliss.

"If any servant dares or has a right
To call out on his lady or complain,
My dear, I think that I must be that knight.
Consider this: you've now two months remained
Among the Greeks although you first ordained
Ten days would be the limit of your stay.   1350
Two months indeed, and yet you're still away.

"But inasmuch as, dear, I must embrace
What pleases you, I dare not cavil more,
But humbly—sick from sighing, pale of face—
I write to tell you of my sorrows sore.
I hope, and each day stronger than before,
To learn more fully, if you'll grant my prayer,
What you have done and mean to do while there.

"I pray your health and welfare will increase
So that always upward in degree   1360
Their growth will flourish, dear, and never cease.
And just as your heart wishes, lady free,
I pray that God may grant all things will be;
And this as well: that you will look with rue
Upon your humble servant, ever true.

"And if you'd like to know how your knight fares,
Whose woe can't be expressed however he strive,
I can't say more than, fraught with smarting cares
While writing as I do, I am alive.
But death is always ready to oblige,   1370
Which I delay, and will put off, or try,
Until I have the grace of your reply.

"My weary eyes, with which I see in vain,
Bathed in tears, are transformed into wells.
My songs are turned to plaints against my pain;
My good to harm; my days of ease to hells;
My joy to woe. I can say nothing else.
All things are turned—and this, dear, never varies,
My joy, my ease, my mirth—to their contraries.

"All which your coming home again to Troy   1380
Can now redress, and over that increase
A thousand times all I have known of joy.
For never was a heart so strongly pleased
As mine will be the day you give it ease
With your return. But still, if nothing I allege
Can move you, love, I pray, recall your pledge.

"Yet if my guilt is such that I must die,
Or if you'd rather not come back to me,
I've served you in the past, you'll not deny;
And so, I beg you humbly as may be,   1390
Write and tell me now you would go free.
For God's love grant that grace, my guiding light,
So death can make an end of your sad knight.

"And if some other cause makes you remain,
I pray you'll tell me so for my relief;
For though your absence brings me hellish pain,
If you're still true, I can endure that grief.
Your letter will sustain my firm belief.
Now write, my sweet, don't leave me in despair.
With hope or death deliver me from care.   1400

"Certainly, my dearest, sweetest heart,
I think when we meet next that you will see,
I've lost such health and color for my part,
Criseyde herself won't know who I may be.
In brief, my heart's true day, my lady free,
I'm so athirst your beauty to behold,
I'm halfway dead and cannot be consoled.

"I say no more, though I have much to say—
Far more indeed than I have room to tell.
But live or die, my dear one, either way,   1410
I pray to God this finds you safe and well.
Goodbye, my fair, who holds me in her spell.
You can make me live or die, as I profess.
It all depends upon your faithfulness.

"To you such health as you once wished to me,[47]
And if you don't again, I'll shortly die.
It lies with you to say how things shall be—
Just choose my day of death and I'll comply.
But then you're just as able to untie
All my diseases, all my pain and smart.   1420
And so farewell again, my dear sweetheart!

     "Le vostre T."[48]

When Criseyde got the letter Troilus sent,[49]
Her answer to him in effect was this:
Full piteously she wrote of her intent,
That soon as may be, if she didn't miss,
She would return to mend his injured bliss.
But then she added at the very end
That though she'd come, she still could not say when.

Her letter was so filled with soothing speech,
It was a wonder. She swore she loved him best.   1430
But there was nothing sound in all she preached.
Now, Troilus, you may journey east or west,
Or pipe in an ivy leaf or take your rest!
Thus goes the world. God shield us from mischance,
And every faithful, loving wight advance!

Troilus' woe increased from day to night.
He mourned Criseyde, yet she stayed away.
His hope began to dwindle, and his might,
For which he laid him down in bed to stay,
Refusing meat or drink in sorrow's sway.   1440
Always thinking Criseyde was untrue,
Half mad with anguish nothing could subdue.

---

47. This stanza does not appear in Boccaccio.

48. Your T.

49. This and the following thirteen stanzas (through line 1519) do not appear in Boccaccio, where there is no return letter from Criseyde at this point and Cassandra does not interpret Troilus' dream of the boar. She merely remarks that it is a shame that the lowborn Criseyde has disappointed him.

His dream, which I recounted here and glossed,
Never left his sad, tormented mind.
He thought Criseyde now was surely lost,
And that great Jove, intending to be kind,
Had sent the dream, whose meaning he must find,
Of her untruth and how his trust was broken.
All seemed to turn on what the boar betokened.

So he for his foreseeing sister sent—   1450
Cassandra,⁵⁰ as they called her all about—
And told his dream and what he thought it meant,
And asked her to resolve his scalding doubt,
To name the boar if she could tease that out.
After a pause and some brief signs of strain,
She settled down beside him to explain.

She smiled at him and said, "O brother dear,
If you desire to know the truth of this,
You must listen to a few old stories here
That tell how Fortune toppled from their bliss   1460
Some lords of old, through which, unless I miss,
You'll learn who this boar is, and in what way
His people trace their past, as old books say.

"Diana⁵¹ once was wrapped in dreadful ire:
For Calydon withheld her sacrifice—
They would not pile rich incense on her fire.
O no! They set her at too low a price,
So she revenged herself in wondrous wise.
She sent a boar as big as any ox
To spoil their wheat and grapes and fright their flocks.   1470

"To slay this boar they called the country out.
And with the rest who answered to their plea

---

50. One of King Priam's daughters and twin sister of Helen of Troy. Like her twin, she was uncommonly beautiful, so much so that Apollo tried to seduce her with the gift of prophesy. When she refused him, he turned the gift into a curse: she would prophesy truly, but no one would believe her. Cassandra's stories come from Ovid (Meleager and Atalanta) and the Roman poet Statius' *Thebaid,* a retelling of *The Seven Against Thebes.* See also the note to Book 3, line 410.
51. Huntress goddess of the moon.

Came a maid,[52] a matchless girl, no doubt,
And Meleager,[53] lord of that country.
He so loved this peerless maiden free
That with his manly courage, stout and sure,
He slew the boar, and sent its head to her.

"This act, as ancient stories tell us,
Raised a great dispute and evil thoughts.
From Meleager[54] descended Tydeus,   1480
Or those old authors' words must go for naught.
But how this Meleager's mother brought
His death about, I cannot tell you now,
For that would make my tale too long, I vow."

She told him, though, how Tydeus later went
Unto Thebes, a city strong and fair,
To claim the kingdom, which he thought was meant
For Polynices, who'd been exiled from there.
Eteocles,[55] his brother and co-heir,
Wrongfully held the city all alone.   1490
All these ancient doings she made known.

She told as well how Maeon[56] by his art
Escaped when Tydeus killed his company.
Then all the details, which she had by heart,
Of how those kings with all their panoply
Besieged the town so no one there could flee,

---

52. Atalanta, a famous heroine and later mother of Parthenopaeus, who was one of the Seven Against Thebes.

53. *Mel-ee-AY-ger*. The country was Calydon.

54. At Meleager's birth the Fates proclaimed his life would last only as long as a certain piece of wood then burning in the hearth. Overhearing them, his mother, Althaea, snatched the brand from the fire and put it away for safekeeping. According to one version of the story, in the quarrel over the boar's head Meleager killed two of his uncles, Althaea's brothers, and she retaliated by throwing the brand into the fire and ending his life.

55. *E-TEE-a-clez*.

56. *ME-an*. One of fifty warriors sent to kill Tydeus, who slew all of them except Maeon.

And of the holy serpent and the well
And of the Furies, she went on to tell.[57]

She told of Archemorus'[58] funeral pyre and games,
And how Amphiaraus[59] fell into the ground,
How Tydeus was slain,[60] a thing of shame,
And how Hippomedon[61] came to be drowned,
And how Parthenopaeus[62] was found
Dead of wounds, and of Capaneus[63] the proud
Who died to pay for what he rashly vowed.

And then she told him how those warring brothers,
Polynices and Eteocles as well,
Met in a scrimmage where each one killed the other,
And how Argia[64] wept at what befell,
And how they burned Thebes' fated citadel.[65]

---

57. The holy serpent was a snake or dragon who killed Archemorus, the infant son of King Lycurgus of Nemea, when the seven kings stopped there for water. The baby's death was held to portend the failure of their expedition. The Furies are only tangentially related. When the islanders of Lemnos neglected her worship, Venus sent the Furies to enflame the women there to kill the men. One woman, Hypsipyle, saved her father and fled with him, later becoming Archemorus' nurse. All these details come from the *Thebiad.*

58. *Arch-ee-MOR-us.*

59. *Am-phee-a-RAY-us.* One of the Seven Against Thebes. Jove caused the earth to swallow him to keep him from being killed in battle.

60. He was mortally wounded by Melanippus, whom he killed. Amphiaraus, blaming Tydeus for starting the unsuccessful war with Thebes, cut off the head of Melanippus and brought it to Tydeus, who drank the brains. This barbarous act offended Athena, who decided to withhold the immortality she had planned to give him.

61. *Hi-POM-a-don.* One of the Seven, like the two in the following notes. He pursued a band of Thebans into the local river and was overwhelmed by the water at the request of Ismenis, the nymph of the river, whose son he had killed.

62. *Par-then-o-PEE-us.*

63. *Ka-PAIN-e-us.* He vowed to take Thebes even if Jove defended it and was killed by a bolt of lightning while climbing a siege ladder.

64. *Ar-GI-a.* Poynices' wife.

65. The burning of Thebes is not part of the original story according to Statius.

And so she worked down from these tales of old
To Diomedes; then this is what she told:

"Diomedes is the man meant by this boar,
Tydeus' son, for both these are descended
From Meleager, who smote the beast so sore.
This means Criseyde, whatever she intended,
Gave Diomedes her heart. And that cannot be mended.
Weep if you like, or don't. Without a doubt,
This Diomedes is in, and you are out."

"That isn't true!" he said, "You sorceress,   1520
With all your lying, ghostly prophesies!
You hope to be a famous seer, I guess!
You're nothing but a fool for fantasies,
Passing on such slanderous lies as these.
Away with you, and may Jove give you sorrow.
Time will prove you wrong. Perhaps tomorrow!

"You might as well taint Alcestis[66] with your lies—[67]
Of all the good, kind creatures ever known,
That noble wife and lady took the prize!
For when her husband was to die alone   1530
Unless she'd buy his life back with her own,
She chose to die for him and go to hell,
And so she did, as all the old books tell."

Cassandra left, and he, full cruel hearted,[68]
Forgot his woe for ire at what she said.
Up from his bed all suddenly he started
As if some dose had raised him from the dead.
He looked at things behind him and ahead
To winnow out truth with all his care,
And thus lived out the end of his affair.   1540

---

66. *Al-CEST-is*. As Chaucer says, she volunteered to die in place of her husband,
King Admetus of Pherae in Thessaly, but Hercules later rescued her from the
underworld.

67. This stanza does not appear in Boccaccio.

68. This and the following five stanzas (through line 1575) do not appear in
Boccaccio.

Fortune, through a power to her committed
By heaven's king, controls the permutations
Of things on earth—all that is permitted
Beneath the rule of Jove's predestination—
Among the rest the fall of mighty nations.
And now she plucked the feathers of bright Troy,
To leave her stripped of power and bare of joy.

Amid all this the end of Hector's life
Came on apace, full eager to arrive.
For Fate would pare his soul as with a knife,   1550
And had prepared a scene he'd not survive.
Against this plot he had no means to strive.
One day he joined a battle at its height,
But soon, alas, death reaped him from that fight.

For this, I think that every sort of wight
Who uses arms, of right ought to bewail
The death of him who was so fine a knight.
For as he dragged a king by his linked mail—
Intent on this—Achilles with small travail
Struck him through his armor with a spear,   1560
And thus was ended Hector's great career.[69]

For him, as these old books and writers tell us,
Was made such woe as now no tongue can speak.
Among the rest, the sorrow of this Troilus,
Who sat next him on honor's highest peak,
Was bottomless and left his life full bleak;
So scourged with love and now this new unrest,
He bid the heart to burst within his breast.

But nonetheless, though he was in despair,
And dreaded that Criseyde was untrue,   1570
Yet to her his heart would still repair,
And as all lovers will, he thought anew
He'd win her back again, so bright of hue;
And in his heart, so stubborn and contrary,
He'd hold her father Calchas made her tarry.

---

69. This differs from Homer's account, in which Hector was caught outside the
city walls by Achilles and killed in single combat.

Oftentimes he planned in all his rue
To don a pilgrim's outfit for disguise
And go to her; but that would never do:
The Greeks were far too wary and too wise.
Nor could he find a tale that would suffice   1580
If he should go and be discovered there.
And so he wept alone and racked by care.

He wrote and wrote again, and then anew—[70]
He never missed a chance, upon my oath—
Beseeching her because he still was true
That she'd return and thus redeem her troth.
And once, for pity's sake and nothing loth
(As I believe), she wrote him back as well,
And with a new excuse, as I shall tell:

Litera Criseydis[71]

"Cupid's son and fount of honor clear,   1590
O sword of knighthood, source of gentleness,
How may a wretch in such torment and fear
Send word to you except of my duress?
I the sick at heart, I in distress!
Since we can't meet by right, my dear, or stealth,
I cannot send you either heart or health.

"Your many letters have made me acquainted
With your great hurt, which roused my pity here.
And I have noted all you sent were painted
With bitter tears, and your desire is clear   1600
For my return. Yet that can't be, my dear.
But why, lest this letter be found out,
I cannot say and put you out of doubt.

"Grievous to me, God knows, is your unrest—
Your hot repining at the high gods' measures.
You cannot, will not, take them for the best.

---

70. This and the following six stanzas (Criseyde's letter) do not appear in Boccaccio.

71. Criseyde's letter.

No other thing on earth can work your cure,
It seems to me, but only your own pleasure.
Don't disdain me, Troilus, I beseech.
I tarry here for fear of wicked speech.   1610

"I've heard much more than I anticipated
About us two—how far our love has gone—
I'll stay away until that talk's deflated.
Then, too (don't hate me), some have said anon
You only took me up to lead me on.
I know that's false indeed; in you I see
Naught but gentle, loving honesty.

"I'll come to you, but now such is my state,
I'm so in doubt, that what year or what day
That this shall be, . . . I can't supply a date.   1620
But in effect, I pray you, if I may,
Think well of me, and in a loving way;
For truly, lord, as long as life endures
I will be a faithful friend of yours.

"I pray as well you won't hold me in spite
That I'm so brief in what I say to you.
I hardly dare, here where I am, to write,
Nor can I write as well as others do.
Yet words can wield great weight although they're few.
The meaning's all, and not the letter's length.   1630
And now farewell, and may God lend you strength!

        "La vostre C."[72]

Troilus thought this letter passing strange.
Each line he read brought out a doleful sigh.
He thought her words betrayed a hidden change.
But then he'd argue to himself, or try,
Her pledges were too strong to be put by.
It's hard for earnest lovers to believe
Their love is false, though doubt may make them grieve.

---

72. Your C.

But nonetheless a man will at long last,
In spite of everything, see what is what.   1640
And so poor Troilus did, and that full fast.
He came to understand his sorry lot—
That she was not as true as he had thought.
And finally he knew without a doubt,
He'd lost the only thing he cared about.

One day as he stood sadly by and sighed
In fear that she was false, his dearest joy—
The one for whom he gladly would have died—
It happened that throughout the streets of Troy,
Men carried to incite the hoi polloi   1650
A captured *cote-armure*,[73] as often done,
A trophy that Deiphebus had won.

This was Diomedes' cloak, my author, says.[74]
Deiphebus had captured it that day,
And when it fell beneath Prince Troilus' gaze,
He saw that it was neatly made and gay,
Embellished top to bottom, every way.
But as he took the fabric up to hold,
Full suddenly he felt his heart grow cold.

Before him, on the collar, he found pinned   1660
A brooch he gave Criseyde on that day
She rode away from Troy so sore chagrinned,
In memory of his love and sad dismay.
She swore to him her love could not decay.
She'd wear it always! Now he knew for sure
He was betrayed. There was no trust in her.

At that he made his way straight home to send
For Pandarus, and of this newest sleight
And of the brooch, he told him to its end,
Complaining that Criseyde's heart was light   1670

---

73. An embroidered tunic worn over armor and bearing the wearer's heraldic
device (a medieval, not a Greek, style).

74. In the original, Chaucer again names his fictitious source, "Lollius," here.
See note to Book 1, line 394.

In spite of his long love and trust and right.
And next he cried full piteously for death
To come and end his sorrows with his breath.

And then he said, "Criseyde, lady mine,
Where is your promise? Say, where has it gone?
Where are your love, your trust, your pledges fine?
Are you with Diomedes now? Is he the one?
I never thought you'd do as you have done:
Although your truth and honor you'd betray,
I scarcely thought you'd toy with me this way!   1680

"Who shall believe again in any oath?
I never would have thought, as I insist,
That you, Criseyde, could renounce your troth!
Unless I'd sorely sinned, gone far amiss,
I'd never thought you'd be so cruel as this.
To slay me thus! Alas, your honesty
Is ravaged now as all can clearly see.

"Was there no other brooch you could forgo
To deck your newest lover's cloak," he cried,
"But that one I, in tears as you must know,   1690
Gave you to hold and cherish till you died?
I think you must have meant to spite my pride
By spurning it; then too you must have meant
To openly proclaim your new intent.

"By this I see that I am truly cast
Clean from your mind—and yet I have no way,
For all the world, my heart is so harassed,
To unlove you a quarter of a day!
Cursed from birth, even now I'm forced to say
That of all creatures it's you whom I love best—   1700
The very one who dooms me to unrest!

"Now God," he said, "bestow on me this grace:
That Diomedes and I may meet upon the field!
If I have might and meet him face to face
I'll make him swim in blood until he yield.
O God," he said, "who should uphold and shield

Honesty and truth, and punish vice,
Why don't you make this traitor pay some price?

"O Pandarus, who reviled my trust in dreams,
Upbraiding me, as you were wont to do,   1710
Now you must unsay all that, it seems.
Your lovely niece Criseyde is untrue!
By sundry signs that we must all construe
The gods attune our sleep to joy and pain.
My dream has shown the truth of this again.

"Now certainly—there's nothing else to add—
From this time forth I'll labor as I may
To die in arms. My death will make me glad.
It can't come soon enough, my fatal day.
But Criseyde, sweet as ever, I must say,   1720
Since I've done all you asked and never swerved,
Your lack of faith is wholly undeserved!"

This Pandarus, who heard all Troilus said,
And knew full well he spoke the truth of this,
Could think of no fit answer on this head.
He sorrowed for his good friend's shattered bliss
And blamed his niece who'd done so much amiss.
His wits, so much at fault, were overthrown.
Without a word he stood as still as stone.

But at the last he roused and spoke his piece: 1730
"My brother dear," he said, "you wring me sore.
What can I say? I hate my traitor niece,
And as God knows, I will forevermore!
All the things you asked from me of yore,
With no regard for my good name or rest,
I did for you and wished them for the best.

"If I did aught at all to ease your smart,
I'm glad of that. But of her treason now,
God knows it throws a weight upon my heart.
And, Troilus, to restore your ease, I vow,   1740
I'd do what that might take, but don't know how.
Yet from this world, almighty God I pray,
Will reap her soon. That's all I have to say."

Troilus' sorrow and his plaints were piteous,
But Fortune held her course as I have told.
Criseyde now holds dear the son of Tydeus,
And Troilus must lament out in the cold.
So goes the world. Look well and you'll behold
There is no worldly state where hearts can rest.
God grant us grace to take all for the best!   1750

In many a cruel battle, out of dread,
Troilus showed his prowess as a knight.
As all the tales in ancient books have said,
He fought with knightly bearing and great might.
Propelled by flaming anger, day and night,
He trounced the hated Greeks to great acclaim,
But meeting Diomedes was his aim.

And oftentimes, I find that those two met
With bloody strokes and clashing words of spite.
They soon found out how well their spears were whet,   1760
And as God knows, with all his cruel might
Troilus banged him on the helm and made him sweat!
But nonetheless Dame Fortune did not will
That either's hand had force enough to kill.

Now if my foremost task here was to write[75]
The tale of Troilus as a fighting man,
I'd undertake his battles to endite.
But that is not the story I began.
I've told his love as truly as I can.
Whoso wants his warlike deeds to hear,   1770
Read Dares,[76] where the bulk of them appear.

I pray to every lady bright of hue
And every gentle woman who may be,
Albeit this Criseyde was untrue,
If I say so, you won't be wroth with me.

---

75. This and the following four stanzas (through line 1799) do not appear in Boccaccio.

76. *DAR-ez*. Dares the Phrygian, one of Chaucer's old authors, a Greek writer of doubtful authority on the Trojan War.

Her guilt is plain in other books, you see.
I'll write more gladly, if you would,
Of Penelope's faith and Alcestis, true and good.[77]

Nor do I write for disappointed men,
But more for women who have been betrayed   1780
By lying folk—God give those grief, amen!—
Who with their wit and words so nicely weighed,
Win them from good, then choose to act dismayed!
This moves me now to warn you once again—
Hear what I say: you must beware of men!

Go, little book. Go, my tragedy.
May God permit thy poet ere he die,
To find the skill to make a comedy!
Don't envy others' work, however high,
But bow before the great ones, slight and shy,   1790
And kiss the footsteps, humbly as thou can,
Of Virgil, Ovid, Homer, Statius, Lucan.[78]

And since there is so much diversity
In English and the writing of our tongue,
I pray to God no scribe miscopies thee
Or leaves thy meter halting or unstrung,
And that wherever thou are read or sung
Thou may be understood, dear God, I pray!
. . . But back again to what I meant to say.

Troilus' wrath, as I once said to you,   1800
Cost the Greek invading host full dear.
For he killed thousands of that hostile crew,
And fought like one who never knew a peer—

77. Penelope was the faithful wife who waited twenty years for the return of Odysseus. Alcestis gave her life to save her husband Admetus. See the note to Book 5, line 1527. Chaucer went on to write of Alcestis in his unfinished *Legend of Good Women*.

78. Virgil, Homer, and Statius treated war and other themes with more or less epic gravity, as did Lucan, whose *Pharsalia* recounts the civil war between Julius Caesar and Pompey the Great. Ovid is a very different sort of writer, whose view of war is generally dispassionate and often mocking.

Save Hector—in his time, from all I hear.
But then, alas, although it was God's will,
Fierce Achilles left him cold and still.[79]

Yet as his body lay in all its gear[80]
His weightless spirit rose and, blissful, went
Up to the place below the utmost sphere,[81]
Leaving behind each drossy element.[82]   1810
And there he saw beneath his late ascent
The wandering stars, and heard the harmony
Of heaven voicing its great melody.

And looking down he held before his eyes
This little spot of earth girt by the sea,
And found it now full easy to despise
This wretched world, where all is vanity
In light of heaven's true felicity

---

79. Troilus' death comes abruptly here, as it does in Boccaccio. According to
Dares, Troilus was killed after his horse was wounded and fell, entangling him in
its trappings. Other accounts have Achilles ordering Troilus' throat cut after he has
been captured, ambushing Troilus at a well, or killing him in the temple of Apollo.

80. This and the following two stanzas do not appear in Boccaccio.

81. Ancient and medieval authorities often thought of the universe as a system
of nine hollow, crystalline spheres moving around the earth, starting with one
each to carry the moon and the sun and then Mercury, Venus, Mars, Jupiter, and
Saturn, the five known planets. Outside these seven was an eighth sphere housing
the fixed stars, and the whole system moved in various ways under the influence of
a ninth sphere—the Primum Mobile—that was turned by God. The sun, moon,
and planets were called wandering stars because at different times they seemed
to take different routes across the sky, while the fixed stars were so called because
they always appeared in the same positions with respect to one another (think of
the constellations). Meanwhile, the friction between the moving parts produced
"the music of the spheres." Outside the Primum Mobile was the Empyrean, a world
of light and the home of God. Troilus's soul ascends to the eighth sphere—the
sphere of fixed stars. Beneath him are the earth, sun, moon and planetary system.
Overhead are the Primum Mobile and Empyrean.

82. *Elements* could refer to earth, air, fire, and water, which were not thought
to exist beyond the sphere of the moon, or to the planets, which were sometimes
called elements. The planetary meaning may be more likely in view of Chaucer's
source in Boccaccio. The whole description of this spiritual journey comes from
Boccaccio's *Teseida,* a poem on which Chaucer later based "The Knight's Tale."

That God maintains above; and then at last,
To where he died his downward look he cast.   1820

And to himself he laughed to see the woe
Of them who wept for his demise so fast,
Condemning all our work that follows so
On purblind lust, which nothing can make last,
When all our hearts on heaven should be cast.
And forth he went—here's all that I can tell—
Where Mercury[83] ordained that he should dwell.

So ended was this Troilus' love of late!
So ended was his splendid worthiness!
So ended was his pomp and royal estate!   1830
So ended was his lust and nobleness!
So ended was this false world's brittleness!
For so his love, Criseyde, won his heart,
And so he died when they were set apart.

O young, fresh folks, every he or she,[84]
In whom love grows as you advance in years,
Come home!—Away from earthly vanity.
Direct your hearts and minds above the spheres
To God, who fashioned you and all your peers,
And think this world is but a tawdry fair   1840
That passes like the flowers ere we're aware.

Give Him your love, He who Himself for love
Died on a cross for our blotched souls to pay.
He died and rose and sits in heaven above.
He won't be false to anyone, I say,
Who's fixed on Him and never thinks to stray.
Since He is best to love, so mild and meek,
What need have you some falser love to seek?

See here the use of pagans' cursèd rites!
See here how far their gods extend their aid!   1850

---

83. One of Mercury's roles was to guide the souls of the dead.

84. Boccaccio addresses his corresponding stanzas to young men only, advising them to beware the fickleness of girls. Nothing he says has a religious bearing.

See all the good of worldly appetites!
See here the use of all that wretched trade
Of Jove, Apollo, Mars—that whole charade!
See, too, the form of tales the old clerks told,
Their poetry as found in books of old.

O moral Gower,[85] this book I now direct[86]
To thee, and thee as well, my learned Strode,[87]
To read and, where you see the need, correct,
I count on you for help, so long bestowed.
And then to Christ, who bravely walked death's road.   1860
With all my heart for mercy, Lord, I pray,
And to Thy Godhead I have this to say:

Thou never-ending One and Two and Three[88]
Who reign forever, Three and Two and One,
Uncontained, while all's contained in Thee,
Help us here our spirits' foes to shun.
Defend us, Lord, as you have ever done.
Lead us, Jesus, so that Thy love we find,
For love of your dear mother so benign. Amen.

Explicit liber Troili et Criseydis[89]

---

85. John Gower, Chaucer's contemporary and friend, who wrote with equal facility in Latin, French, and English.

86. This and the following stanza do not appear in Boccaccio.

87. Ralph Strode, a controversialist and authority on logic who upheld free will against the theologian and Bible translator John Wycliff.

88. The Trinity of Father, Son, and Holy Spirit. Lines 1863–65 are translated from Dante's *Paradiso,* XIV, 28–30.

89. The end of the book of Troilus and Criseyde.